My Collection of Original Desserts

The Art of Creative Baking

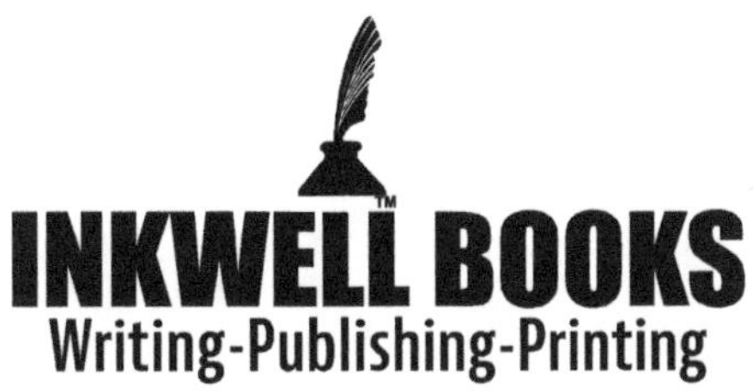

ISBN: 978-0-578-66486-6
Library of Congress Control Number: 2020905379

Published by Inkwell Books LLC
10632 North Scottsdale Road, Unit 695
Scottsdale, AZ 85254
Tel. 480-315-3781
E-mail info@inkwellbooksllc.com
Website www.inkwellbooksllc.com

Layout and design by
Thomas Rodriguez, TJR Designs, LLC
480-940-7767
www.tjrdesigns.com

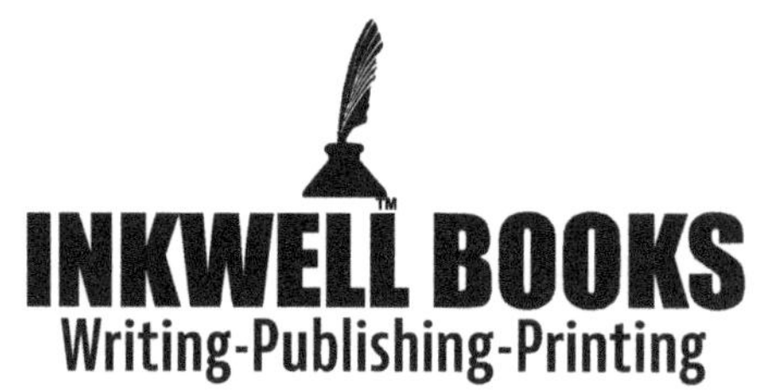

My Collection of Original Desserts

The Art of Creative Baking

Nikos Ligidakis

New Edition

Including Recipes for Healthy Diets

Dedication

To my wife Helene and my children Lisa and Steve

"Let food be thy medicine and medicine be thy food"

Hippocrates 460-370 BC

The Three Principles and the Symphony of Flavors

When I decided to become a chef, I understood that cooking for the public comes with great responsibility. I contemplated my options before opening the doors of my first little restaurant. I decided that my new journey's priority should be about a culinary exploration of new tastes. My initial thoughts were to focus on three principles: I wanted my food to be Fresh, to be Wholesome, and to have Character. I was not so naive as to think that amidst the grueling, high-pace restaurant activity, I would have the time to perfect all my goals at first. My dilemma was how much you compromise while trying to maintain your principals. I was confident that I could manage the freshness, that was the most natural part. I defined wholesomeness to be about healthy, nutritious foods. I understood that this was an ongoing process since the research about foods was updated continuously. I also realized that to develop the character of my foods would be a never-ending process. My definition of "food character" included the essence of flavors and the perception of tastes. Research in those days was difficult. After the long daily shifts in the kitchen, there was not much time to spend on research. I had to rely on experience and memories, what I had learned working in restaurants, and what I remembered growing up.

It is a fact that the behavior of each food changes according to what it is blended with. Balancing the flavors of foods is an old trade. In book II, On the Soul, Aristotle discusses the perception of taste. He establishes four basic tastes that the tongue is sensitive: sweet, sour, bitter, and salty. In my opinion, those are the four tastes that allow you to balance food flavors. Early Hippocratic doctors, following their teacher's theories, practiced a healthy diet as a form of medicinal treatment and the maintenance of good health. The ancient doctors emphasized that their patients use local resources to prepare simple, flavorful foods. Fruits and vegetables that were particularly potent with intense flavors were considered to be a reflection of nutrition value. The ones with a milder taste were important for the body as well but needed flavoring. Therefore, balancing the flavors of foods became a culinary issue. I mentioned in another note that my parents knew things because of common sense and folk wisdom, but eventually, we had scientific research. We were becoming aware that there are functionalism and undeniable truths about how some foods are harmful to your health. Slowly I began to limit or to eliminate food items that seemed to be unhealthy.

Shortly after I open my little restaurant on McDowell street, the five food items written on the blackboard at the opening multiplied into a nice size menu. However, looking at my dessert case, the three lonely items in it, Sweet Chocolate Death, New York Cherry Cheesecake, and Rum Apple Pie, needed some company. By now, the frantic dance of the herbs and spices in my head had subsided a bit, and food recipes were unfolding easier; I knew it was time to develop my baking skills. I often mentioned that very few chefs could master both cooking and baking. It is because they require two different mindsets. With cooking, you can use a bit more herbs and spices, and you can free-poor some more wine or broth to adjust the recipe to your taste. You can taste-and-correct the flavoring during the process. But, with baking, you must be precise; once you put your item into the oven, you are giving up the control of consistency and taste.

I remember the struggle at first trying to blend flavors in my head. There were sleepless nights and many disharmonic ideas that they had to be rejected. But once I was able to master the symphony of flavors, the size of the menu increased into hundreds of items, and the small glass case with the three cakes multiplied into many large display cases full of desserts. There was so much to explore, so much to learn. Creativity indeed unfolds by adding to familiar tastes. Therefore, to develop my creativity, I had to travel back into familiar grounds: my childhood.

Near my father's taverna in my hometown of Kiato, there were other restaurants and bakeries with windows full of luscious pastries and wholesome breads. There were shops for ice cream, snacks, yogurt, and coffee, all to entice children and adults alike. Beyond the food scents of my father's cooking, there were tempting aromas of various foods that draped the neighborhood. There was the exquisite fragrance of chocolate from the pastry shop and the addictive aroma of freshly made bread from the bakery. Walking down the main street of my hometown, exotic scents of cinnamon and honey, blended with smells of garlic, roasted nuts, and freshly brewed coffee filled the air. The tastes of my parent's cooking, the culture I grew up with and the fusion of aromas pervaded my young mind and slowly awakened a mortal fever for food flavorings. Imagination proved to be a reliable partner in creating new tastes.

For centuries humanity has stretched its ingenuity in search of delicious fragrances, always with the hope of creating the scent capable of granting the user the power of obsolete seduction. The art of fabricating heart-stopping aromas is complex. The chemistry of mixing ingredients that produce results requires imagination and experience. Creativity is more difficult in culinary art than any other because it involves the satisfaction of all the senses and the involvement of thousands of ingredients. All senses must come together when tasting foods.

The most memorable foods are the ones you touch during preparation or while you eat them. When you squeeze the lemon, you feel the tartness on your fingers. When you wash the vegetables, you sense their crispness. To determine the thickness of the body of the sauce, you feel it with your fingertips before you taste it. The direct contact with food, like breaking bread or eating a cookie, brings you closer to the reality of the taste. Listening to the crunch when you bite an apple, break lettuce, eat a cracker or nuts; these are sounds that establish freshness. The sight of the actual food can also be important. Usually, people will not believe that something that looks bad, or does not have a familiar color will taste right.

The smell is the most sensual of the senses. The aroma of various foods haunts and manipulates the senses. The nose is capable of detecting thousands of fragrances and sends them to the brain where the mind distinguishes what to eat. To create new tastes, we must determine the aromas of foods. The most obvious are coffee, chocolate, cinnamon, or baked bread. When these aromas register in the pages of our brains, they are unforgettable. Then we must try to identify the other aromas less potent: vanilla, basil, butter, eggs, adding to the collection of flavors. Eventually, we will be able to identify the smell register among the plethora of other ingredients in our mind. You will be able to single out the tomato smell from the stew, distinguish the vanilla in the pudding, the pistachio in the ice cream, the anise in the biscotti, and the nutmeg in the pie. Before you know it, you will be able to strip every ingredient from the dish or cake and savor each taste individually in your palette. A symphonic taste of every ingredient used will be under your control.

I do not regret one minute of the years I spent secluded, sculpting recipes before and after opening my restaurant, the endless hours dreaming of recipes included in this book. Conceived in my mind and born in the kitchen, this book is purely an act of passion and creativity. My desire to always learn and my passion for creating new tastes was not restrained after leaving the restaurant business. Nearly forty-years after opening the first restaurant, I am still learning and creating. Knowledge of how to prepare natural foods and the study of flavor profiles is so vast; it is impossible to learn it all in a lifetime. Learning about the amazing benefits of preparing your own foods is no different; we start with the basics, and we learn from our mistakes. In no time, you will be creating your recipes in a way you might not have thought possible.

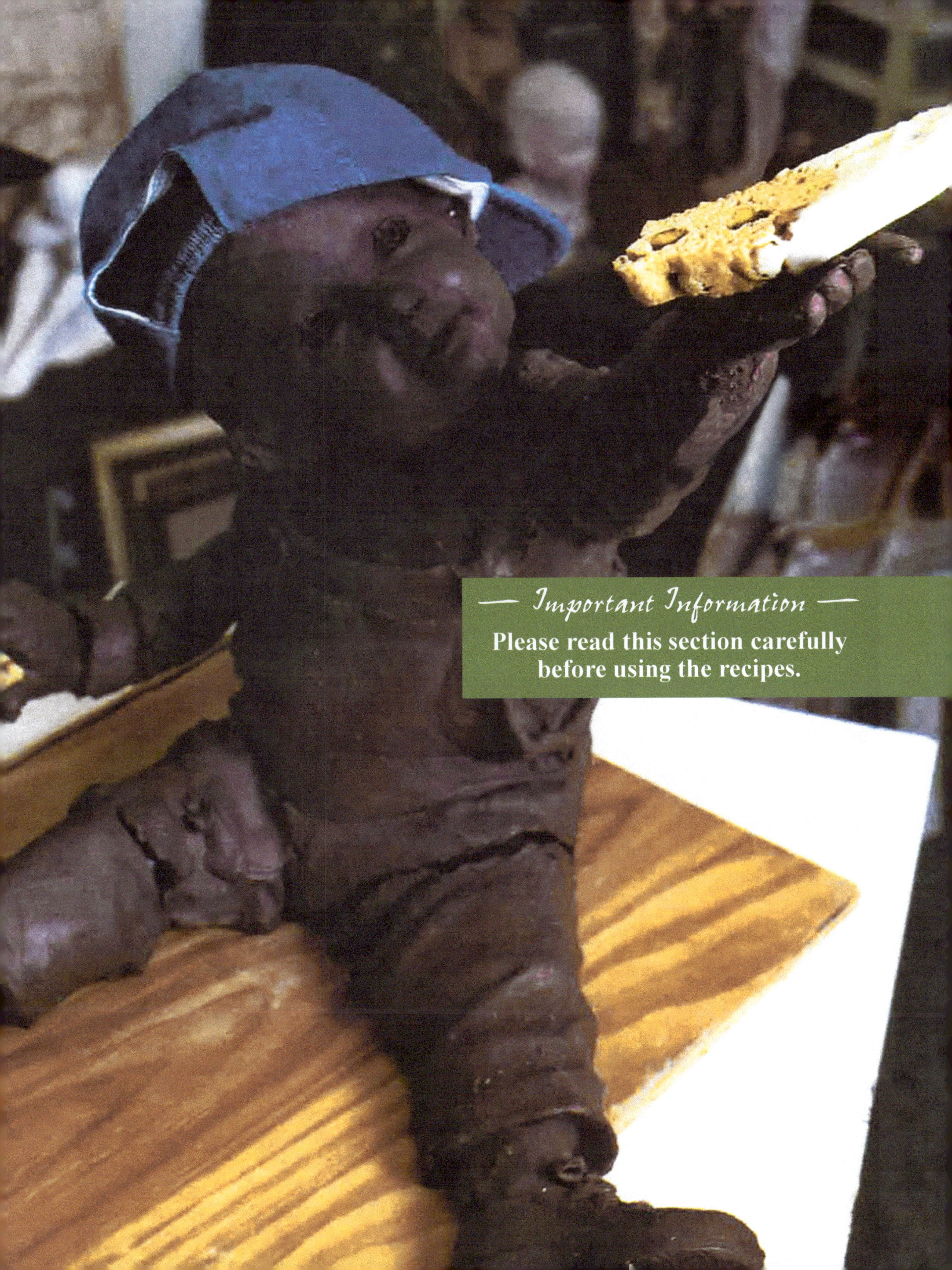

— Important Information —

Please read this section carefully before using the recipes.

Recipe Format

More than a few times, people have asked me to explain recipes written in various cookbooks or magazines. Even someone like me, who has spent most of my life in the kitchen, gets confused with the multiple formats and additional long explanations. In my previous cookbooks, I created a recipe format to follow; the recipes are in a step-by-step format which avoids repeating annoying details. I list the ingredients and, indented directly below, is the necessary step on how to use these ingredients.

This section of the book contains detailed information about various techniques on how to handle some of the common components of multiple recipes, such as how to melt chocolate, whip cream, make rosettes, and much more. Also, in this section, you will find valuable information about baking, quality ingredients, and more. Please read the recipe before using it so you can understand the steps and so you can have all the items necessary for the completion of your recipe.

Times Have Changed

Back in the day, when I wrote a recipe containing flour, it meant the use of white flour, unless I wanted to specify using whole wheat. Occasionally there was rye flour, semolina, durum wheat, and a few other unusual flours but none were gluten-free. Back then, if you looked for a gluten-free flour in the grocery store, there wasn't any. And then, it all changed. The selection of gluten-free flours displayed in the grocery stores now is overwhelming. In general, we've used wheat flour to create structure in baked goods or to occasionally thicken soups or sauces. Before the invasion of gluten-free flours, there was no interest in knowing how wheat flour worked. When you work with gluten-free flours, the first challenge is to understand the profile of each gluten-free flour. Thus, begins the journey of trial-and-error baking with gluten-free flours. The problem is that not a single gluten-free flour behaves precisely like wheat flour; therefore, you must use a blend of various gluten-free flours to achieve your goal of baking without wheat flour. The various gluten-free flours produce a different consistency and flavor. As it is true with wheat flour, the liquids used in recipes with other flours can affect the texture of the mixture. For example, the size of an egg or the origin and type of an oil will affect the consistency, and most likely, alter the result of your recipe. It is essential, in baking, to be familiar with the constancy of various mixtures. Familiarity with the consistency, allows us to add a bit more flour or some more liquid, to bring your mixture to your desired consistency. Wheat flour is known for its texture and taste. It is the taste where gluten-free flours have an advantage – they all have a different flavor; therefore, the tastes you can create with gluten-free flours are endless. The question is, which blend of gluten-free flours is best? It depends on what you want to bake. Some flours have a strong flavor, others are sweet, and some are nutty. When you start the fascinating journey of baking with gluten-free flours, you must be flexible and try as many as you can. The texture is the biggest challenge for gluten-free baking. Even since I began the writing of this book, new flours have appeared on the market. Therefore, there is a lot more information about the combinations of flours and additives. Because of its texture and taste, the most common flour used in gluten-free baking is the white rice flour. The white rice flour has a very mild flavor, which allows for other flours to be mixed in to create the various gluten-free baked products.

Challenge Yourself

I know many baking and cooking methods have been done in a certain way for a long time. It is natural to assume that this is the only way. Finding a simpler way is the challenge for this art. Complicated recipes are the norm of my work, yet I try to simplify things without compromising the taste. Why take unnecessary steps and use complicated methods if you can avoid it? In my baking, I have broken many rules. The only rule I have not broken is the final result of my work. I found that breaking up some of the old tired techniques sometimes improves the final taste. The simple truth about baking as well as cooking is this: take pride in your work and use the best ingredients available. Use your judgment about changing or substituting ingredients. You can only fail once, but the lesson learned from the experience is invaluable.

Never be intimidated. Develop your own style and techniques with this great art. If you develop a true love for baking, it will show in every morsel of your creation. Do read carefully through all the recipe ingredients and instructions before beginning. Follow directions carefully. Most of my desserts rely on the marriage of many complicated tastes and textures. Be sure to read the recipe before beginning to understand the method used. Directions follow each list of ingredients. It will be beneficial to read through the entire book for facts, information, history, and other tips. Above all – enjoy yourself!

Substitutions for Healthier Choices

Sweeteners

Even though refine sugar and artificial sweeteners are under increased scrutiny because of their unhealthy impact and side-effects, their general consumption is on the rise. It is a puzzling fact since there is research to back the claims of the damage they do to our health. Some sweeteners must be used when it comes to desserts, some breakfast items, and drinks – there is no way around it. However, for those who follow a healthy diet or must avoid unhealthy sweeteners for medical reasons, the most frequent question is what kind of sweetener to use in order to avoid refined sugar, some artificial sweeteners, or high fructose corn syrup. The answer is that there are plenty of healthy alternatives. Sugar is overly processed and high quantities of it will do much damage to your health. Natural sweeteners are sugar sources that are somewhat in a pure state. The less refined products maintain their vitamins, minerals and antioxidants, and some fiber. Plus, some of these natural sweeteners like banana puree, date paste, and natural fruit jams provide fruit-health benefits. Following a healthy lifestyle does it mean that we must give up the sweetness entirely. You can substitute unhealthy artificial sweeteners and high fructose corn syrup with various natural sweeteners.

Sugar adds texture and volume to baking. Substituting sugar with fruits can be a bit tricky. Here is where the knowledge of food chemistry and texture comes in handy. If you liquidate the fruit, your baking goods' center will remain unbaked; It is best to chop the fruit in small pieces. Also, if you have to adjust the consistency, you might have to add a bit more flour. If you have to add moistness, add another egg or a bit of applesauce or yogurt. It is good to know that egg yolks adds moisture and egg whites dry our your baking goods. Typically gluten-free flours absorb more moisture than wheat flour. It is the main reason most gluten-free baking recipes used applesauce or yogurt. In general, nut flours such as almonds or coconut flour absorb large amounts of liquid.

The best fruits to be used for sweeteners, Bananas, Mangoes, Apples, Pears, or Dates, to name a few. My favorite sweetener is coconut sugar for its taste and consistency.

HEALTHIER ALTERNATIVES

Natural Fruit Sweeteners

On top of my list are the natural fruit sweeteners. The prominent fruits to be used as sweeteners are dates and bananas. Dates are loaded with potassium, copper, iron, manganese, magnesium, and vitamin B6. They are easily digested and help to metabolize proteins, fats, and carbohydrates. To use dates as sweetener, you must make a date paste, soak dates in hot water until soft, for about an hour. Add the soaked dates to your food processor, along with a little water and blend until smooth. Add a bit more water if needed to create a thick paste. Date paste can be used in many recipes. Use it in cookie, muffin, pie, or cake recipes to reduce sugar and boost the nutrients. Usually, a half cup of date paste will substitute 1 cup of sugar. The drawback with dates is that they are high in calories. One dry date contains about 65 calories. Bananas are sweet with a subtle flavor making them an excellent natural sweetener. To make a banana puree, place them in your food processor with a bit of water and blend to the consistency of applesauce. To give the banana puree an extra flavor, substitute the water with lime juice. Bananas can be used as an equal amount to sugar. For 1 cup of sugar, replace it with 1 cup of banana puree. One cup of bananas contains about 200 calories. Berries, apples, pears, and grapes are great sweeteners either as fruit or pure fruit jam. You can make fruit jamwith no sugar or pectin. Fruit jams can be used as an equal amount; 1 cup of sugar replace it with 1 cup of fruit jam. Using fruit sweeteners as an alternative to sugar will change the consistency of your recipe. You either have to use less liquid or more thickener to bring your recipe to desired consistency. It takes a bit of practice, but it is well worth the effort to not only produce a healthier food for your family but to create new tastes. The fruit sweeteners will boost the flavor of your recipe.

Honey

Diluted honey, thinned out with other elements, has always been around. However, since health-conscious people are looking for a healthier alternative and honey was the first choice on the list, its popularity lately has sky-rocketed. With the increased demand in the last few years, some honey producers invented many adulterate and sophisticated methods to produce honey. Therefore, the impurity of honey has become more complicated. Pure honey is packed with enzymes, antioxidants, iron, zinc, potassium, calcium, phosphorous, and vitamins B6, niacin and riboflavin. Once the honey is refined, it loses most of the health benefits. A pure label on the honey jar does not guarantee at all that it is not diluted with water and further sweetened with other syrups. It is relatively safe to buy local raw honey directly from a trusted beekeeper. Local honey comes from the bees that live in your neighborhood and may be helpful to improve seasonal allergies. It is believed that the darker the honey, the richer the flavor and the greater the health benefits. Unfortunately, you cannot cook with honey in high temperatures. Some people believe that heating honey in high temperatures can be toxic. That is simply a myth. The main reason you do not use raw honey while baking in high heat is that it changes its make-up and destroys the enzymes, minerals, and vitamins. It is essential to look for raw, organic, unfiltered honey, and treat it like sugar when it comes to measurements. One tablespoon of raw honey contains about 65 calories. Raw honey is a superfood.

Coconut Sugar

My attraction to coconut sugar as a natural sweetener is about its low glycemic index and rich mineral content. Coconut sugar is made from the sweet nectar of flower buds of the coconut palm. It is packed with polyphenols and phytonutrients. Coconut sugar contains iron, zinc, calcium, potassium, antioxidants, and phosphorous, Coconut sugar is versatile and now available in many markets. I like coconut sugar because of its appealing taste. It comes with hints of date and caramel flavors, which gives an added flavor into your recipe. Another reason I like coconut sugar is that it is not as sweet as regular sugar. One of the reasons my desserts had an influential flavor is because the sugar was not the overbearing factor in the taste. I have used limited amounts of sugar or other flavors, like potent flavor fruits, vanilla, or cinnamon to balance the sugary aftertaste. The measurement of coconut sugar in recipes is just like traditional sugar. It is a bit coarser than regular sugar and if you like a more delicate texture, pulse it in your food processor a couple of times. Coconut sugar is hands down my first choice to use as a dry, granulated form. It is more expensive than other natural sweetens but well worth the price. One tablespoon of coconut sugar contains 45 calories.

Xylitol

Xylitol is a sugar alcohol with implanted sweetness. Xylitol contains neither alcohol nor sugar; it is a powder, typically extracted from birch wood; hence the word xylitol, from the Greek roots Xylo - which means "wood" and "–itol" signifying sugar alcohols. Researchers first discovered its oral health benefits decades ago. It was first used in Finland and it has been used as a sweetener in European countries. Xylitol has a pleasant sweetness ideal as a sugar substitute and quickly becoming an excellent choice for a sweetener. Whereas some sweeteners may cause health risks, studies show that xylitol has real health benefits. It doesn't spike blood sugar and eliminates the bacteria in your mouth. If you are looking for a healthier alternative to regular sugar, xylitol is one of the best choices. Xylitol is a white crystalline substance that looks and tastes like sugar. It can be used the same way you would use sugar teaspoon for teaspoon. Xylitol has 30 calories per tablespoon.

Alternative Flours

Tapioca Flour

Tapioca flour is now a staple for the gluten-free diet. Tapioca is low in all types of fats, protein, fiber, and essential vitamins or minerals. It tastes mild and slightly sweet. Tapioca is extracted from cassava roots, and even though will not provide the essential nutrients using tapioca makes it possible to recreate recipes without the use of all-purpose flour. Tapioca's presence in gluten- free diets is to be a thickening food agent. Tapioca has decent amounts of calcium, potassium and phosphorus. It contains low amounts of iron, magnesium and selenium

Arrowroot Flour

Arrowroot flour is made from a starchy substance extracted from a tropical plant known as Maranta arundinacea. It is a versatile flour and can be used as a thickener or mixed with other flours for gluten-free baking. Arrowroot gives a crispy texture to baking products. Because it is a starch-based flour it can be a good thickener for creamy soups and sauces. It could also be used to thicken the fillings for fruit pies. Arrowroot is a rich source of vitamin B9, calcium, potassium, magnesium,and phosphorus. It also contains low amounts of zinc and iron, as well as vitamins B1 and B6.

Coconut Flour

Coconut flour is another low-carb, gluten-free baking alternative flour. Its superior texture is suitable for baked goods and can even be added to smoothies to increase nutrition. The caution with coconut flour is that a small amount of flour will absorb a considerable amount of liquid; because it is so absorbent, it tends to have a drying effect on baked goods. The fact about glutenous flours is that the ones with higher protein content absorb more liquid. It is the same with gluten-free flours. Coconut flour has a high protein content, therefore, consumes high amounts of liquid. To control the drying effect when baking with coconut flour, use liquid or soft foods that are difficult to be absorbed, like plenty of eggs, honey, Greek yogurt or bananas. The egg whites help to provide structure to baked goods while the yolks offer moisture. It is always a good practice to beat your eggs separately. Separating the eggs improves the structure of many baked goods, mainly when you use coconut flour. Coconut flour is also a good source of fiber, and iron.

Almond Flour and Almond Meal

Almond flour is becoming a popular alternative to wheat flour. The difference between almond flour and almond meal is that almond flour is made from blanched and peeled almonds and almond meal contains the almond skin. Without the skin, almond flour is ideal for lighter texture foods, like cakes and muffins and the coarser almond meal is better suited for denser foods like biscotti, cookies or even pizza crusts. Pure almond flour and almond meal have just one ingredient – almonds. The extra fat in both almond products adds some excess moisture and richness to the recipes. The oil in the almond flour makes it safe to be baked in high temperatures. Almonds don't contain gluten. Therefore, a dough made with it doesn't act like a traditional dough; it will not rise with yeast. Almond flour combines well with mild spices and grated Parmesan cheese. The drawback with almond flour is that it is expensive. Almond meal is a bit less expensive, but they are worth the high price. Be careful though, if you find an inexpensive almond flour/meal, most likely it is not pure – it contains other flours as fillers.

Brown Rice Flour

Brown rice flour is one of the best substitutions for wheat flour. Even though brown rice flour contains much oil, it absorbs a lot of moisture. If you are using it for baking to compensate for the lack of gluten and to achieves a smoother consistency, adding additional liquid, like eggs or extra oil, is essential. If you are using a rising agent, like arrowroot powder, with brown rice flour, it tends to rise quickly. Gluten-free flours need to be baked in lower temperatures than recipes that contain wheat flour. It helps to refrigerate the gluten-free dough or batter for about an hour before using it. Although brown rice flour is an excellent replacement in baking, because of its darker color and flavor, it can be used as a thickening agent. Because the bran of brown flour is milled with the endosperm, brown rice flour has a higher level of fiber, iron, B vitamins than white rice flour. It is also high in protein, as all types of rice flour are.

Oat Flour

You can easily make your oat flour by putting dried oats into your food processor and pulse them into a fine powder. Oat flour adds moisture into baked goods. Therefore, it is an excellent choice for making cookies, quick breads, cakes or muffins. The mild flavor and light texture of oats do not overpower your baking items. Oats gives a chewy texture to cookies and moistness to breads, cakes and muffins. Also, it lends thickness to brownies and pancakes. Bottom line, oat flour is a useful flour for gluten-free baking. It is also one of the healthiest flours. Oat flour is high in fiber and many vitamins and minerals. It is high in potassium, phosphorous, magnesium, iron, manganese, calcium and reasonable amounts of calcium, zinc and selenium.

Fruits Used in the Recipes of This Book

Apples

You might want to re-think before removing the skin from the apple. The skin of the apple contains large amounts of vitamin C, potassium, calcium and fiber. The skin of many other fruits and vegetables also contain various nutrients. The problem with the skin of fresh produce is the pesticide. It is one of the many reasons that many fruits and vegetables we eat should be organic. Apples are a good source of fiber and several antioxidants. Apples used in salads, smoothies, cooking and baking. Apples pairs well with almond, walnuts, caramel, cinnamon, raisins, ginger. The tree originated in Central Asia and have been grown for thousands of years around the world.

Bananas

Bananas contain vitamins B6, C, A, as well folate, riboflavin, niacin, manganese, potassium, magnesium, iron, protein and fiber. Bananas have been part of our diet for about two-thousand five hundred years. Bananas are the most popular fruit in the world. The origin of bananas is placed in Southeast Asia. From there it spread to the Philippines and Africa. Bananas are the perfect snack; they are nutritious, inexpensive and safe, protected by its thick skin. It is excellent in smoothies, bread, cakes, with pancakes and oatmeal, and of course with peanut butter.

Blueberries

This super-fruit has an impressive nutrition profile. Blueberries have the highest antioxidant content of the most commonly consumed fruits. Flavonoids appear to be the blueberries' antioxidant with the most significant impact. They contain high amounts of fiber, vitamin C, vitamin K and manganese, and decent amounts of folate, choline, vitamins A and E, and manganese. Blueberries are versatile in the kitchen. They can be used in salads, smoothies, with yogurt, in baking, or just eat them by the handful. Native Americans used blueberries for centuries. They ate blueberries fresh and dried them to preserve them for the winter. Blueberry juice was used by Native Americans for medical reasons and to dye their clothes and baskets. Its leaves were used to make a medicinal tea. English settlers tried unsuccessfully to cultivate blueberries since the early sixteen-hundreds, but it wasn't until 1910 that farmers were successful in growing blueberries. Finally, in 1916, blueberries made their way to the American

Cherries

Cherries are a good source of vitamin C, vitamin A, calcium, protein and iron and very high in potassium. It seems like cherries have been present around the globe since ancient times. The Chinese, Greeks and Romans used cherries for centuries. Cherries pits were brought to America by French colonists in the sixteen-hundreds. The French grew cherries along the Saint Lawrence River and the Great Lakes. Today, cherries grow into different colors and tastes. The tart cherries are bright red, and the most common sweet cherries are the bing cherries. Bing cherries come in various colors as well. They are mostly dark, and sometimes are black or purple. Because of its different flavors, today's chefs find creative ways to use them. Cherries can be used in sweets, smoothies, breakfasts, in sauces, desserts, and with some grains. In this book, I have a pancake recipe made with buckwheat flour, cherries and pears.

Figs

Figs are rich in minerals including potassium, calcium, magnesium, iron and copper and a good source of the antioxidant vitamins A, E and K that contribute to health and wellness. Firmenich, the world largest privately owned fragrance and flavor company, named the fig as the 2018 flavor of the year. Because of this, it expected hat more people, outside the Mediterranean, are about to discover the tremendous nutritional value, remarkable versatility of the complex sweet, smooth and silky tasting fig. The history of figs is as fascinating as is its taste. The word sycophant, from the Greek sykophantes; from sykon "fig" and phainein "to show, make known." Many stories have been created over the years to give sense to the composition of this word. Whatever reason, this word was created for those who illegally exported figs did not pay taxes for the fig sales or harmed the fig trees.

As stories evolved, figs and the word sykophantes described shady people. Figs were loved in ancient Greece so much that sycophant offenders were arrested and prosecuted. The love of the fig has not changed much over the years in the Mediterranean. Firmenich used over ten flavors trying to describe the taste of fig. These descriptors will not make sense unless you've eaten fresh figs at peak ripeness. I get it. Growing up in Greece, I had the privilege to consume tons of figs during the hot summer months. Figs can be used as appetizers, salads, and in both cooking and baking. In Greece, the ultimate compliment to a chef when asked about the taste of the food is to say, "It was just like a cold fig."

Mango

Mangos are high in vitamins C and A. They contains goodly amounts of vitamins B6, K, folate, potassium,calcium, copper and iron, as well as antioxidants and beta-carotene, and small amounts of protein. Mangoes are native to India. They were cultivated for the first time around five thousand years ago. Fortunately, the cultivation of mangoes spread to all tropical regions of the world. Because of their exquisite and unusual flavor mangoes are regarded as the king of the tropical fruit. Mango can be used to make a sweet and sour salsa and chutney; it is great with yogurt and in smoothies. In this book, I have a fruit relish recipe with mango and pineapple. Also, I use it in a salad with quinoa, yogurt and other fruits. While in the restaurant, I created a white cake with mango mousse and kiwi white chocolate. Today it is the most requested cake for family birthdays

Pears

Pears are high in vitamins C, K, and potassium. They have small amounts of calcium, iron, magnesium, riboflavin, vitamin B-6, and folate. Pears are popular as appetizers and desserts. They can be served with hard or soft cheese and salads. Their subtle, distinct flavor works well with dark chocolate, sweet sauces and baked goods. There are thousands of pear varieties grown in countries with temperate climates. Like bananas, pears are not tree-ripened, they are sold when firm, but to get their full flavor they must be ripened before serving. Pears are one of the world's oldest cultivated fruits. In The Odyssey, Homer praises pears as a "gift of the gods." The Roman farmers documented extensive pear growing and pears have been a muse in the works of Renaissance masters. Pears are versatile and have a long storage life.

Raspberries

Raspberries are rich in vitamin C and K and contains good amounts vitamin E, iron, potassium, manganese and lesser amounts of thiamin, riboflavin, niacin, pantothenic acid, vitamin B-6, calcium. Natives of Asia Minor and North America collected raspberries as a food source for centuries. By the Middle Ages, wild raspberries had many uses. Artists used raspberry juice in paintings and physicians recommended the fruit, leaves, and roots for various medical reasons. When the first European settlers migrated to America, Native Americans were drying raspberries to preserve them. Since the early eighteen-hundreds raspberries are made into preserves and syrups. Raspberries seem to have originated in Asia. Since then, raspberries have been widely bred, with a multitude of varieties. Raspberries were long considered a luxury, as only the rich were able to enjoy this delicate fruit. Today, raspberries rank high on the list of the world's most popular berries. Raspberries are extremely versatile fruits and can be used in sauces, jams, smoothies, ice cream, salads, pies, cakes, or pancakes. I use raspberries for my baking – they partner well with dark chocolate. Some decades ago I created a recipe for breakfast called Raspberry Stuffed Toast. It is a staple in every one of our family gatherings for brunch.

Strawberries

Strawberries contain iron, copper, magnesium, phosphorus, vitamin B6, vitamin K and vitamin E. Strawberries are a good source of vitamin C, manganese, folate and potassium. Strawberries are the most cultivated berry in the United States. Most commercial strawberries in the United States are grown in California or Florida, where the climate helps to extend the strawberry growing season. The best strawberries are brightly colored, plump and have fresh green caps attached. Strawberries do not ripen after being picked, so if you buy the partly white ones, it means that they were not ripe when picked. Here is a good time to talk about pesticides. For the past three years strawberries have topped the Environmental Working Group's dirty dozen list of fruits and vegetables with the most pesticide residues. While others, including the alliance for food and farming, view the report with skepticism. Following the dirty dozen list is spinach in which most of the samples contained pesticide residues. Among the fruits and vegetable making a list are some other favorite items, including apples, grapes, tomatoes and cherries.

Natural versus Chemicals

Adding color to the icing or the filling of cakes with natural foods provides a boost in the taste and transparency to the appearance. The artificial food colors include none of the above. Most of the artificial colors are harmful to your health and visually unpleasantly, clad with unnatural, vibrant colors. Do your research before using chemicals in your food. There are several fruits and other food items to use as prime for coloring. The fruits commonly used in baking are raspberries for their various red or purple shades, blueberries for light blue, strawberries for pink, blackberries for lavender, cherries or pomegranates for pink or red. For various brown shades use coffee and cocoa or even a bit of cinnamon, especially to white chocolate or cream cheese.

For fruit color: Place one cup of water and half a cup of fruit in a small saucepan. Bring to a boil, reduce heat and simmer for 2 to 3 minutes, then place the mixture in a food processor and pulse a couple of times. Strain the mixture using a fine-mesh sieve and use the liquid for coloring. You can adjust the shade of the color by the cooking time. The longer you cook, the deeper the color gets.

About Nuts

Most nuts are high in omega-3 fatty acids. Also, nuts contain high amounts of fiber, protein, Vitamin E, and a variety of essential minerals. Raw nuts contain the highest numbers of these healthy nutrients. Roasting nuts reduce the antioxidant content and can reduce the amount of healthy fats. Nuts are a common snack food and can be used as a vegetarian protein source. Because nuts are quite high in calories, they are a naturally compact source of energy, which is perfect for traveling. Since ancient times, grounded nuts were used, in some cultures, to thicken various sauces. I use this method in some of my creamy sauces.

Almonds

Almonds deliver a massive amount of nutrients: Fiber, manganese, magnesium, vitamin E,copper, riboflavin and phosphorus.

Chestnuts

Chestnuts are high in manganese, vitamin C, vitamin B6 and copper and vitamin C.

Hazelnuts

Hazelnuts are high in magnesium, calcium andvitamins B and E.

Pecans

Pecans are high in healthy unsaturated fat. They also contain vitamins A, B, and E, folic acid, calcium, magnesium, phosphorus, potassium, and zinc.

Pistachios

Pistachios are extremely rich in potassium. They are high in protein, fiber and antioxidants.

Walnuts

Walnuts contain good fats. They also contain iron, selenium, calcium, zinc, and vitamin E.

Macadamia Nuts

Macadamia nuts are high in manganese, thiamine and copper. They contain good amounts of magnesium, iron, vitamin B6, protein and fiber.

The ancient Greeks and later the Romans used finely ground nuts, especially walnuts and almonds, for food thickeners and used various nuts to extract oil.

SPICES

Cinnamon

The healing superspice. Cinnamon is another good healing superspice that contains large amounts of highly potent polyphenol antioxidants. It is so powerful that cinnamon can be used as a natural food preservative. Cinnamon also includes a small amount of vitamin E, niacin, vitamin B6, magnesium, potassium, zinc and copper. Sweet, aromatic and spicy flavors. Cinnamon is both sweet and spicy which is the reason it does well in both baking and cooking. It is extremely aromatic as well. Cinnamon is a personal favor.

Cloves

Cloves contain fiber, vitamins and minerals. Among them vitamin K and C, calcium, magnesium and potassium. Cloves have a bitter, intense aroma and fruity, woody undertones. Cloves contain high consternation of oil which during cooking or baking time releases a sweet warm flavor.

Fennel and Anise

When it comes to cooking and baking, anise is not to be confused with fennel. Some believe that those two are interchangeable in recipes. This is incorrect. While the aroma is similar, the taste is not. The fronds of fennel have leaves resembling dill, the bulb is citrusy, and the seed is extremely licorice; all parts of fennel can be used for cooking. From the anise plant, you can only use their seed for flavoring. The anise seed has a distinct flavor that is at once spicy and sweet with a mild licorice accent. Fennel is a plant whose parts carry several different flavors and anise is a seed with a more intense flavor, especially the licorice.

Ginger

Ginger is an excellent natural source of vitamin C, magnesium, potassium, copper, and manganese. Ginger is fierce and peppery with lemon/citrus aroma undertones. When cooked has a mild sweetness with warm flavor. Its complex flavor makes ginger versatile for both baking and cooking.

Shredded Coconut

Shredded Coconut is available both sweetened and unsweetened. Sweetened coconut has been combined with sugar. The sweetened coconut is best to use for toasted coconut. When toasted, it loses most of its sweetness. Toasted coconut is an excellent addition to baked goods and salads. There are two ways to toast coconut.

*Place coconut in a saúte pan and cook over low heat, frequently stirring, until the flakes are golden brown.

*Preheat oven to 300-degrees. Spread coconut flakes on a baking sheet and bake. Stir coconut frequently to ensure even color. Coconut will toast quickly, 5 to 8 minutes.

The method of balancing flavors; using mild spices for the potent foods and strong herbs and spices for the poor tasting ones, is the fundamental principle of creating recipes and the formula used by today's creative chefs to make up new recipes with harmonious flavors. The primary objective is to create a taste so that all flavors "dance" in your mouth rather than just one particular taste overpowering all others.

Working with Chocolates

Cocoa butter, the natural fat of the cocoa bean, contributes to the aroma, making the difference in the taste of the chocolate. The cocoa butter adds to the difficulty of working with chocolate and sometimes makes it unpredictable. If it is overheated, it sometimes turns to lumps, sometimes is dull, sometimes shiny. If added to another mixture with a different temperature, it may become gritty. White chocolate is even more delicate to work with because of its high milk content. Always handle chocolate gently when you work with it, especially the melting process.

The quality of the chocolate depends on the raw material and the handling of the different stages of preparation by the manufacturer. It is essential to roast and crush the cocoa beans and mix them with sugar or other ingredients. Good chocolate should be shiny brown, free of bubbles, white specs, and should break cleanly. It should melt like butter, have the true aroma of chocolate rather than cocoa powder, and is neither sticky nor greasy. The more cocoa butter it contains, the creamier it becomes when melted.

The best way is to melt chocolate is in a water bath, in low heat, uncovered. You do not want to cook the chocolate but melt it. The low heat will melt, eventually, every type of chocolate It may take longer for some than others, you have to pay attention to the process. I found that chocolate melts faster and smoothly if done in very low heat. It helps if the chocolate is cut into smaller pieces. There are a couple of reasons if chocolate transforms from smooth and shiny to a mass of dull paste. One is that the chocolate is burned from too much heat. Another reason is that if it is mixed with a cold liquid; the cold substances immediately hardens the chocolate and forms gritty particles. Do not mix warm chocolate with cold creams. Whatever you do – handle chocolate with care.

Semisweet Chocolate

Good semisweet chocolate contains 60 to 75% cocoa butter and is easier to work with compared to other types of chocolates. Unsweetened chocolate is 100% chocolate and challenging to work with it. Milk chocolates contain only 10% cocoa butter and 50% sugar. When mixed with other ingredients it loses most of its character. My favorite chocolate to work with is semisweet chocolate. It has some sweetness to limit the added sugar use and it is bitter enough to maintain the chocolate characteristics.

White Chocolate

It is made with cocoa butter, milk, sugar, and oil. The more cocoa butter that is used, the more addictive this white wonder becomes. It is difficult to find quality white chocolate. The best white chocolate is that of an ivory color. White chocolate does not tolerate high heat. White chocolate is one of my weaknesses.

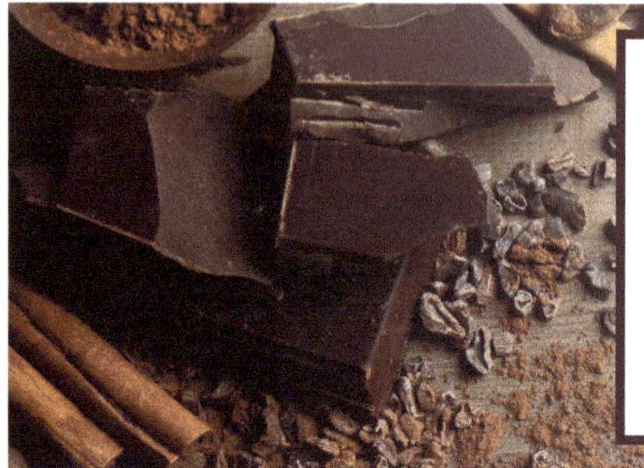

The cocoa tree grows only in tropical regions, approximately 20 degrees of the Equator. This wide branching tropical evergreen tree is found mainly in the great cocoa plantations in South and Central America and Africa. It produces fruits, which contain between 30 to 50 seeds. These are the cocoa beans. Once they are pick, they are left for about one week to ferment and develop the cocoa aroma. Then they are dried and sent to chocolate manufacturing companies.

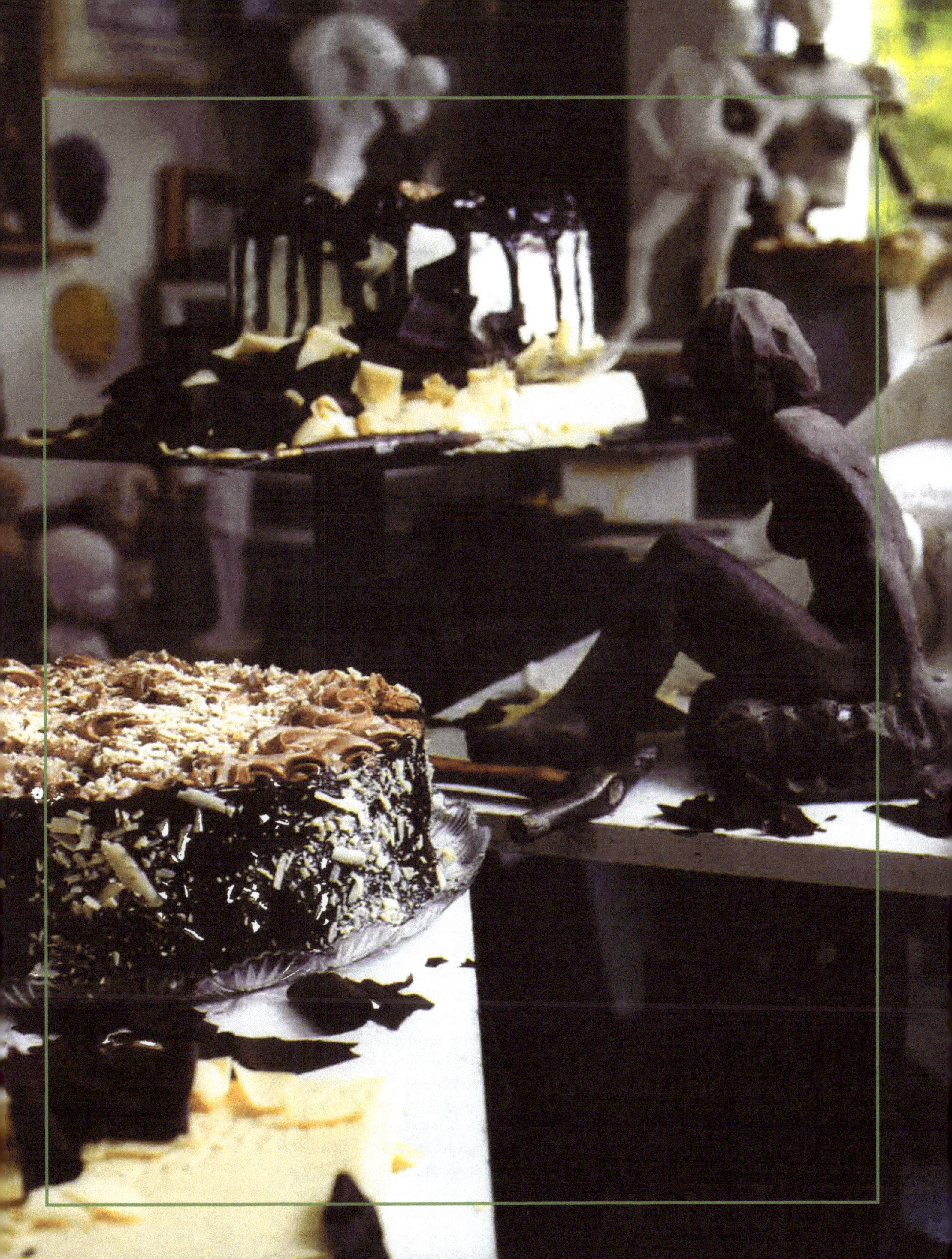

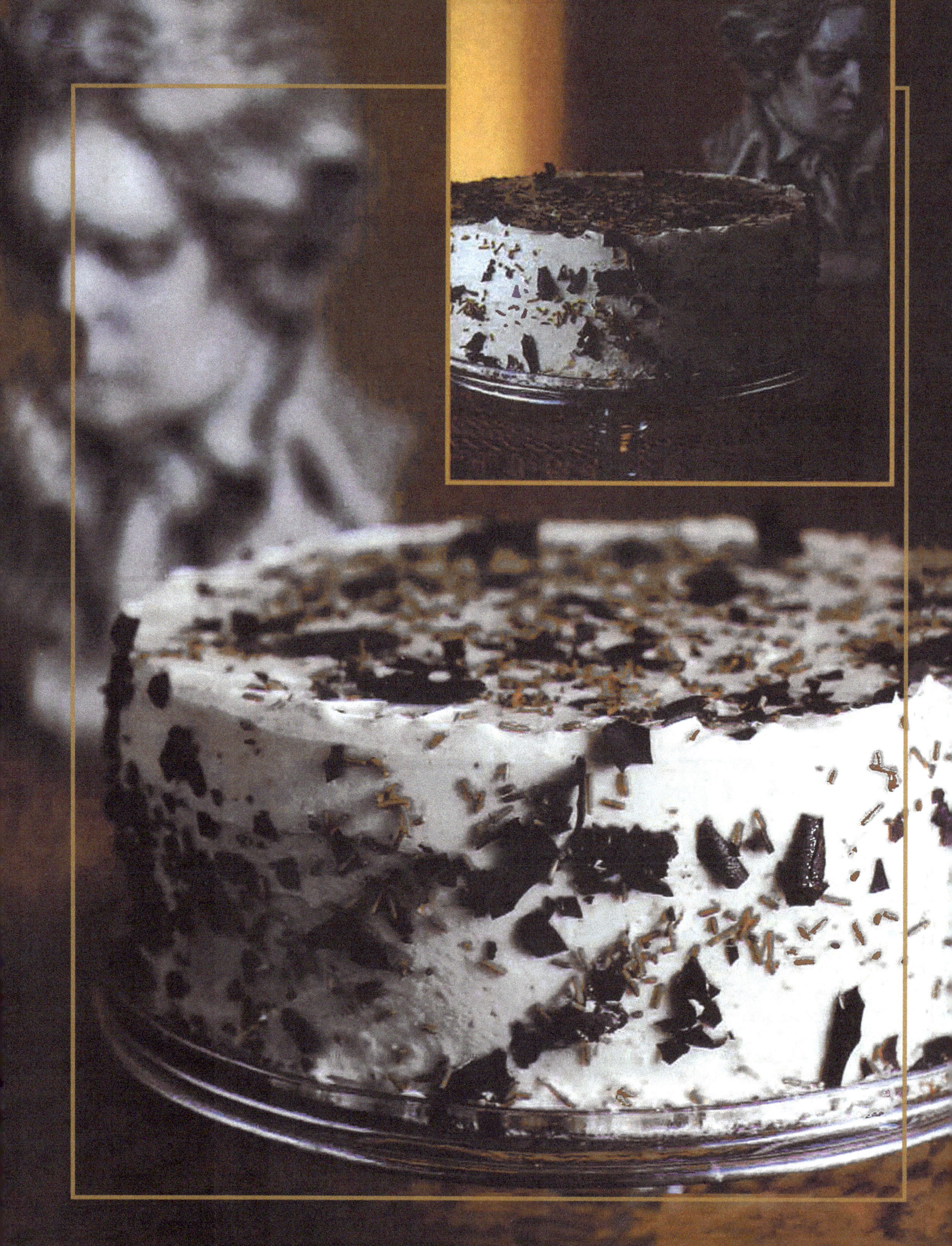

The Chocolate Addiction

At the beginning of the 4th Century AD, a group of people came down from Alaska to occupy the peninsula located between Guatemala and Mexico. Those people were the Mayas and the peninsula was Yucatan. This remarkable civilization existed in the 5th Century; It built pyramids, temples, and paved roads. Suddenly for an unknown reason, the Mayans went into the virgin forest and never came out, leaving behind the abandoned cities they had built. Some were even left halfway built. In the forest, the Mayans discovered a tree that had grown about 10 meters tall. This tree became the tree of the Mayan gods. The trees' seeds were an offering to their gods. The seed of the cocoa pod, which later was named "bean" was roasted and then crushed between two stones. It was then boiled in water and the Mayans drank it, thanking their gods for being good and allowing people to share their sacred food. This boiled liquid was named "tshacabouku". Before they went to war, for additional calories and energy, they mixed the boiled powder with maize or honey and musk and drank it. They attributed this energy to their gods. In the early 15th Century, when the Spanish reached Central America, there was nothing left of the Mayan, but their forgotten cities and few primitive tribes who called themselves Mayans.

By this time, the Aztecs occupied this territory, replacing the Toctecs who came after the Mayans. The Aztecs came down to this territory from North America. In their need for provisions, they went into the forest and were forced to fight the Mayans for everything they brought out. The most precious possession was the bean of the tree so that the Aztecs could make the liquid for the gods. They named this liquid "tchocoalt". There is a myth that claims that the decision of the Mayans to enter the forest and never come out was caused by the departure of the bearded god Quetzalcoatl who disappeared going east in the great ocean towards the rising sun. It was to him that this tree, "cacabuaquchtl" was dedicated.

Throughout the centuries, people would whisk the powder of this bean with boiling water into a froth and drink as much as possible, awaiting the return of their god. Finally, their god arrived. He was a strange bearded creature clad in iron that came from the East across the great sea. People were delirious with joy and hailed him as their god. This "god" was none other than the conquistador Hernando Cortez who, on his quest for gold, took advantage of the unexpected welcome and asked for their treasure. They led him into plantations where he at first was greatly disappointed but eventually realized that the mountains of cocoa were as valuable as mountains of gold.

A few years earlier, Columbus, in his fourth voyage into what now is Nicaragua, sent cocoa beans to Spain. However, nobody knew how to rid them of their forbidden bitterness. Hernando Cortez, who had tasted chocolate as a liquid, brought back the knowledge of how the Aztecs treated the bean. By the time Cortez and his crew went back home a couple of years later, they were so addicted to the chocolate drink that they kept pots full at all times and some of them even lost the urge to drink alcoholic drinks.

Voyages were made to Central America for this chocolate to convert people to Christianity, and also to bring back the chocolate. By now, the flavoring had changed to sugar, vanilla, and cream. In the late 15th Century, the first full cargo reached land in Europe and, despite the high price, was sold in just a few hours. The Spanish ladies developed a passion for cocoa and drank it flavored with cinnamon.

It even became an issue of the church. The ladies had this liquid served in the communion table, claiming that liquid does not break the fast. Pope Clement VIII, who liked cocoa, was given the task of resolving whether drinking chocolate broke the fast. A few years later, a group of priests in Madrid opposed this idea along with the idea of drinking chocolate before celebrating the mass.

In the early 16th Century, this Spanish specialty was brought to Naples, and its addictive taste spread all over Italy. It was then introduced to the Netherlands and France, where it became a great success with high society. Later, it was introduced to Germany. In the late 16th Century, the English finally gave in to the chocolate temptation, which they, up until now, had turned up their noses due to anti-Spanish political reasons. By now, Europe was addicted to chocolate. In the middle of the 17th Century, the addiction would spread to America. Throughout the centuries, the chocolate addiction would grow as the technique of forming the liquid chocolate into solid form and flavoring it with creative flavors continued to improve.

The 350-degree Protocol

Why all baking authorities insist on baking cakes at 350-degrees? In just about every cookbook, the 350-degree is the standard temperature to bake cakes. What is it about that number? Is it going to be a national disaster if the oven's dial is a few numbers off?

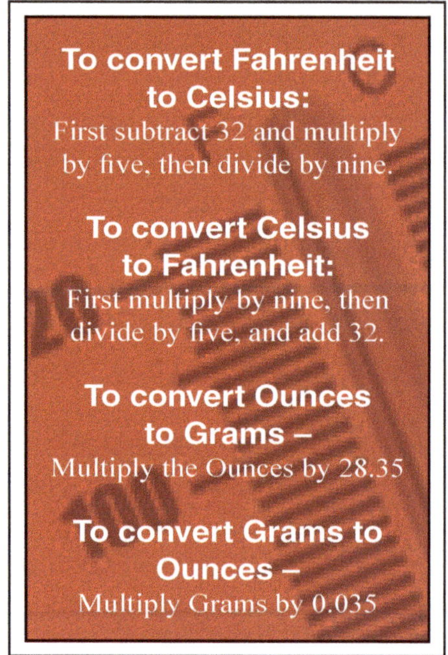

To understand the over-temperature obsession, we must realize what is going on during the baking of a cake – when a gooey batter transforms into an irresistible delight. There is a chemical reaction during the complex process of transformation, and that reaction is based on the oven temperature. In lower temperatures, these chemical reactions occur slowly. The batter's rise begins at the outer crust and gradually reacts towards the center of the dough. In higher temperatures, the process moves on at a fast pace; therefore, there is an uneven distribution of temperature to all parts of the dough. Consequently, a cake baked around 300 to 325-degrees is much lighter, but the crust of the cake will be relatively soft. A cake baked between 375 to 400-degrees will have crusty edges and dried texture.

Baking your cake in 350-degrees is the ideal temperature to bake a light in texture with a firm crust. However, a few degrees, more or less, will not make much difference. The point is that every oven is deferent.

You must pay attention to the accuracy of your oven to predict the outcome of your cake. If you do not get the results you like, adjust the temperature of your oven. The 350-degree oven is the benchmark to start baking cakes, but you can adjust the temperature dial-up or down a bit.

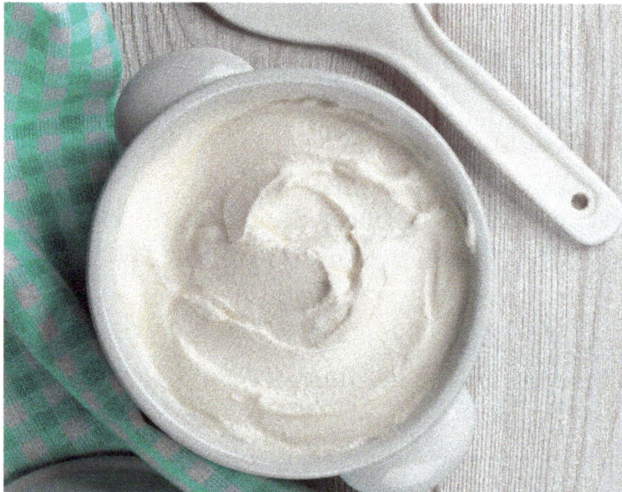

Sour cream adds fat to your baking goods for a richer, creamier, and thicker cake. Cakes without any fat tend to be drier. Also, sour cream activates the raising agents and helps the browning of the cake. The acidity of sour cream will reduce the sweetness of your cake and create a smoother taste.

THE CONVENIENT TRUTH ABOUT CONVENIENCE

Unhealthy cookware and cluttered kitchen

For several decades I've been using stainless steel sauté pans. The main reason I used them is that stainless steel heats up very fast and holds the heat well. Also, it is durable and lasts for a long time. I still have and use for home cooking, some of the stainless steel pans used in my restaurants. My children have a few of them and will most likely hand them down to their children. I was pleased to discover that stainless steel is one of the healthiest cookware to use several years after using stainless steel cookware. Today I use cast iron stock pots as well. Cast iron cookware is probably the safest and most effective cookware in the kitchen. While cast iron is relatively heavy and takes a while to heat up, it holds heat very well and is oven-safe.

LIQUID MEASURE

1 tsp	⅙ oz	5 grams
1 tbsp	½ oz	15 grams
1 cup	8 oz	227 grams
2 cups (1 pint)	16 oz	454 grams
4 cups (1 quart)	32 oz	907 grams
⅔ tbsp	3 ½ oz	100 grams
1 cup plus 1 tbsp	8 ½ oz	250 grams
4 ⅓ cups	2.2 lbs	1000 grams (1 kilo)

EGGS

1 large egg = 2 oz
1 large egg white = 1 ¼ oz
1 large egg yolk = ¾ oz

Glass cookware tends to be mostly for baking and is entirely non-toxic. Glass isn't the most dynamic cooking material and it's somewhat limited in its use in the kitchen. However, to be used as baking dishes, there aren't many more safe and affordable materials than heatproof glass. Ceramic cookware is non-toxic as well, as long as they are correctly glazed with a glass-like surface. Glass and ceramic are durable and versatile. They could be moved from the stovetop to the oven and the refrigerator or freezer. For convenience, using non-stick cookware, such as Teflon, is most likely the most dangerous cookware to use. The non-stick properties of Tefl on cookware are coated with polytetrafluoroethylene (PTFE), a plastic polymer that leaches toxins when heated on high heat. Aluminum and copper cookware can be very toxic when used in high temperatures also. These heavy metals are released into foods during cooking and end up in your body. Please do your research about the cookware you are using.

During my years in the restaurant business, everyone in the kitchen knew my fixation about having an organized, clean, and decluttered kitchen. Organization in your kitchen, knowing where everything is, allows you to speed up your cooking process and keep an inventory of foods. I don't like my kitchen to be crowded with gadgets that I will use once in a long while. Why do I need things like a garlic peeler, strawberry huller, citrus zesters, food chopper, melon ballers, or a banana slicer? There is nothing these things can do that I cannot accomplish with my knives. Not sure why I would need an egg separator, or a rice cooker or an electric steamer. Besides the obvious items, like knives, mixing bowls, serving spoons, etc., the equipment which are used continuously in my kitchen are my food processor and stand up mixer.

Essential kitchen tools needed using this book

- Stand Up Mixer with various attachments: The flat edge beater is the all-purpose attachment for various mixtures. The wire whip uses it for whipping cream and the dough hook for bread.
- Food Processor: Pulsing allows you to regulate the texture of your food. The pulsing function on a food processor works by turning the blade a few turns at the time. Pulsing in a food processor for one second is about the right time. Any longer, the food is either mashed or liquefied.
- 10" x 3" springform pans: I use springform pans not only for cheesecakes but also for round chocolate cakes. It is easier to remove the cakes from it. For layer cakes that have to be refrigerated for their filling to set, I use springform pans as well. It keeps the cake uniformed and it is easier to ice the cakes.
- For birthdays and other special occasion cakes, use a 10" x 3" square pan. It holds the same amount of batter as the 10" x 3" springform pan.
- For Barcakes, use the same recipe for an approximately 11" x 4" x 3" loaf pan.
- For larger birthday or other special occasion parties, use an approximately 14" x 14" pan and double your recipe.
- For Quick Breads, I use 8" x 4" x 2 ½" glass or ceramic baking pan.
- For regular breads, I use 9" x 5" x 2 ½" glass or ceramic loaf pans.
- For muffins, I use a 12-cup muffin pan.
- For pies, I use a 9" deep glass plate.
- Pastry bags, I use large and small bags with a large and small star and straight tips.
- Baking trays for cookies, biscottis, and other uses. Large and small mixing bowls, rolling pin, plastic heat-resisting spatulas, decorating spatulas, wire whip, measuring cups, pastry brush.

WEIGHTS

Flour

½ oz	2 grams	1 tsp
¼ oz.	6 grams	1 tbsp
1 oz	33 grams	⅓ cup
3 ½ oz	100 grams	1 cup
16 oz (1 lb)	454 grams	4 ½ cups
2.2 lbs	1000 grams (1 kilo)	10 cups

Butter

1 pound = 2 cups or 32 tbsp or 424 grams

Sugar

1 cup = 8 oz or 454 grams

No Compromise on Quality

The use of quality ingredients is essential in both cooking and baking. The purity of ingredients and "old-school" techniques used is almost unprecedented today, an epoch of convenience and ready to use fillings and creams. For best tasting results, there should not be any artificial flavoring, no ready to use mixes, absolutely no compromise with quality. With little practice, you can master fundamental techniques. If you are comfortable using a knife to slice a cake, handle a spatula with a firm hand, release the cream from the pastry bag, you can also be celebrated as a true craftsman – a dedicated pastry chef.

Food extracts

There is nothing more unpleasant than the overpowering taste of a food extract in a baking item, especially that of almond extract, which tastes nothing like almonds. The pure almond extract is extracted from bitter almonds. All imitation and most natural extracts are chemically synthesized. The only extract I use is the pure vanilla extract. Every other extract can be substituted with natural flavors. For the almond extract, I grind almonds and use them for flavor and as a thickener. The same applies to any other nut flavoring. For orange or lemon flavors, I use the juice and the zest. For fruits such as the banana, raspberry, strawberry, mango, place the fruit in your processor, pulse 2 or 3 times and use the pulp for a natural fruit flavor for mousse, cream, or icing.

Pulsing

Pulsing allows you to regulate the texture of your food. The pulsing function on a food processor works by turning the blade a few turns at the time. Pulsing in a food processor for one second is about the right time. Any longer, the food is either mashed or liquefied.

About Double Boil

Fill a boiling pot to about one-quarter full. Turn heat to low. Place the chocolate in a bowl that fits the top of the boiling pot. Make sure the bowl does not touch the simmering water. Occasionally stir the chocolate with a heat-resistant spatula. Do not add cold heavy cream or whipped cream to the hot chocolate. Let the cream cool down to room temperature. Turn off the heat and let the chocolate cool off a bit before adding any cold substance.

Unsalted Butter – always

It is essential in baking to use unsalted butter. Salt is a mineral that can alter the chemistry of foods drastically. With unsalted butter, you have complete control of the overall flavor of your recipes. The difference between salted and unsalted butter is obviously the salt. Salt is also a preservative, which gives salted butter much longer shelf life. The unsalted butter is fresher since it has a shorter shelf life.

Melting Butter

Melt in a saucepan on low heat. Combining the hot butter with the batter is critical because melted butter tends to sink in the bottom of the saucepan while baking if not mixed thoroughly with the rest of the batter.

*"When it comes to cheesecakes at Nick's,
nothing succeeds like success. These are some of the
most decadent cheesecakes in the planet."*

— Best of Phoenix

*White Chocolate Pistachio
Cheesecake should only be served
in the presence of paramedics.*

— Best of Phoenix

"One ought to be acquainted with the power of juices, and what action each of them has upon man and their alliances towards one another. What I say is this. If a sweet juice changes to another kind, not from any admixture but because it has undergone a mutation within itself, what does it first become? Bitter? Salty? Austere? or Acid? I think acid. And hence, an acid juice is the most improper of all things that can be administered in case in which a sweet juice is most proper. Thus if one should succeed in his investigations of external things, he would be the better able always to select the best; for that is best which is farthest removed from that which is unwholesome."

— Hippocrates 460 - 370 BC

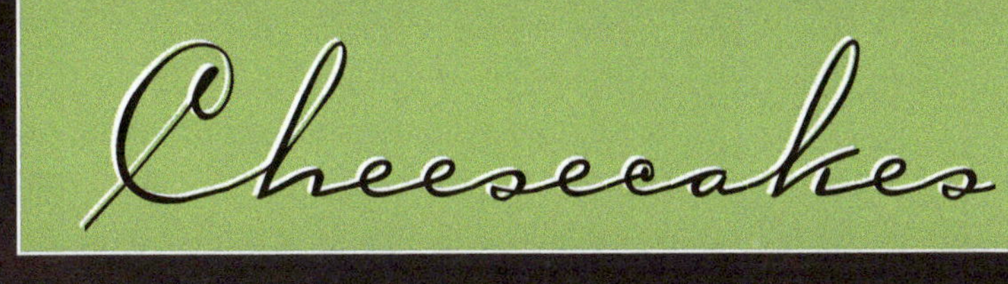
Cheesecakes

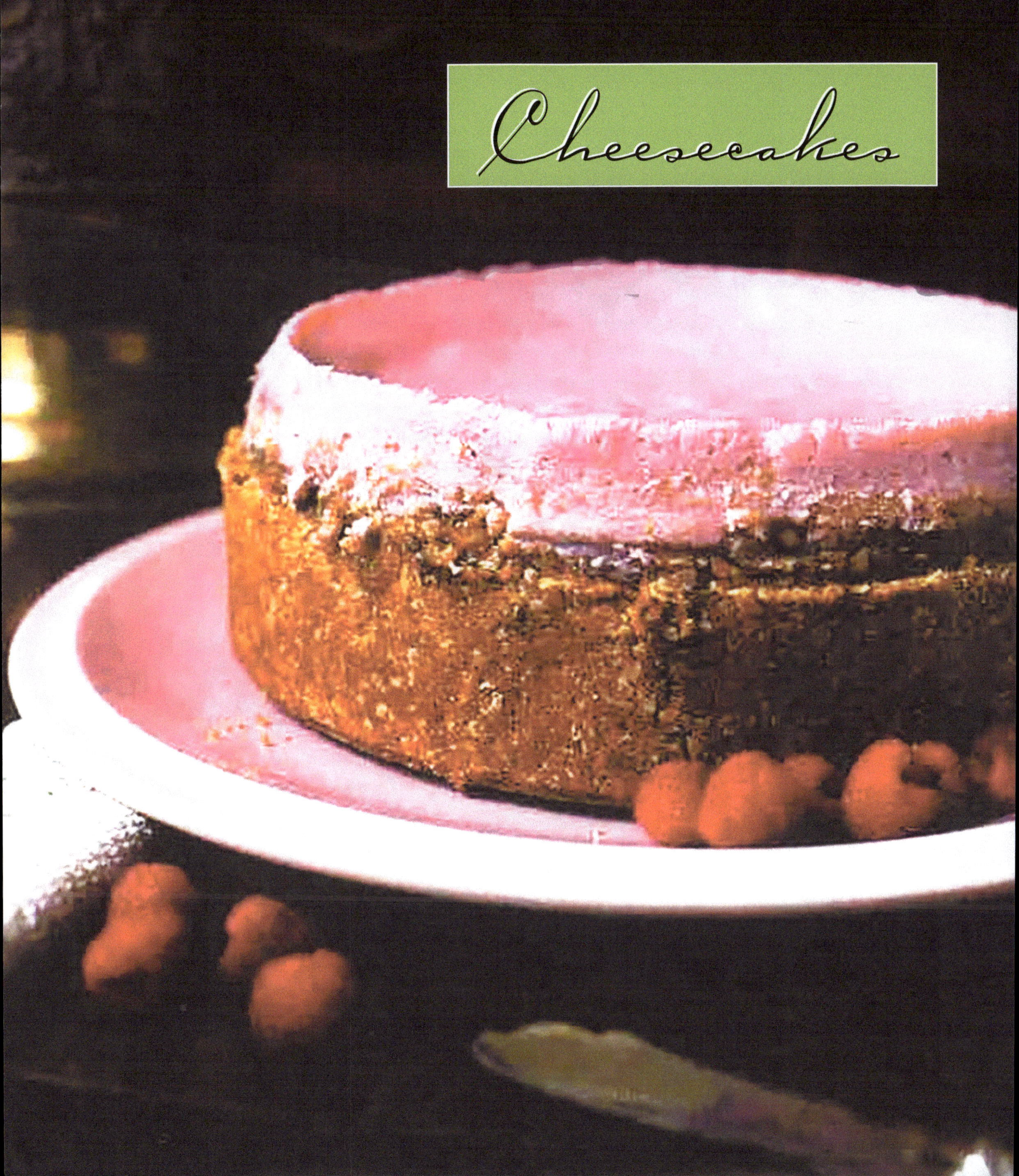

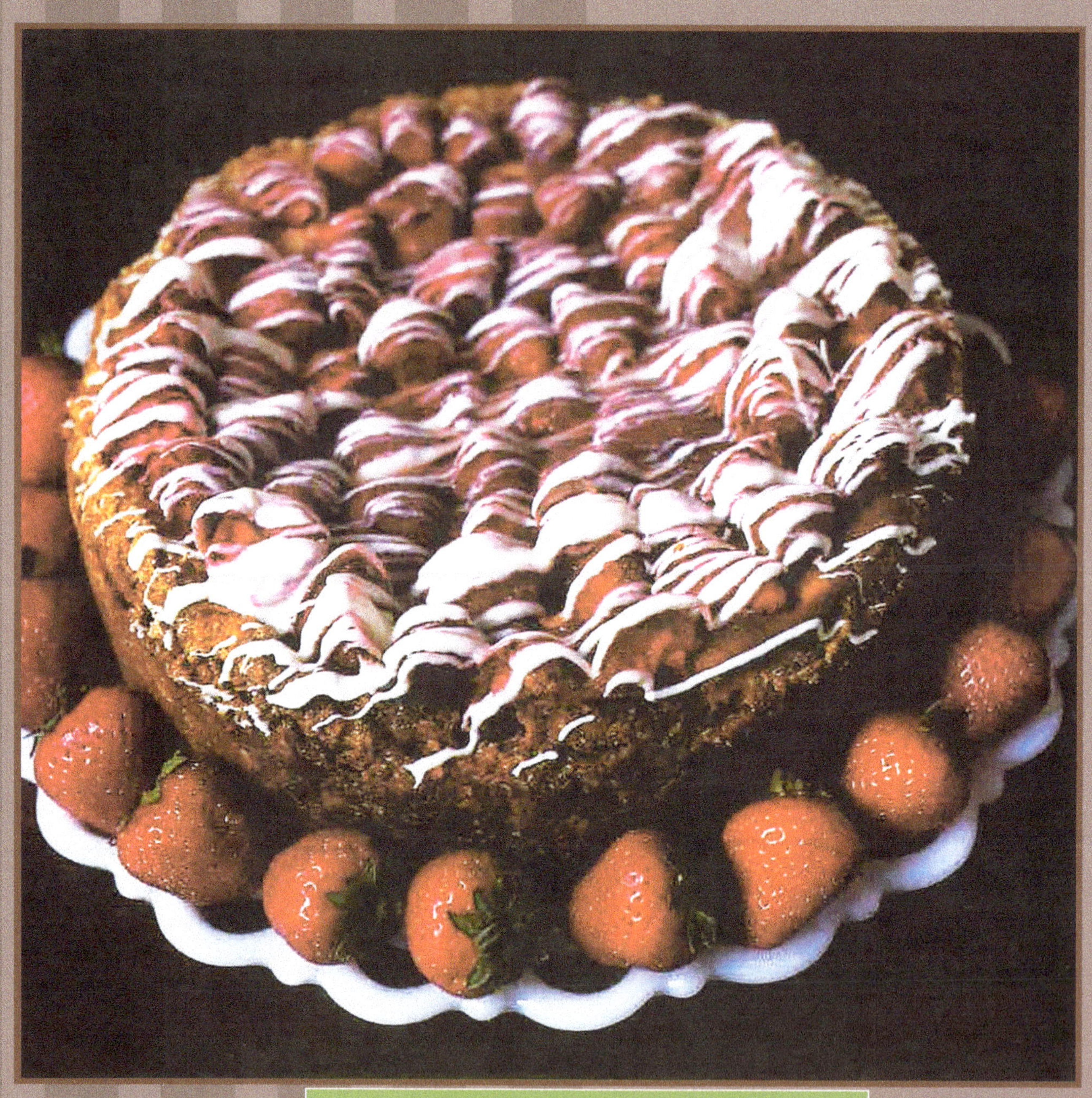

Strawberry Cheesecake

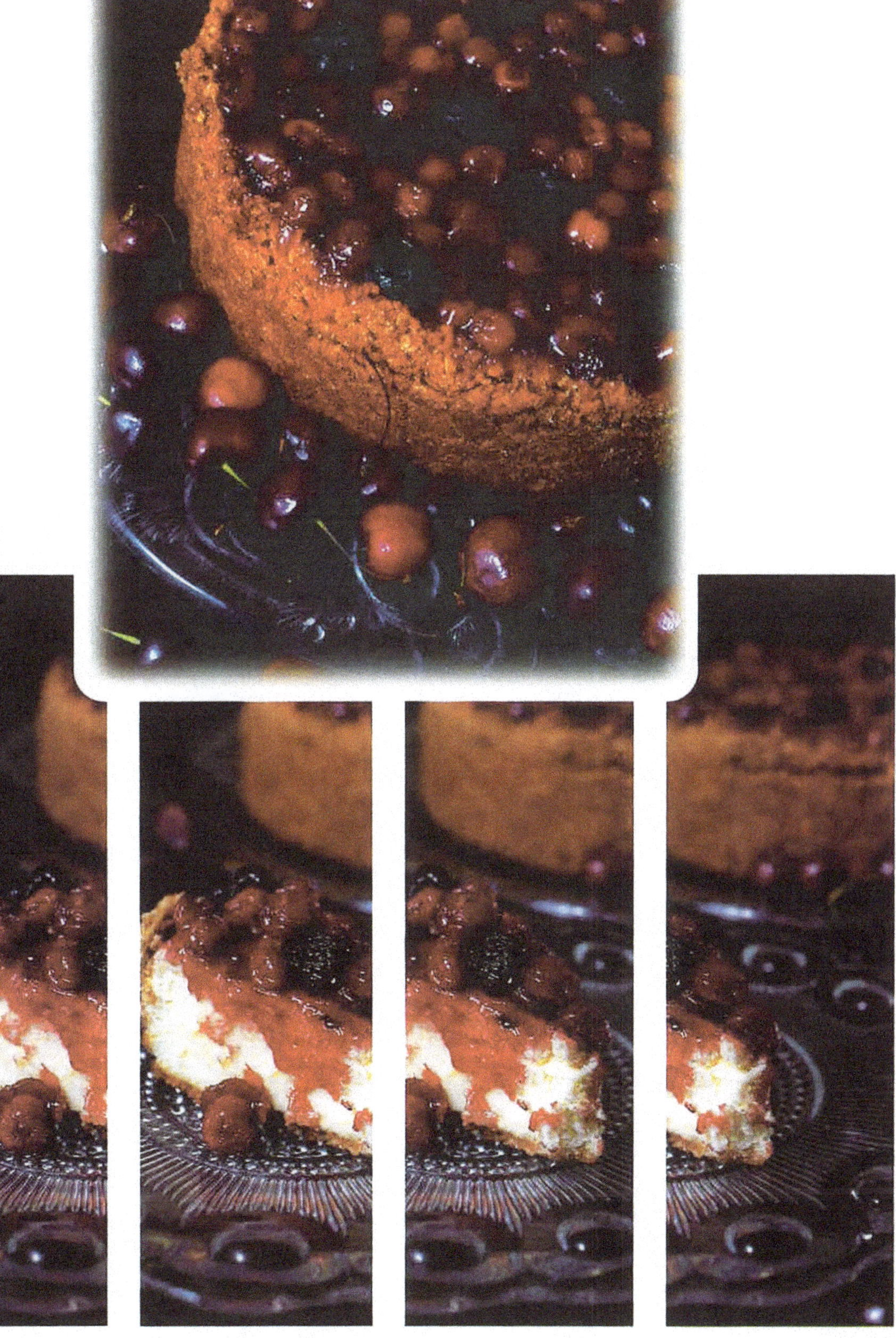

Peanut Butter Cheesecake

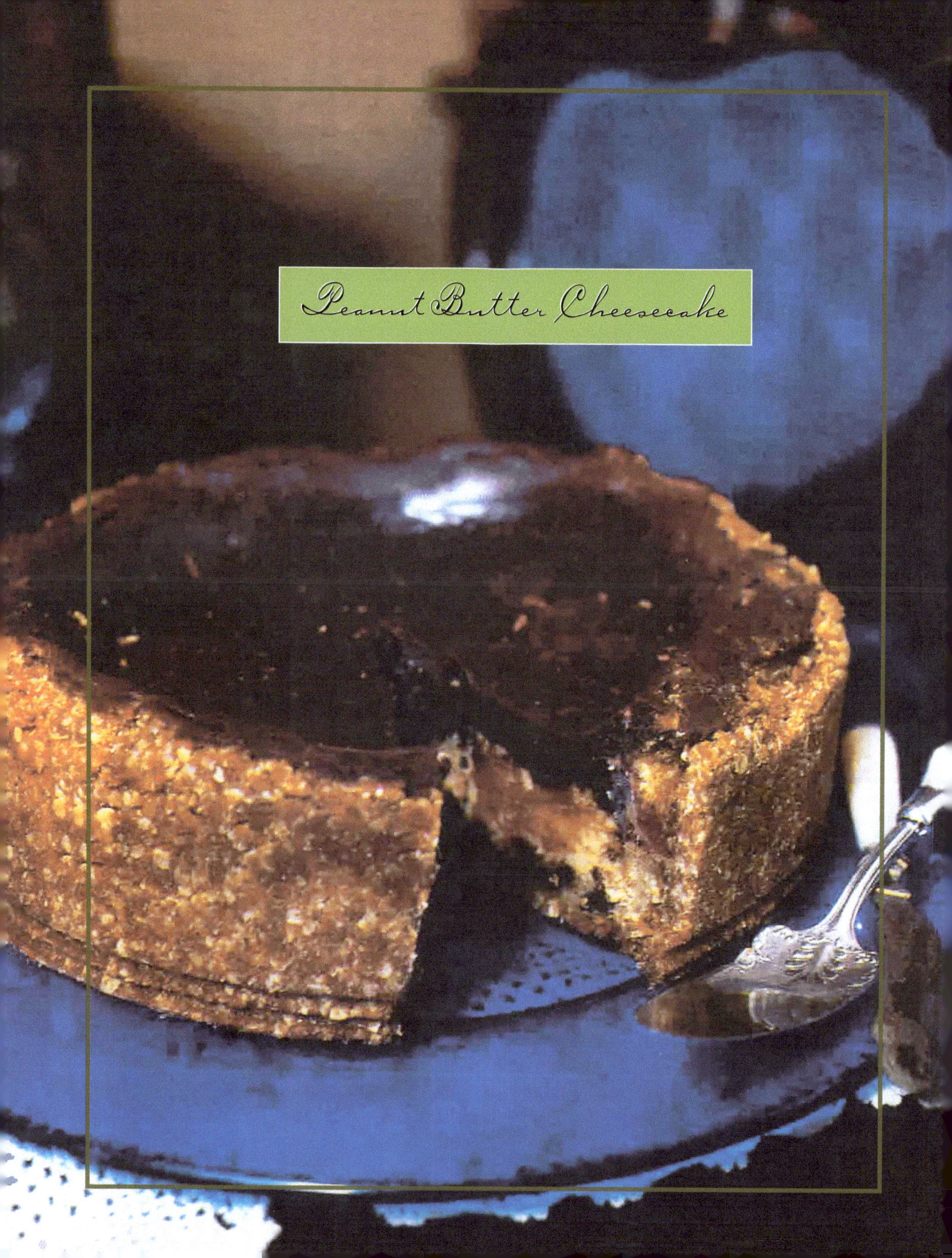

Crust Recipe for Cheesecakes

1½ cups rolled oats
1½ cups graham cracker crumbs
1 cup of sugar
8 oz unsalted butter, melted

Mix well in a mixing bowl.

Lightly butter a 10" springform pan and press mixture against the sides and the bottom of the form.

Gluten-Free Graham Crackers

Preheat oven 350-degrees
¾ cup almond meal
1 cup brown rice flour
½ cup arrowroot
½ cup coconut sugar
1 tsp baking powder
¼ tsp vanilla extract

Mix in a mixing bowl and then place it in the food processor.

⅓ cup low-fat butter, cold

Add the cold butter in the food processor and pulse 2 times.

The mixture should be coarse. Remove and return mixture to the mixing bowl.

⅓ cup almond milk
2 tbsp honey

Add to the bowl and stir with a wooden spoon to mix thoroughly. Dust lightly with brown rice flour a large piece of parchment paper (about 12" x 18")

Place dough on top and press to flatten.

Dust the top of the dough with brown rice flour lightly and cover it with another piece of parchment paper. With a rolling pin, open the dough to a rectangle, about ¼" thick. Remove top paper and transfer dough, with the bottom paper into a 12" x 18" baking pan.

Score dough into small rectangles.

Bake in the preheated oven for 18 to 20 minutes, until crackers are lightly brown. Remove, cool completely, and break crackers along score lines.

For a Creamy, Silky Cheesecake

The three main components to a creamy texture in the cheesecake are the critical process of creaming the cream cheese with the sugar, the baking time, and protecting the cake interior from excessive heat.

Before adding the eggs, the cream cheese/sugar mixture has to be smooth. Add the eggs one at a time. I bake in 350-degrees for an hour, then turn the oven off and let the cheesecake in the oven for another half an hour. Your baking time could fluctuate a little since various ovens cook at different times. The 30 minutes in the oven gives a change for the cheesecake to set and to cool off a little. The cheesecake might crack if overcooked and cooled too fast. I use crust on the sides of the springform pan to protect the delicate cake from the heat. I also place the cake on a baking sheet to protect the bottom part.

I use a 10" springform pan and wrap the bottom with aluminum foil. The foil will make it easier to get the cake off the bottom pan.

Some ovens cook differently to make sure your cheesecake is done, check the outer ring of your cheesecake. It should be slightly puffed and set. The inner-circle should be just a little bit softer. Cracks that show up after baking are mostly cosmetic and not a sign of failure. Your cheesecake will taste good if you follow your familiar recipe. Most cheesecakes require a topping, which will cover the cracks. It is best to prepare the cheesecake a day before serving it. And to keep it in the springform, refrigerated until the next day.

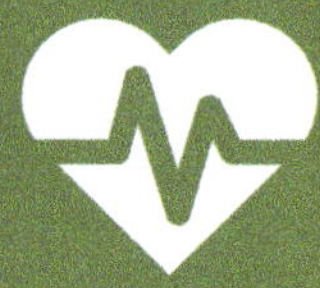

For a healthier choice

Substitute the 1 cup of sugar with ½ cup of coconut sugar
Substitute the butter with a healthier butter substitute. For Gluten-Free cheesecakes, use gluten-free graham cracker crumbs.

Peanut Butter Cheesecake

Preheat oven to 350-degrees

Prepare the crust

Lightly buttered a 10" springform pan and line it with the crust (page 31)

Filling

16 oz cream cheese
1 ½ cups sugar

Place in your mixer and beat on medium speed until smooth and creamy.

1 ½ cups creamy peanut butter

Add to the mixer and blend well.

5 eggs
1 cup sour cream
Juice of ½ small lemon

Add to the mixer, reduce speed and blend well.

1 cup of chocolate chips

Add and mix gently.

Pour filling into the springform pan.

Bake in the preheated for one hour.

Turn oven off and remove cake.

While the cake is baking prepare the topping:

Topping

1 cup semisweet chocolate chips

Melt in a double boil.

1 cup sour cream
½ cup sugar

Turn off the heat and add sour cream and sugar to the melted chocolate.

Mix with a spatula until smooth.

Spread topping evenly on the top of the cheesecake and return the cake to the oven (oven should be turn off) for 30 minutes longer.

Refrigerate for at least 8 hours before removing from pan.

New York Cherry Cheesecake

Preheat oven to 350-degrees

Prepare the crust

Lightly buttered a 10" springform pan and line it with the crust (page 31)

Filling

24 oz cream cheese
1 ½ cups sugar

Place in your mixer and beat on medium speed until smooth and creamy.

6 eggs
2 cups sour cream
Juice of ½ lemon
2 tbs cornstarch
1 tsp vanilla extract

Add to the mixer, reduce speed, and blend well.

Pour filling into the springform pan. Bake in the preheated oven for one hour.

Turn off the oven and leave cake in for 30 minutes. Remove cake from the oven and refrigerate for at least eight hours.

Topping

8 oz can of cherry pie filling
4 oz canned dark cherries
Juice of ½ lemon
1 tsp. orange peel, grated

Place in a mixing bowl and blend well with a spatula.

Remove cake from pan and cover the top of the cheesecake with the cherry mixture.

Red Berry Cheesecake

Preheat oven to 350-degrees
16 oz white chocolate
Melt in a double boil.
Prepare the crust
Lightly buttered a 10" springform pan and line it with the crust (page 31)
Filling
24 oz cream cheese
1 cup of sugar
Place in your mixer and beat on medium speed until smooth and creamy.
4 eggs
Juice of ½ lemon
½ tsp vanilla extract
1 cup whipping cream
1 cup sour cream
The melted white chocolate
½ cup raspberries
If you are using frozen, drain well.
½ cup boysenberries
If you are using frozen, drain well.
Add to the mixer, reduce speed, and blend well. Pour filling into the springform pan.
Bake in the preheated oven for one hour.
Topping
¼ cup frozen raspberries
Defrost and ran raspberries through a fine sieve. Discard the seed and save pulp and liquid.
6 oz white chocolate
Melt in a double boil.
1 cup sour cream
½ cup sugar
Add to the melted chocolate.
Mix with a spatula until smooth.
The raspberry pulp and liquid
Add and mix until smooth.
Spread topping evenly on the top of the cheesecake and return the cake to the oven (oven should be turned off) for 30 minutes longer.
Refrigerate for at least 12 hours before removing from pan.

White Chocolate Pistachio Cheesecake

Preheat oven to 350-degrees
16 oz white chocolate
Melt in a double boil.
Prepare the crust
Lightly buttered a 10" springform pan and line it with the crust (page 31)
Filling
24 oz cream cheese
1 cup of sugar
Place in your mixer and beat on medium speed until smooth and creamy.
4 eggs
Juice of ½ lemon
½ tsp. vanilla extract
1 cup whipping cream
1 cup sour cream
½ cup pistachios, finely chopped
The melted white chocolate
Add to the mixer, reduce speed, and blend well. Pour filling into the springform pan. Bake in the preheated oven for one hour.
Topping
¾ cup white chocolate
Melt in a double boil.
1 cup sour cream
½ cup sugar
½ cup hazelnut, finely chopped
Add to the melted white chocolate.
Mix with a spatula until smooth.
Spread topping evenly on the top of the cheesecake and return the cake to the oven (oven should be turned off) for 30 minutes longer.
Refrigerate for at least eight hoursbefore removing from pan.

"The Cinnamon Stick cake is a crazy combination of cheesecake and baklava that silenced each of us"
— The Tribune newspapers

Chocolate Truffle Cheesecake

Preheat oven to 350-degrees

16 oz semisweet chocolate,

Melt in a double boil.

Prepare the crust

Add ¼ cup cocoa powder and 2 extra oz of unsalted butter to the cheesecake crust recipe (page 31)

Lightly buttered a 10" springform pan and line it with the crust.

Filling

24 oz cream cheese

1 ½ cup sugar

Place in your mixer and beat on medium speed until smooth and creamy.

5 eggs

¼ cup whipping cream

The melted semisweet chocolate

Add to the mixer, reduce speed, and blend well. Pour filling into the springform pan.

Bake in the preheated oven for one hour.

Topping

1 cup semisweet chocolate

Melt in a double boil.

1 cup sour cream

½ cup sugar

Add to the chocolate.

Mix with a spatula until smooth.

Spread topping evenly on the top of the cheesecake and return the cake to the oven (oven should be turned off) for 30 minutes longer.

Refrigerate for at least eight hours before removing from pan.

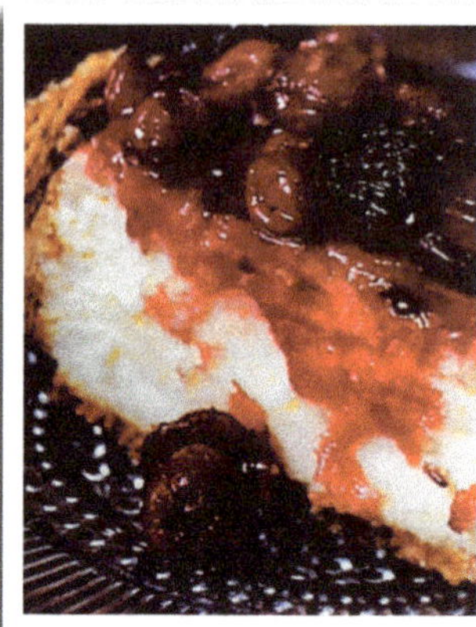

Cherry Cheesecake

Pumpkin White Chocolate Cheesecake

Preheat oven to 350-degrees

16 oz white chocolate

Melted in a double boil

Prepare the crust

Lightly buttered a 10" springform pan and line it with the crust (page 31)

Filling

16 oz cream cheese

1 cup of sugar

Place in your mixer and beat on medium speed until smooth and creamy.

4 eggs

Juice of ½ small lemon

1 tsp. vanilla extract

1 cup pumpkin purée

The melted white chocolate

½ cup sour cream

¼ cup whipping cream

Add to the mixer, reduce speed, and blend well. Pour filling into the springform pan.

Bake in the preheated oven for one hour.

Topping

¾ cup white chocolate

Melt in a double boil.

¾ cup sour cream

½ cup sugar

½ cup pumpkin purée

Mix with a spatula until smooth.

Spread topping evenly on the top of the cheesecake and return the cake to the oven (oven should be turned off) for 30 minutes longer.

Refrigerate for at least eight hours before removing from pan

1 cup whipped topping

Beat in your mixer on high speed for about three minutes, until topping is stiff.

Use a pastry bag with a star tip to make rossettesaround the top edges.

1 tbsp chocolate sprinkles

Sprinkle the top of the cake.

Strawberry Cheesecake

Preheat oven to 350-degrees
8 oz white chocolate
Melt in a double boil.

Prepare the crust
Lightly buttered a 10" springform pan and line it with the crust (page 31)

Filling
24 oz cream cheese
1 cup of sugar
Place in your mixer and beat on medium speed until smooth and creamy.
4 eggs
2 cups sour cream
Juice of ½ lemon
1 tsp. vanilla extract

The melted white chocolate
Add to the mixer, reduce speed, and blend well.

2 cups strawberries, cut into large pieces.
Cut strawberries into large pieces
Blend the strawberries into the mixture with a spatula. Pour filling into the springform pan.
Bake in the preheated oven for one hour.
Tum off the oven and leave cake in for 30 minutes.
Remove cake from the oven and refrigerate for at least eight hours before removing from pan.

Topping
2 cups strawberries, cut in half
½ cup strawberry jam
Juice of ¼ lemon
1 tsp. lemon peel
1 tsp. orange peel
Blend in a mixing bowl and arrange on top of cheesecake.

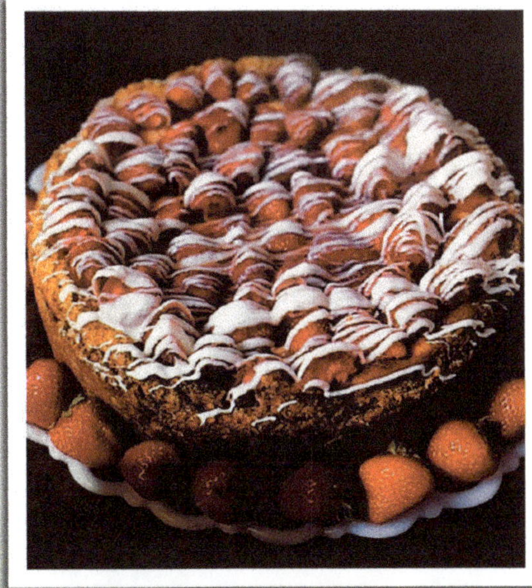

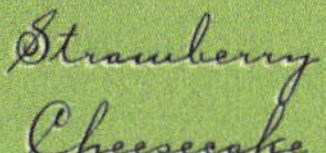
Strawberry Cheesecake

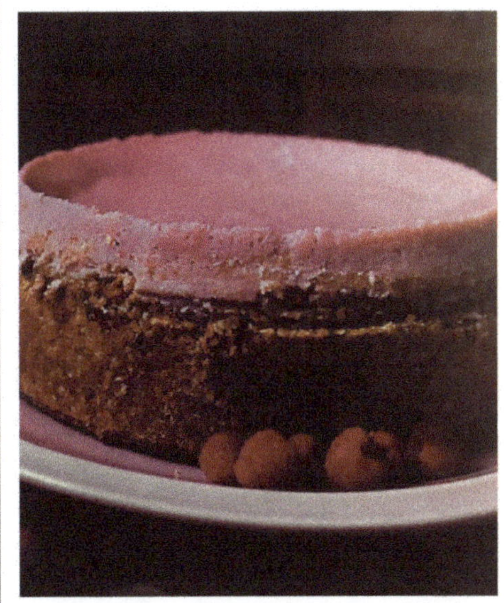

Red Berry Cheesecake

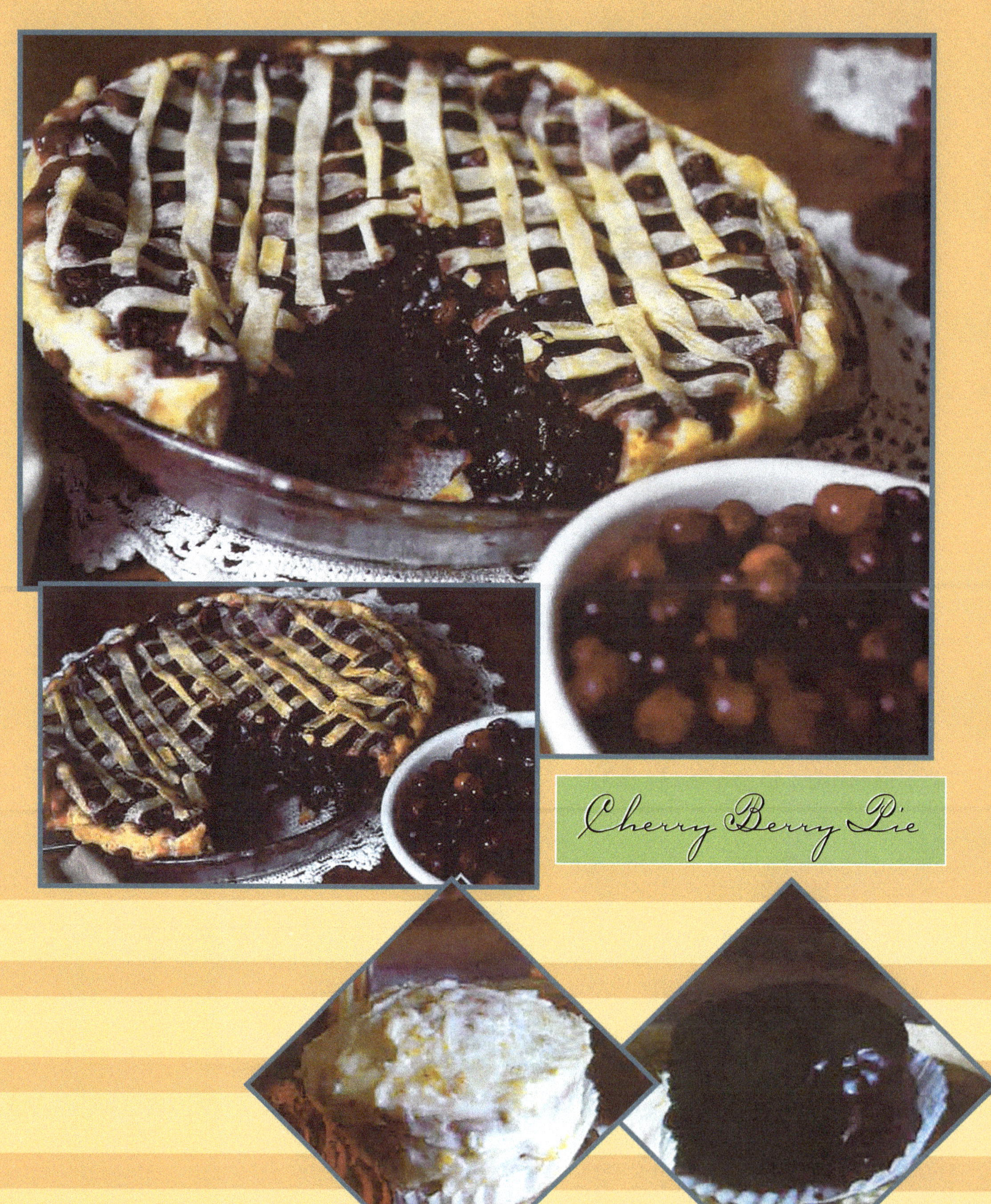
Cherry Berry Pie

Caramel Apple Pie

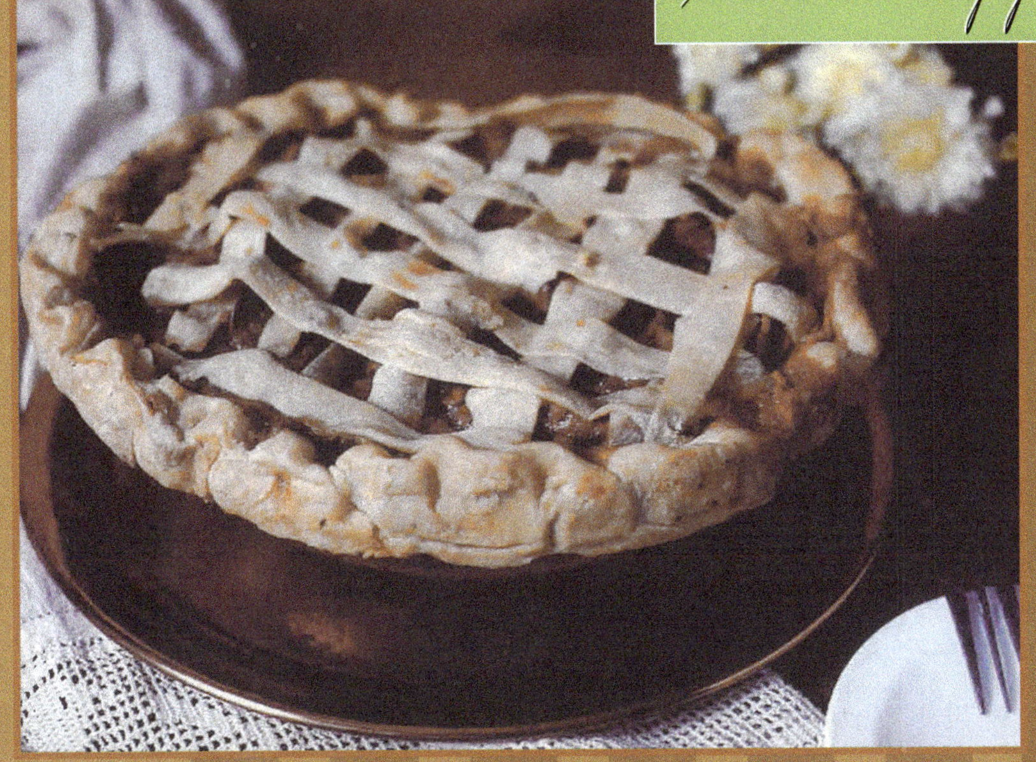

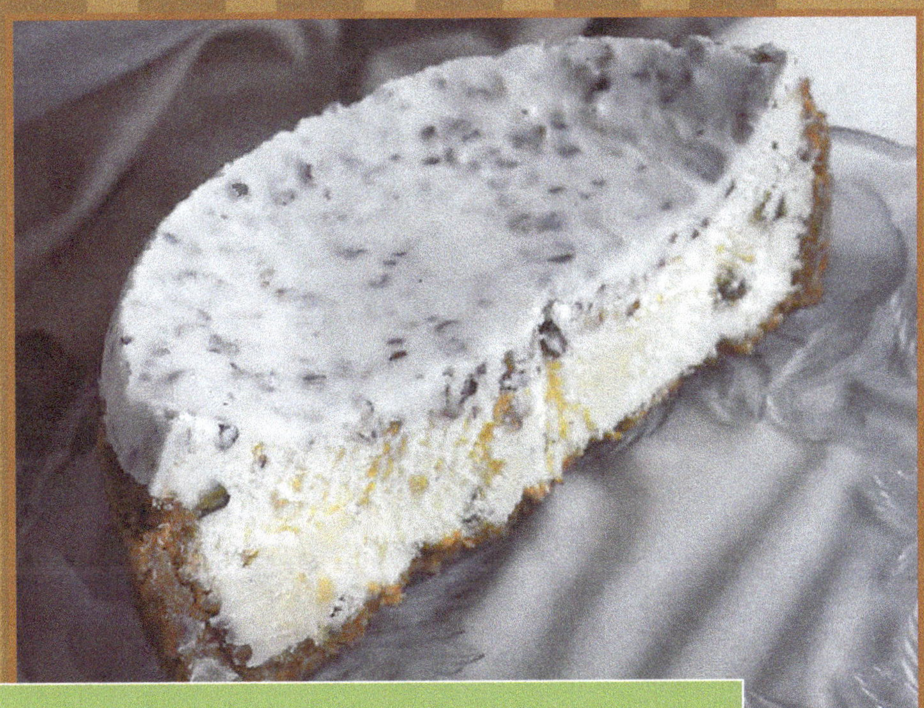

White Chocolate Pistachio Cheesecake

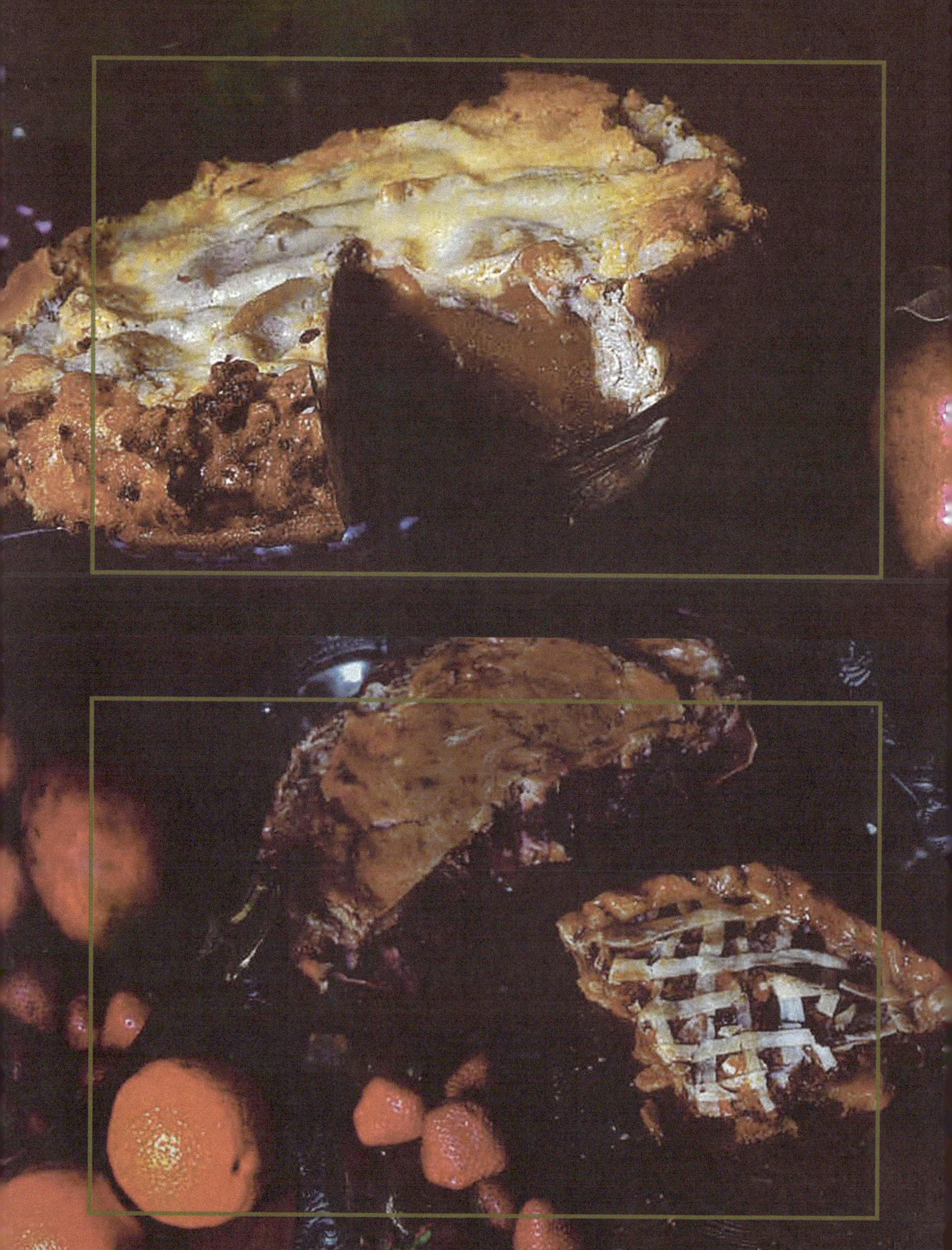

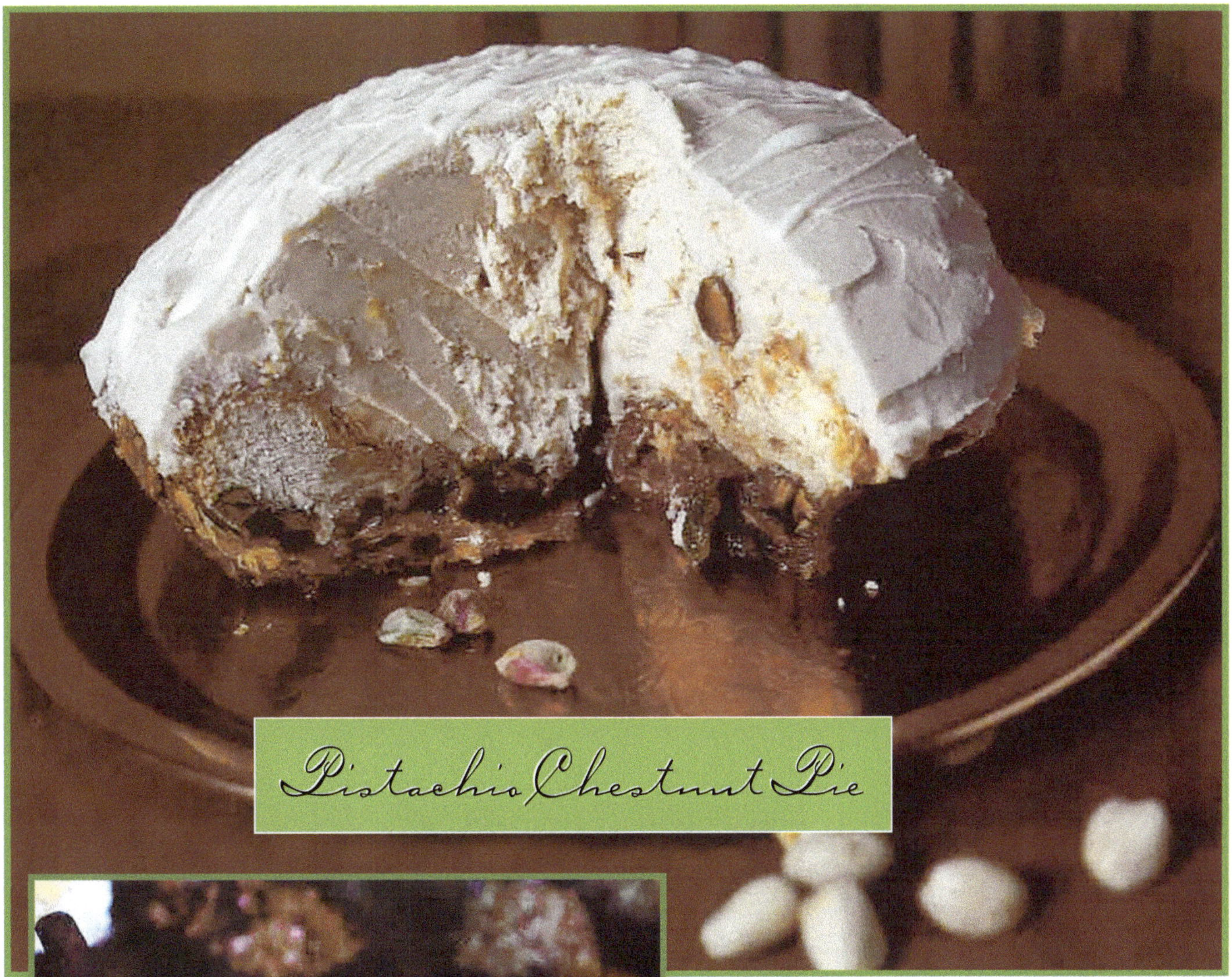

Pistachio Chestnut Pie

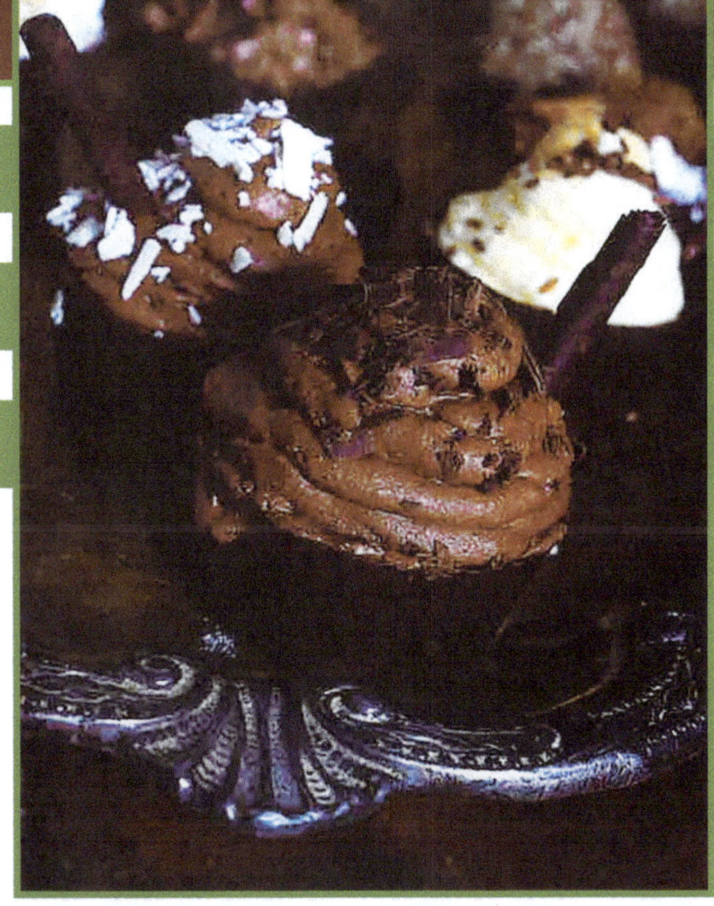

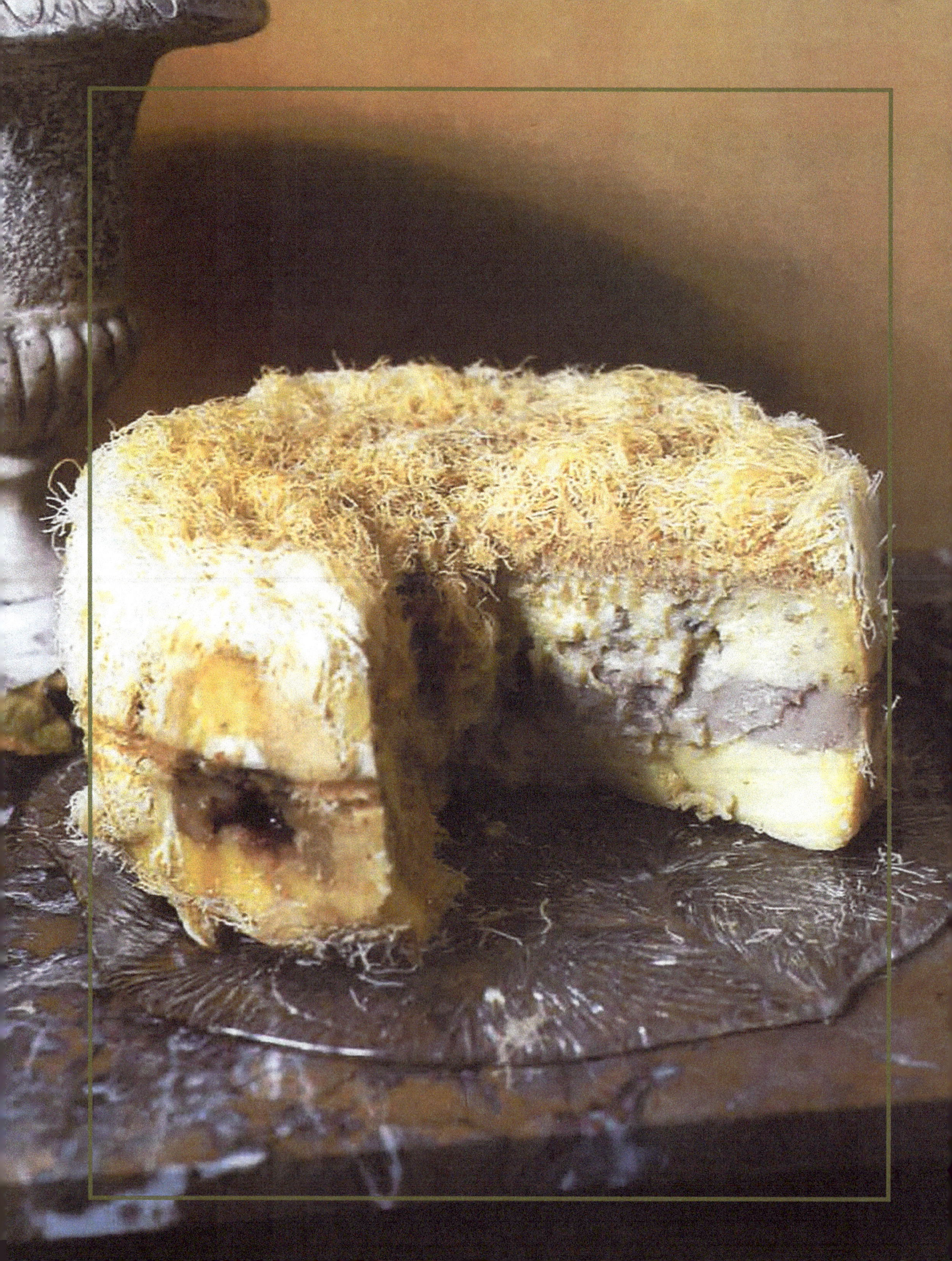

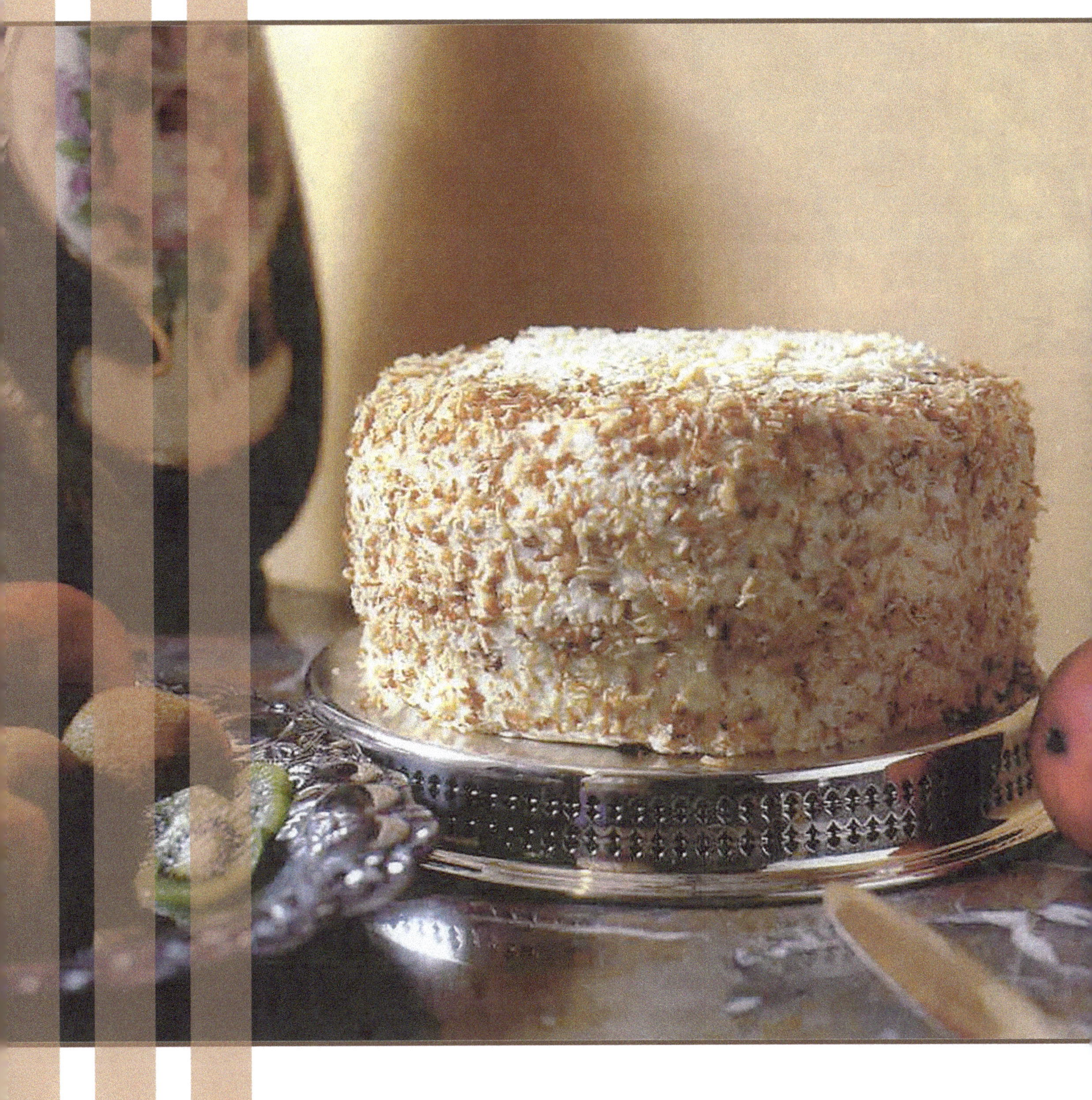

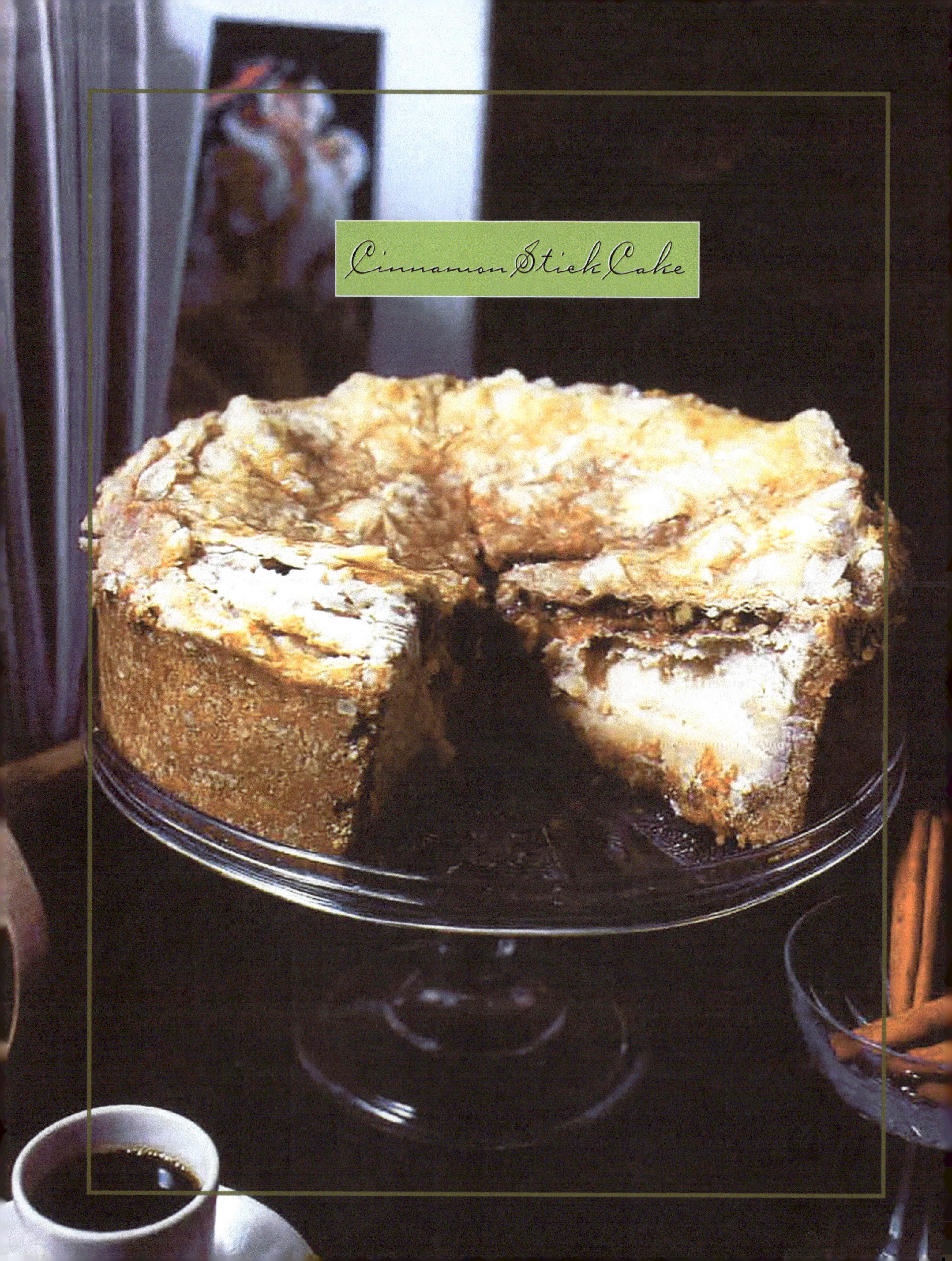

Cinnamon Stick Cake

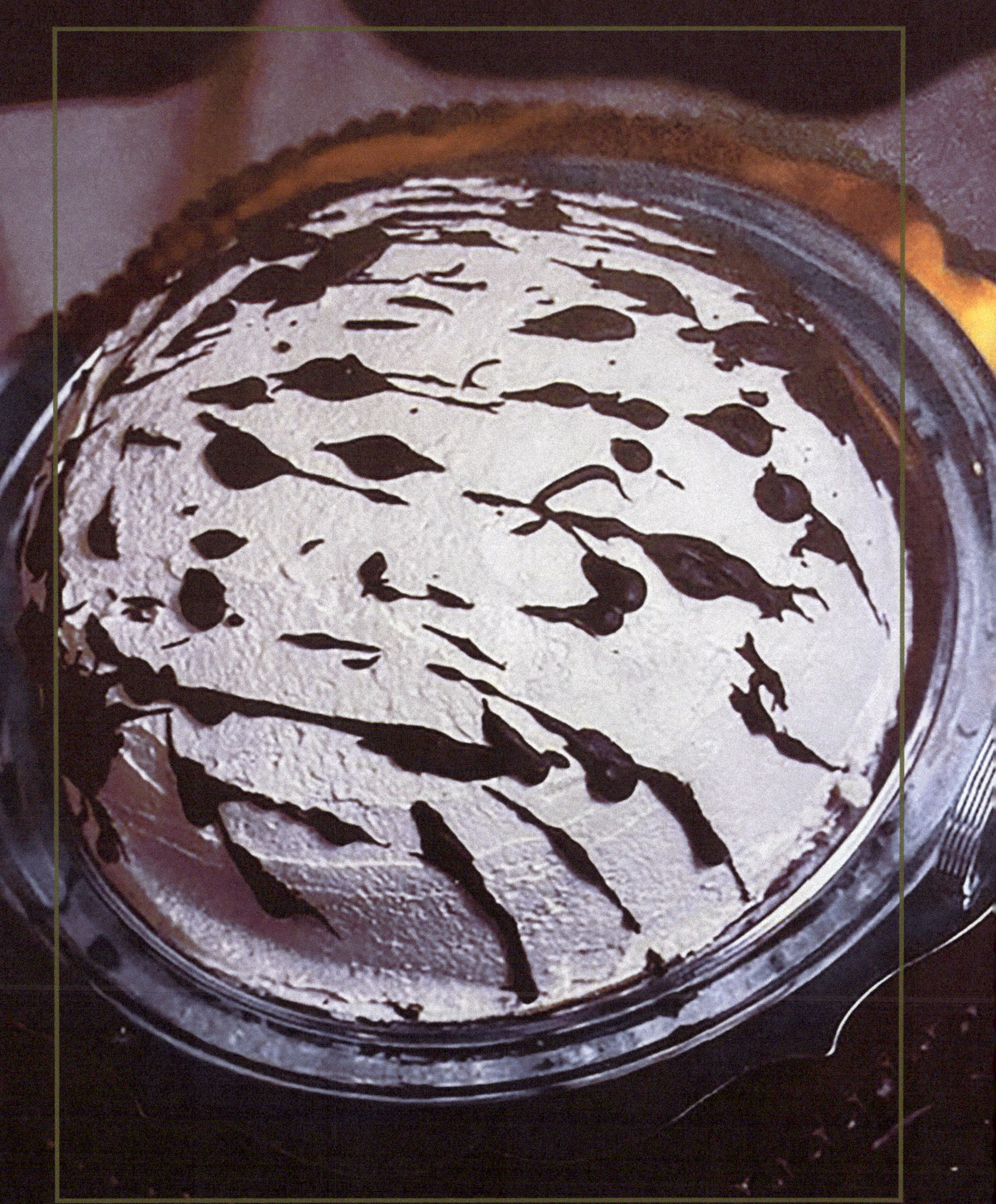

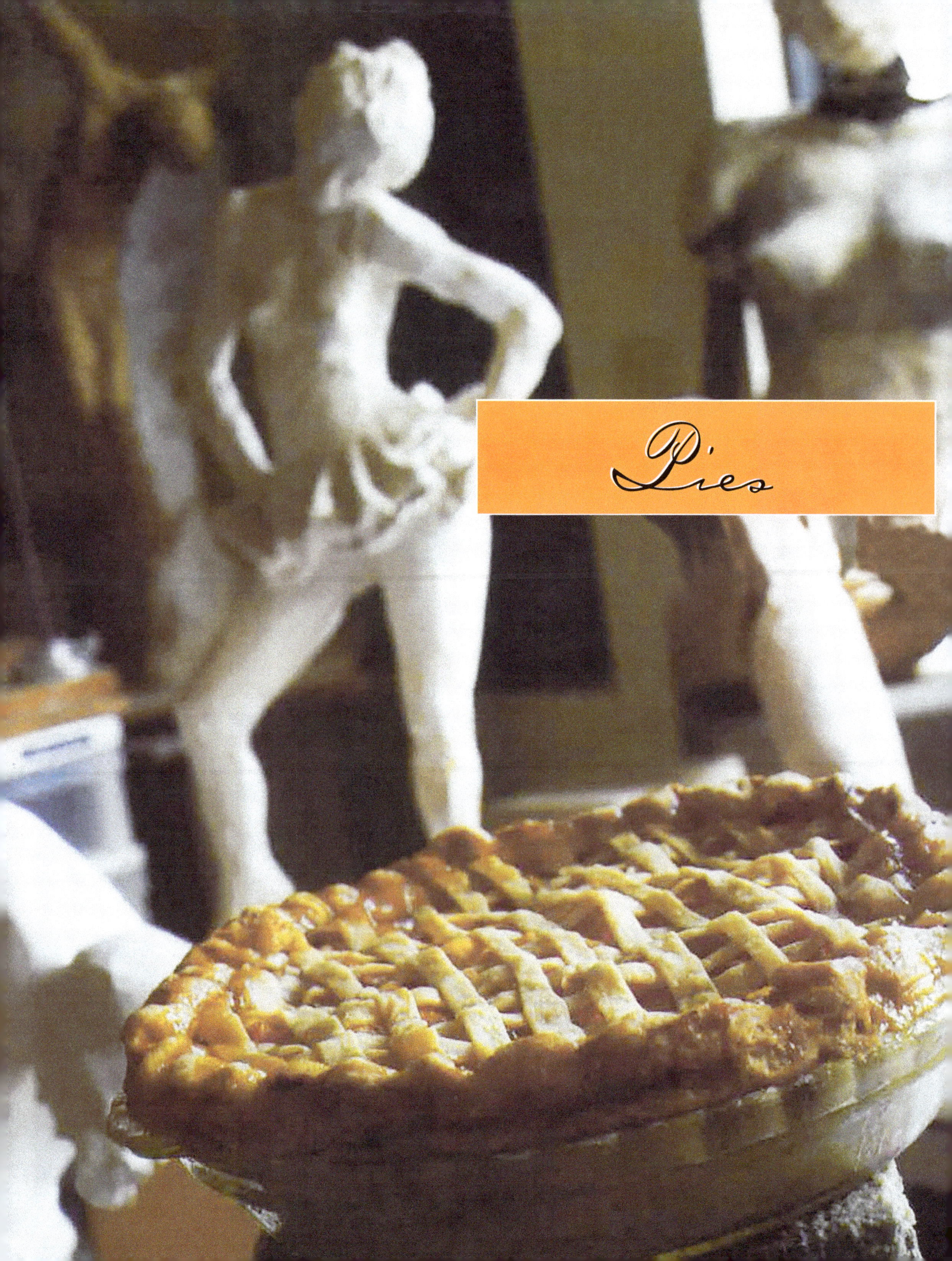

Pies

How to Use the Pie Crust

The following recipe makes dough for two pies. All the pie recipes are designed for a 10" pie plate. Use the deep glass pie plate. You will get better results by baking in the glass.

To make a fluted edge pie crust

Roll the dough into a 12" round. Place it into a lightly oiled pie plate. Press gently into the pie plate. Trim ragged edges with a knife or kitchen shears. Fold the overhanging dough under to create a thick rim. Pinch dough with one hand while pushing against it with the index finger of the opposite hand to flute the edges of the crust.

To make a lattice top pie crust

Divide the pie crust recipe into two parts. Roll the one dough into the desired size. Place it into a lightly oiled pie plate. Press gently into the plate. Roll the remaining dough into a 12" to 14" round. Using a pizza cutter, cut the dough into one-inch strips, or to the desired thickness. Place one strip across the center of the pie vertically. Place another strip across the top to form a cross. Using a weaving pattern, placing a strip across horizontally and another vertically, about one inch apart, complete the lattice pattern. Cut the edges of the strips in about one inch beyond the sides of the pie plate. Fold the bottom crust into the strips and flute the edges. Cut the ends of the strips in about one inch beyond the edges of the pie plate. Fold the bottom crust into the strips and flute the edges.

Class pie plates are the best to use for pie baking. When using a glass pie plate, bake in a slightly lower temperature and bake a bit longer. Glass holds heat better and produces a browner bottom and crusty top.

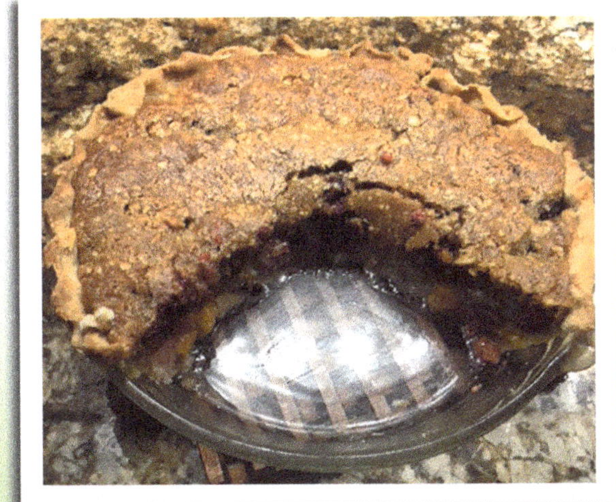

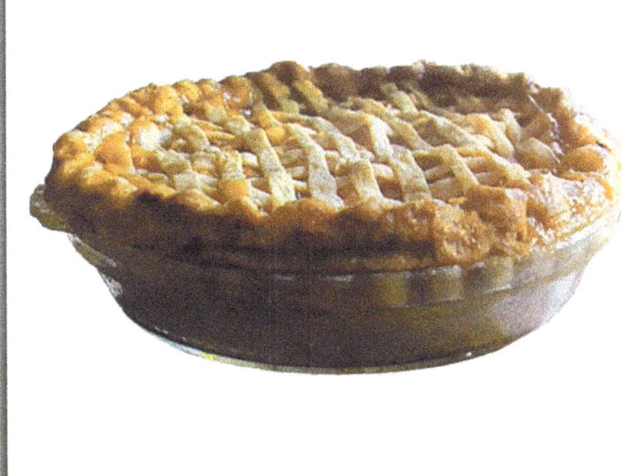

How To Make Chocolate Shavings

Melt chocolate in a double boiler. For a double boiler, Place the chocolate in a mixing bowl. Set the bowl over a stockpot with a small amount of water which is barely simmering. I like to use a mixing bowl larger than the size of the stockpot, so the bottom of the mixing bowl does not touch the water. Occasionally stir the chocolate. Do not overheat. To make the shavings place 3 or 4 tbsp of melted chocolate on a large piece of parchment paper. Cover it with another large piece of parchment paper. With a rolling pin roll out the chocolate into paper-thin. Place it into your freezer for at least 1 hour, or when it's time to use the chocolate shavings. Take out the parchment paper from the freezer, remove the top paper, and break the thin chocolate into preferred pieces.

Pie Crust

4 cups flour
1 tbs sugar

Place in your food processor and pulse 2 to 3 times.

8 oz unsalted butter
1 tbsp olive oil

Add and pulse 5 to 6 times until the butter is in small pieces.

2 tbsp milk
1 tbsp white vinegar
2 egg yolks

Add to the mixer and pulse 2 to 3 times.

¾ cup ice-cold water

Pour the water down the feed tube and pulse until the dough begins to form a ball.

It is best to wrap and refrigerate for the dough for about 30 minutes.

Divide dough into two pieces. Place a healthy amount of flour on a working surface.

Make each pie dough you are using into a firm ball and open it evenly with a rolling pin to about 12 to 14" round. You could freeze the unused dough.

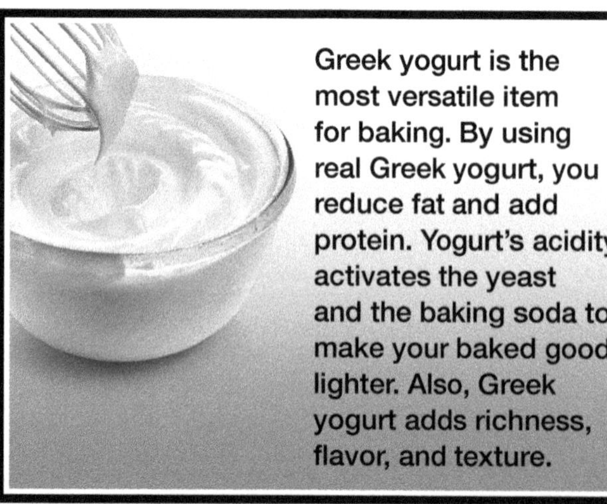

Greek yogurt is the most versatile item for baking. By using real Greek yogurt, you reduce fat and add protein. Yogurt's acidity activates the yeast and the baking soda to make your baked good lighter. Also, Greek yogurt adds richness, flavor, and texture.

Gluten-Free Pie Crust

Makes crust for 2 pies

3 cups gluten-free flour
2 cups brown rice flour
1 tsp xanthan gum
2 tbsp tapioca flour
2 tsp xylitol sugar
1 cup low-fat butter, chilled
1 cup butter substitute, chilled.

Place in the bowl of your mixer and blend on slow speed.

2 egg yolks

Add and mix well.

1 cup of cold water
2 tbsp milk
1 tsp white vinegar

Add and mix gently into a smooth dough.

To make the crust in the food processor

Place flour and sugar and pulse two times.
Add butter and spread and pulse 3 to 4 times.
Add egg yolks and pulse 2 to 3 times.
Add water, milk and vinegar and pulse 2 to 3 times.

To make the crust in the mixer

Place flour, sugar, butter and spread in the mixing bowl and blend on slow speed.
Add eggs, mix well.
Add water, milk, and vinegar, and gently blend into a smooth dough.

Chocolate Pie

4 oz semisweet chocolate
Melt the chocolate in a double boil
Use it to make chocolate shavings (page 46)

Crust
1 cup graham cracker crumbs
1 cup oats
2 tbs cocoa powder
½ cup sugar
4 oz unsalted butter
Mix and press at the bottom and along the edges of a 10" pie plate.
Bake crust in a 300-degree oven for about 15 minutes.
Let crust cool for about 30 minutes. 1/2 cup creamy peanut butter
Spread on the bottom crust.

Filling
12 oz semisweet chocolate
Melt the chocolate in a double boil
¼ cup whipping cream
Whip in your mixer until stiff. Set aside.
8 oz unsalted butter
1 cup of sugar
Place in your mixer and beat on medium speed until smooth and creamy.
3 eggs
1 tsp. vanilla extract
Add to the mixer in and blend well.
The melted chocolate
The whipped cream
Add to the mixer in and blend on low speed until the mixture is smooth.
Place filling in a pastry bag with a large star tip and fill the pie plate to a dome shape.

Topping
Decorate the top with dark chocolate shavings.
Refrigerate 3 to 4 hours before serving.

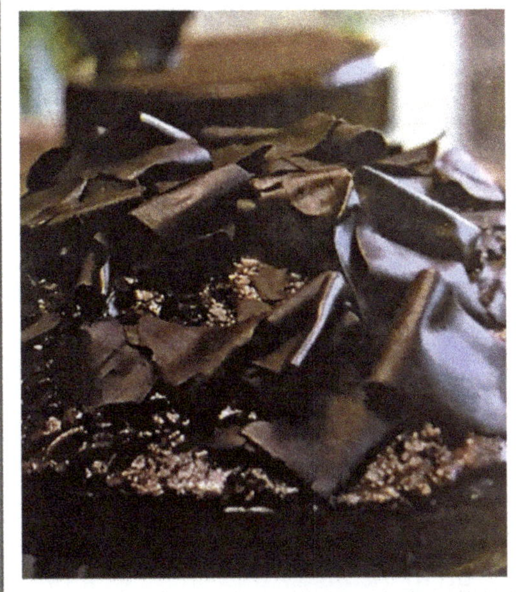

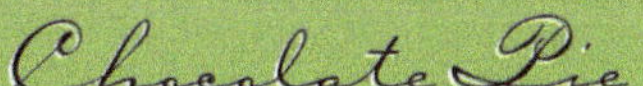
Chocolate Pie

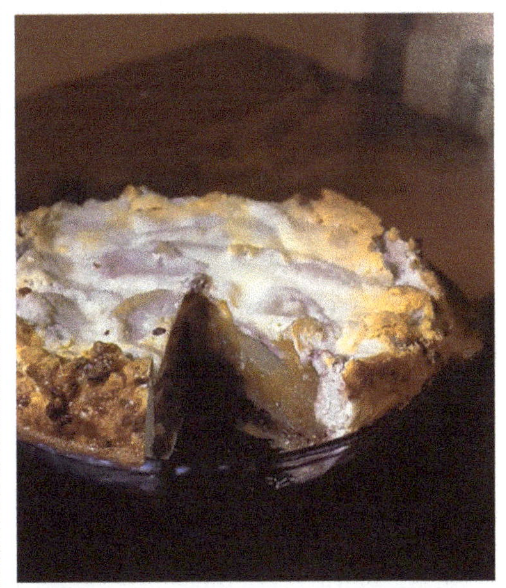

Walnut Pear Pie

Rum Apple Pie

Preheat oven to 350-degrees

Prepare one pie crust (page 46)

Place dough in a lightly buttered 10" glass pie plate.

Fold the excess dough and flute it using your fingers.

Filling

2 ½ lbs. red apples, peeled and sliced
1 cup brown sugar
¼ cup cornstarch
¼ cup dark rum
1 tsp. cinnamon

Mix all ingredients well in a mixing bowl.
Arrange in the pie plate.

Topping

½ cup oats
¾ cup pecan pieces
4 oz unsalted butter, melted
½ cup flour
1 cup brown sugar

Mix well in a mixing bowl.
Spread topping on top of the filling.
Bake the pie in the preheated oven for 1 ½ hours

Pistachio Chestnut Pie

Preheat oven to 300-degrees

16 oz white chocolate

Melt in a double boil.

Phyllo Crust

10 sheets of phyllo dough

Place 6 phyllo sheets in a 10" pie plate, overlapping the plate.

Pistachio Filling

2 cups pistachios, thickly chopped
½ cup coconut sugar
4 oz unsalted butter, melted
1 tsp cinnamon

Mix in a mixing bowl. Place on top of the phyllo in the pie plate. Cover with the 4 remaining phyllo sheets, fold the ends of the phyllo around the edges of the plate – like you would like a pie crust.

Bake the filling in the preheated 300-degree oven for 1 hour. In the meantime, prepare the syrup.

Cinnamon Syrup

1 tbsp sugar
½ cup water
2 tbsp honey
1 tsp juice of a lemon
½ tsp cinnamon

Bring to boil and pour over the baked pistachio filling. Refrigerate for about one hour.

Chestnut Filling

8 oz unsalted butter
1 cup cup of sugar

Place in themixer and beat until smooth and creamy.

1 cup chestnut purée

Add to the mixer and blend well on low speed.

1 tsp. vanilla extract
3 eggs
1 tbsp Kahlua Liqueur – or substitute with black coffee.
The melted white chocolate – Save 3 tbsp for topping

Add to the mixer and blend well on low speed.

Pour filling on top of the crust, forming a dome.

Topping

3 tbsp melted white chocolate
1 tbsp heavy cream, warmed
Mix gently and drizzle on top of the pie.
Refrigerate for at least 2 to 3 hours hours before serving.

Walnut Vermouth Pear Pie

Preheat oven to 350-degrees

Phyllo Crust

10 sheets of phyllo dough

Place 6 phyllo sheets in a 10" pie plate, overlapping the plate.

Walnut Filling

2 cups walnut pieces
½ cup sugar
4 oz unsalted butter, melted
1 tsp cinnamon

Mix. Place on top of the phyllo in the pie plate.

Cover with the four remaining 4 phyllo sheets, fold the ends of the phyllo around the edges of the plate-like you would like a pie crust.

Pear Filling

10 pears, peeled and cut into quarters
2 tbsp cornstarch
1 tbsp vermouth
1 cup brown sugar
1 tsp nutmeg

Mix well in a mixing bowl and pour it into the fillo crust.

Topping

4 oz white chocolate

Melt in a double boil.

1 tbsp sour cream
2 tbsp walnuts, grated
1 tbsp unsalted butter, melted
1 egg, beaten
1 tbsp whipping cream
1 tsp sugar

Mix well in a mixing bowl with the melted chocolate and spread on top of the pear filling.

Bake the pie in the preheated 350-degree oven for 1 ¼ hour.

"Cherry Berry Pie is a unique combination of berries. Lovers of tart pies will adopt this creation as one of their lifetime favorites."

— Best of Phoenix

Cherry Berry Pie

Preheat oven to 350-degrees

Filling

12 oz cranberries
1 cup brown sugar
1 tsp cinnamon
1 tsp. ground cloves
Juice of ½ lemon
¼ cup water

Using a saute pan, simmer for 15 to 20 minutes, until cranberries are soft.

Remove from heat.

8 oz dark cherries, pitted and cut into halves.

Use canned if out of season

8 oz canned cherry pie filling
2 tbsp cornstarch
1 tsp almond extract

Add to the cranberry mixture and mix well.

Set aside.

Prepare pie crust for two pies (page 46)

Line a 10" lightly buttered pie plate with one piece of dough.

Pour filling into the pie shell.

Cut second pie crust into ½" strips.

Criss-cross the pie dough strips on top of the pie filling. Fold the excess dough and flute edges.

Bake the pie in the preheated 350-degree oven for 50-60 minutes.

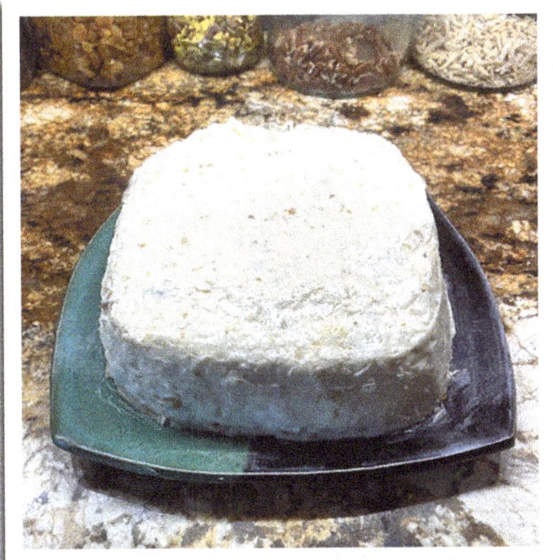

Carrot Cake

White Chocolate Pie

Preheat oven to 300-degree

Crust

1 cup graham cracker crumbs
1 cup oats
2 tbs cocoa powder
½ cup sugar
4 oz unsalted butter, melted

Mix well and press at the bottom and along the edges of a 10" pie plate.

Bake the crust in a 300-degree oven for about 15 minutes.

Let crust cool for about 30 minutes.

6 oz semisweet chocolate

Melt in a double boiler

¼ cup whipping cream

Whip in your mixer until stiff. Set aside.

¼ cup hazelnuts, grated

Combine chocolate, cream and hazelnuts and mix well with a spatula. Spread on the crust.

Filling

8 oz unsalted butter
1 cup of sugar

Place in your mixer and beat on medium speed until smooth and creamy.

3 eggs
1 tsp. vanilla extract
¼ cup whipping cream

Add to the mixer in and blend well.

12 oz. white chocolate, melted

Add to the mixer in and blend on low speed until the mixture is smooth.

Place filling in a pastry bag with a large star tip and fill the pie plate to a dome shape.

½ cup hazelnuts, finely chopped

Sprinkle on the pie.

Fig Berry Pie

Preheat oven to 350-degrees

Prepare one pie crust (page 46)

Place dough in a lightly buttered 10" glass pie plate.

Fold the excess dough and flute it using your fingers.

Filling

12 figs, cut in halves
2 cups raspberries
12 oz semisweet chocolate chips

Place figs on the crust, with the cut, end facing up. Layer with raspberries on top and sprinkle with chocolate chips.

Topping

4 oz cup unsalted butter
½ cup sugar

Cream well in your mixer.

2 eggs

Add and mix on low speed

2 tbs flour
½ cup walnuts, grated
¼ cup whipping cream

Add in and blend well.

Spread topping on top of the filling.

Bake at 350-degree for 1 to 1 ¼ hour, until the top is golden brown.

The Fig Berry Pie is fabulous... Creamy Cinnamon Stick cake is not far behind... scarf up Final Addiction, a rich chestnut cake with coffee laced white and dark chocolate.

— Best of Phoenix Restaurant Guide

As the months went by, the small place on McDowell Road became a Nirvana for dessert-seekers. Its 40 seats were exhausted as customers returned again and again for our cooking. Many asked for a chocolate dessert, a decadence that was already brewing in my head. This creation was, and still is, a favorite of many. I will never forget that one Friday night when two customers fought for the last piece. It was, almost, a fight to the death – *Sweet Chocolate Death.*

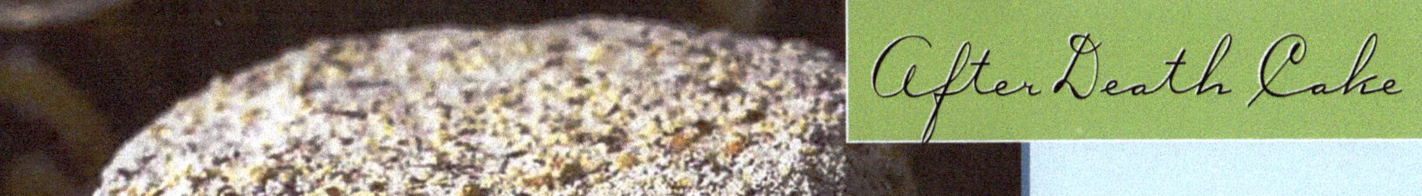
After Death Cake

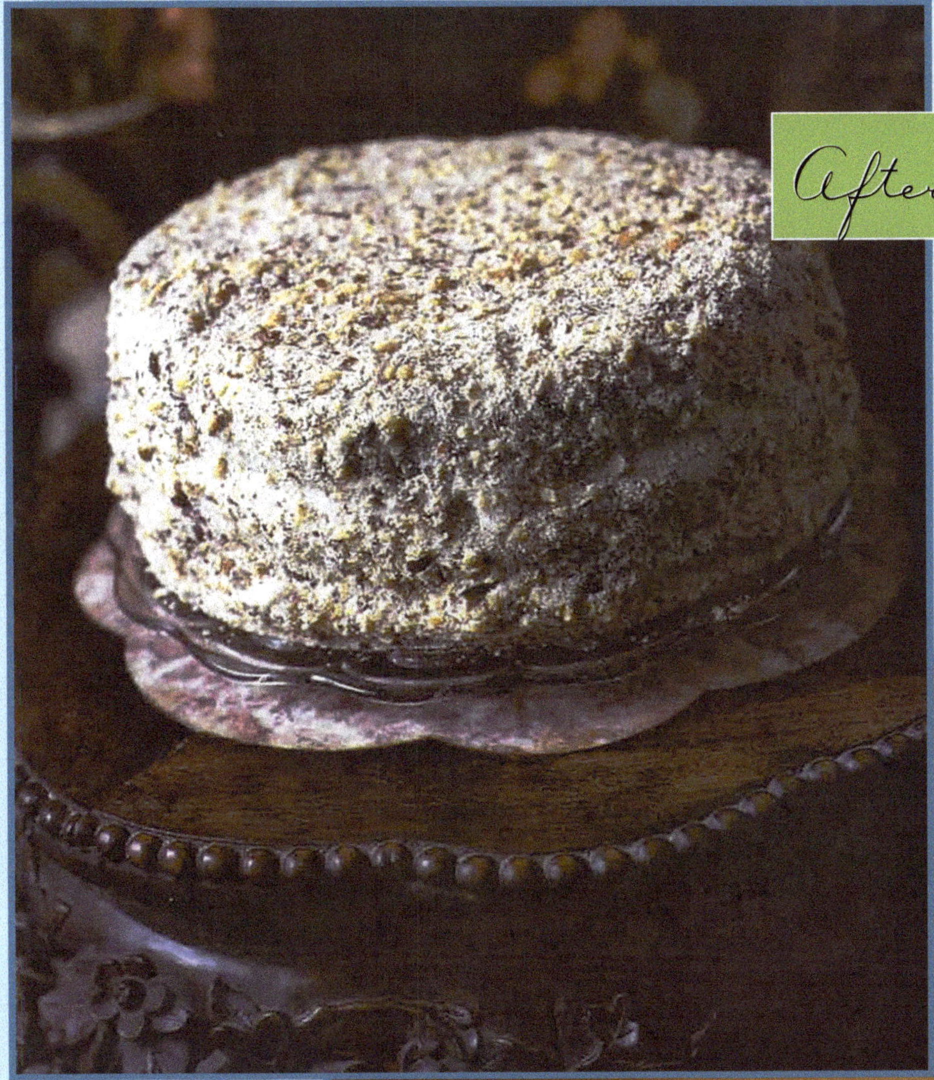

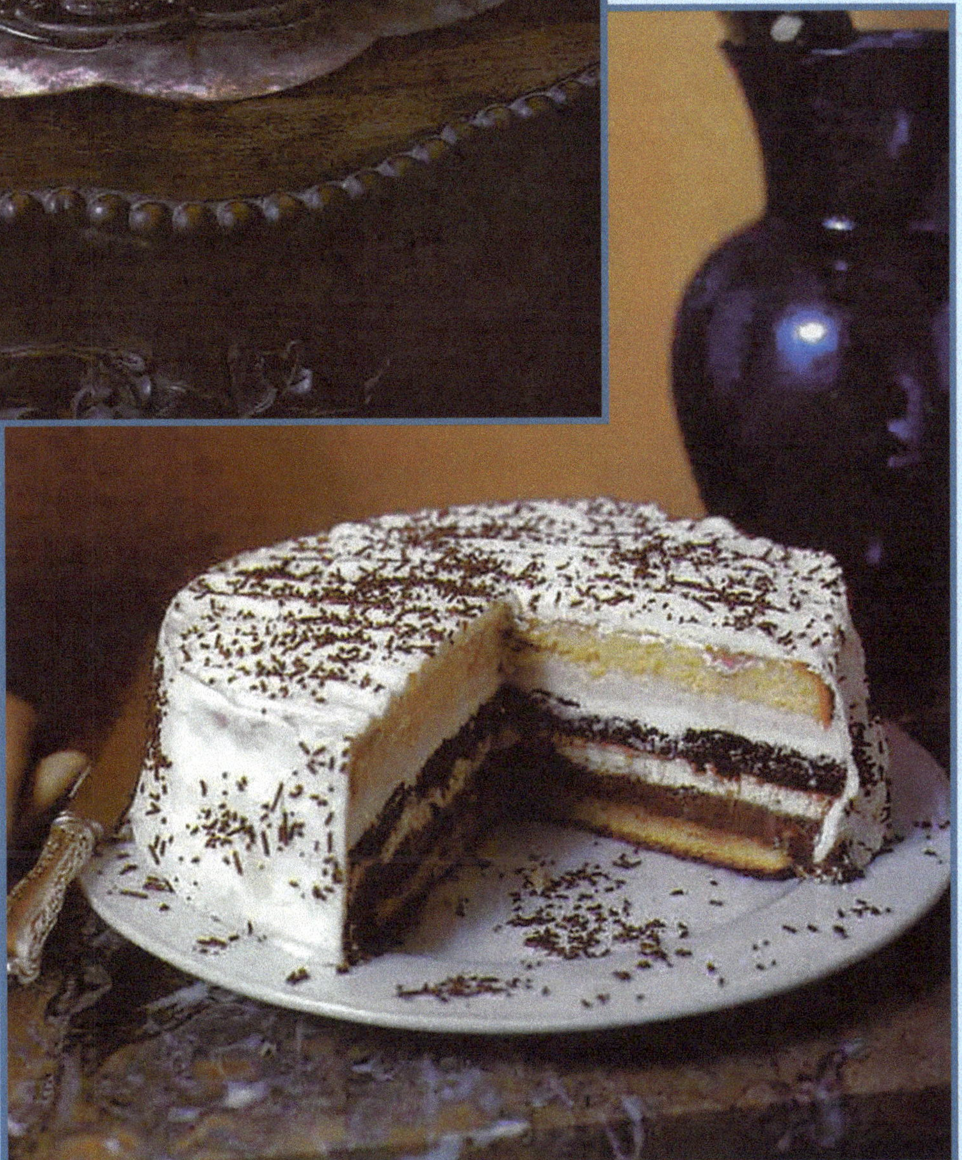

Walnut Vermouth Pear Pie

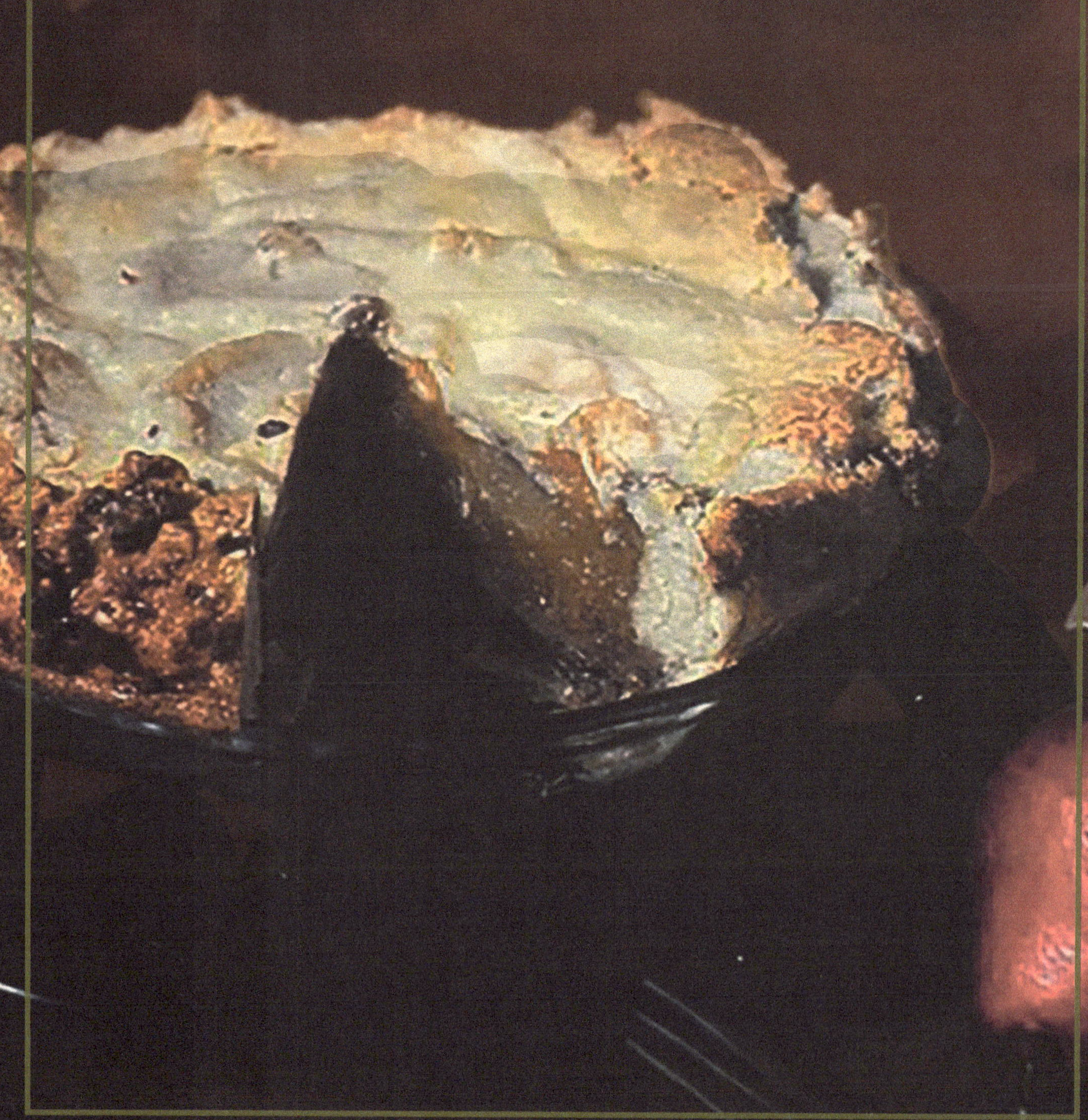

Apple Cherry Pie

Preheat oven to 350-degrees

Prepare one pie crust (page 46)

Place dough in a lightly buttered 10" glass pie plate.

Fold the excess dough and flute it using your fingers.

Filling

8 red apples, peeled and cut into pieces
1 tsp cinnamon
½ cup brown sugar
Juice of ½ lemon

Mix in a mixing bowl and pour it into the pie plate.

8 oz cherry pie filling
8 oz dark cherries, cut in halves

Use canned if out of season

Juice of ½ lemon
1 tsp orange peel

Mix in a bowl and pour on top of the apples.

Topping

2 eggs
½ cup sugar

Blend well in a mixing bowl

1 tsp. nutmeg
1 cup whipping cream
½ cup flour

Add to the bowl and mix well.

Pour on top of the filling.

Streusel

¼ cup flour
⅛ tsp cinnamon
2 tbs brown sugar
2 tbsp unsalted butter, softened

Mix ingredients well.

With your fingers, drop parts of the streusel over the top of the pie topping.

Bake at 350-degree oven for 1 to 1¼ hour, until the top is golden brown.

Strawberry Mango Pie

Preheat oven to 350-degrees

Prepare one pie crust (page 46)

Place dough in a lightly buttered 10" glass pie plate.

Fold the excess dough and flute it using your fingers.

Mango Filling

4 large mango, peeled and cut into pieces
Juice of ½ lemon
¼ tsp nutmeg
¼ tsp. cinnamon
¼ tsp ground cloves
2 tbs. unsalted butter, cut into small pieces

Mix in a mixing bowl and pour it into the pie plate lined up with the crust.

Strawberry Filling

2 lbs strawberries, sliced
½ cup sugar
½ cup brown sugar
2 cups strawberry jam
1 tbsp cornstarch

Mix well in a mixing bowl.

Pour on top of mango filling.

Topping

8 oz cream cheese
½ cup sugar

Place in your mixer and beat on medium speed until smooth and creamy.

1 egg
1 tsp vanilla extract

Add to the mixer and blend well.

2 bananas, cut in small pieces
½ cup sour cream
¼ cup whipping cream
½ cup flour

Add to the mixer and blend well.

Spread on top of filling.

Bake at 350-degree oven for 1 hour, until the top is golden brown.

Peach Boysenberry Pie Gluten-Free

Preheat oven to 350-degrees

Prepare one Gluten-free pie crust (page 46)

Place dough in a lightly buttered 10" glass pie plate.

Fold the excess dough and flute it using your fingers.

Filling

12 large peaches, peeled and sliced

Line along bottom of crust.

4 cups boysenberries

Layer over peaches.

12 oz white chocolate chips

Layer over boysenberries.

Topping

½ cup unsalted butter

½ cup coconut sugar

Place in your mixer and beat on medium speed until smooth and creamy.

2 eggs

Add and blend well

1 cup almond meal

1 cup gluten free muffin mix

Add to the mixer and blend well.

Spread on top of filling.

Bake at 350-degree oven for 1 hour, until the top is golden brown.

NOTE: If boysenberries are not available, substitute with 1 cup raspberries and 1 cup blackberries

Caramel Apple Pie

Preheat oven to 350-degrees

Prepare pie crust for two pies (page 46)

Open dough to about 12" in diameter.

Line a 10" lightly buttered pie plate with one pie dough.

Filling

10 red apples

Do not peel, cut in large pieces. Discard seeds.

Place apples in a large mixing bowl.

2 cups brown sugar

1 cup quick oats

1 cup cornstarch

¼ cup strong coffee

1 tsp. cinnamon

2 cups pecan pieces

1 tbsp lemon juice

3 cups caramel sauce – see page 106

Add to the mixing bowl, mix well with a spatula and pour into a pie plate.

Pour filling into the pie shell.

Cut second pie crust into 1/2" strips.

Criss-cross the pie dough strips on top of the pie filling. Fold the excess dough and flute edges.

Bake the pie in the preheated 350-degree oven for 50-60 minutes.

Harvest Pie

Preheat oven to 350-degrees

Filling

8 red apples, peeled and sliced

6 pears, peeled and sliced

2 cups seedless grapes, cut in halves

1 tsp cinnamon

½ tsp. nutmeg

1 tbs juice from a lemon

2 tsp lemon peel

½ cup coconut sugar

2 tbs arrowroot

Mix ingredients well.

Prepare pie crust for two pies (page 46)

Line a 10" lightly buttered pie plate with one piece of dough.

Pour filling into the pie shell.

Cut second pie crust into ½" strips.

Criss-cross the pie dough strips on top of the pie filling. Fold the excess dough and flute edges.

Bake the pie in the preheated 350-degree oven for 50-60 minutes.

MERINGUES

For a few of my recipes, you will need to prepare baked meringues. When you separate the eggs, make sure there is no trace of egg yolk in the egg whites. Beat the eggs on high speed until stiff.

Egg Whites

The lightness of a cake and a successful meringue depends upon the air beaten into the egg whites. For best results of "stiff" beaten egg whites, here is what you do: Make sure the bowl is clean, free of oils, soaps, and the bowl is at room temperature. Optional; Add 1/4 tsp of cream of tartar to six or seven egg whites. The general belief that the salt "stiffens" the egg whites does not work. Sugar must be added slowly until soft peaks formed. Adding sugar in the early process prevents the whites from achieving maximum volume. If you have over-beaten the egg whites and they seem dry, you can rescue them by adding an egg white to the batch.

How to Pasteurize Eggs

Pasteurizing eggs (or any other foods) is the process of gentle heating the eggs to kill food born illnesses. Since there is a small chance that raw eggs contain salmonella, it is safe to pasteurize before using them. Some grocery stores carry pasteurized eggs. However, it is more cost-effective and convenient to pasteurize your eggs. To pasteurize eggs, pour enough water in a saucepan to cover eggs. Do not place eggs in the water. Heat the water to 140-degrees (eggs usually cook at 142-degrees.) Keep the water temperature at 140-degrees for about 3 minutes. Remove eggs from hot water and rinse thoroughly with cold water. If you follow this process, The eggs still have the consistency of raw eggs, but any harmful bacteria should be eliminated. You can pasteurize a few eggs at a time. You can store the pasteurized eggs in the refrigerator as you would with regular eggs.

Simple Syrup

2 cups of water
¼ cup sugar

Bring to a boil. Reduce heat. Simmer 5-6 minutes.

Use your imagination to flavor this simple syrup and turn it into a fruit or liqueur syrup to flavor your desserts by brushing on top of the cake.

In this book, you will find syrup flavorings of rum, grand marnier, coffee, raspberry, boysenberry. Add the liqueur or the juice of the fruit into the syrup 1 to 2 minutes before removing from heat.

Use between 2 to 5 tbs. of flavoring in the syrup, according to the strength of the liquor or juice.

About Pastry Pride Whip Topping

I used Pastry Pride ready to whip topping for some of my cake recipes. It is versatile, creamy, and easy to work with. Pastry Pride is difficult to find. Pastry Pride is a non-dairy, ready to whip commercial product. You can find it in the frozen section of major wholesale/retail restaurant supply stores such as Smart and Final or Costco. It is popular among many professional pastry chefs for its consistency. When you need it, thaw it in the refrigerator and whip it up cold, just like whipping cream. You can add any flavoring if you wish.

2 cups make 5 cups of whipped topping.

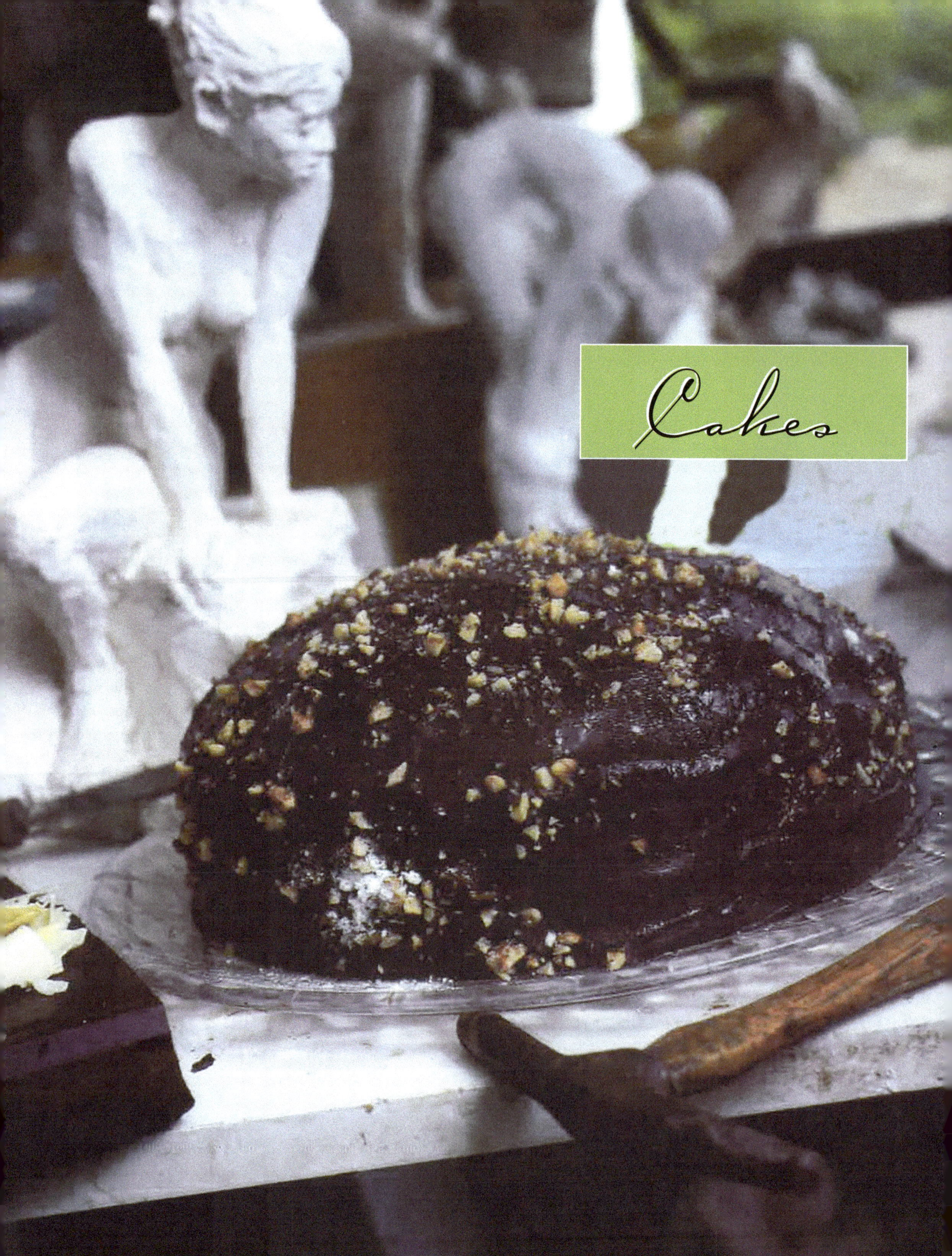

Cakes

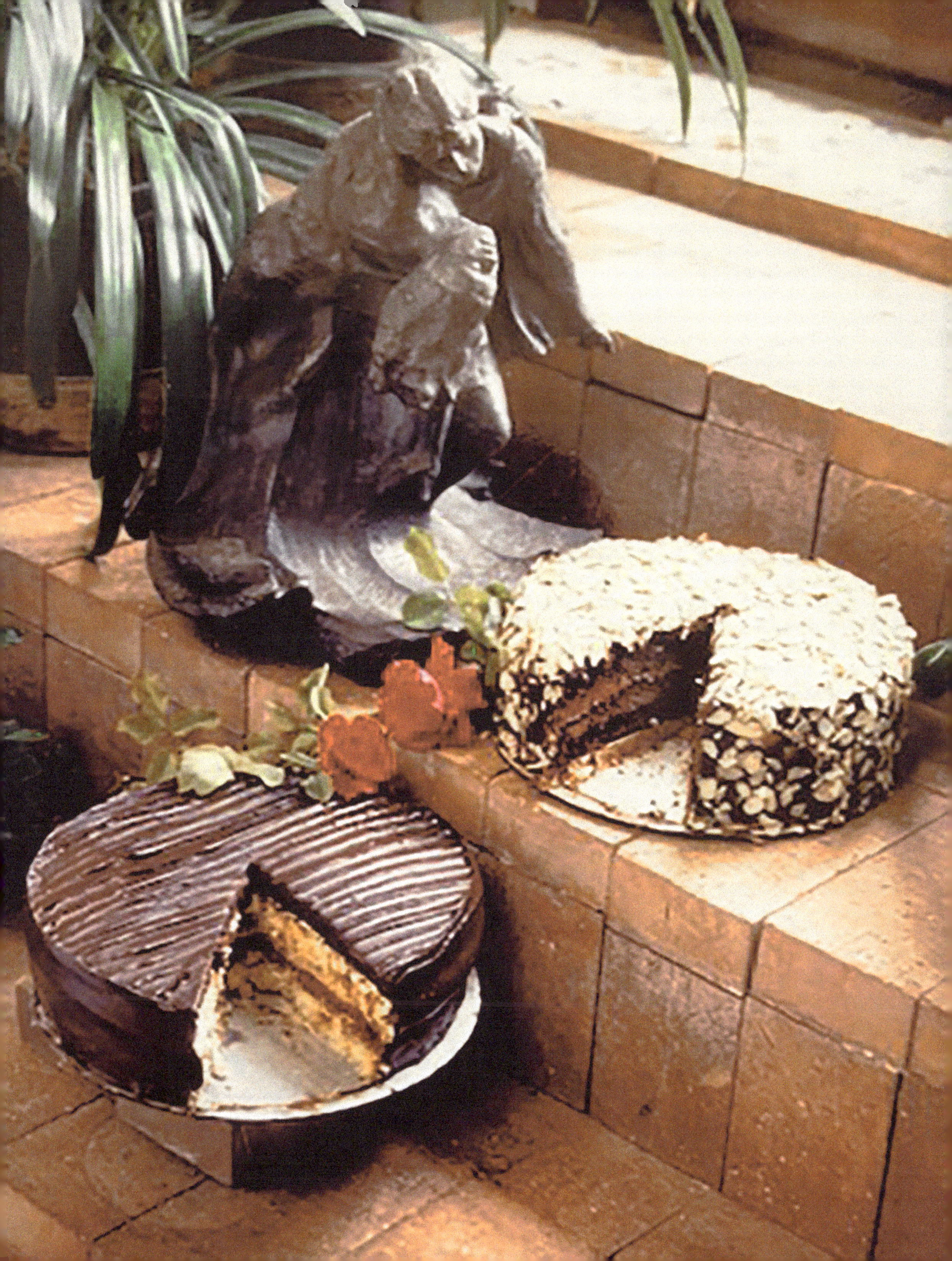

Chocolate Cake

Preheat oven to 350-degrees
2 ¼ cups flour
1 cup sugar
1 cup unsweetened cocoa powder
1 tbsp baking soda
1 tsp baking powder
Place in your mixer bowl and blend in low speed.
3 eggs
1 cup milk
½ cup vegetable oil
1 tsp vanilla extract
Add to the mixer and blend on medium speed.
Turn mixer off
1 cup water
Head in a saute pan on low heat.
2 oz semisweet chocolate
Add to the water and stir to melt.
Start your mixer on low speed. Add the chocolate water and blend well.
Lightly oiled a 10" springform pan.
Pour the chocolate mixture in to the pan and bake in the preheated oven for 30 to 35 minutes.

White Cake

Preheat oven to 350-degrees
¾ cup unsalted butter, softened
1 ½ cups sugar
1 tbsp baking powder
1 tsp baking soda
Place in your mixer bowl and blend in low until smooth.
⅔ cup vegetable oil
1 tsp vanilla extract
Add to the mixer and blend on low speed.
1 cup milk
3 egg whites
1 whole egg
¼ cup sour cream
Add to the mixer and blend on low speed.
2 ½ cups flour
Add to the mixer and blend well.
Lightly oiled a 10" springform pan.
Pour the mixture in to the pan and bake in the preheated oven for 40 to 45 minutes.

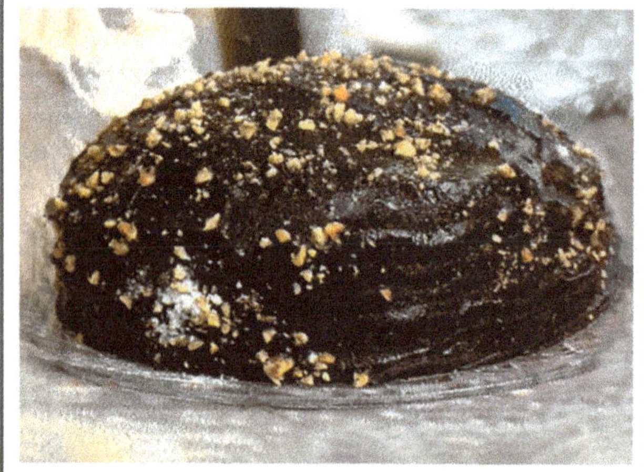

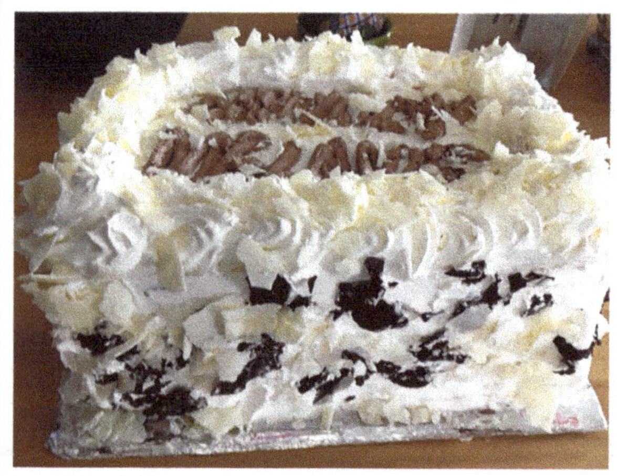

Gluten Free Chocolate Cake

Preheat oven to 350-degrees
1 ¾ cup gluten-free baking flour
1 cup coconut sugar
½ cup xylitol sugar
1 ½ tsp baking powder
1 ½ tsp baking soda
1 cup cocoa powder
Blend well in a mixer.
3 eggs, beaten
1 ¼ almond milk
½ cup pure coconut oil
Add to the mixer and blend well on slow speed.
Lightly oiled a 10" springform pan.
Pour mixture in the pan and bake in the preheated oven for 40 to 45 minutes.
Let the cake cool before removing from the pan.

Genoise

Preheat oven to 350-degrees
1 cup unsalted buttered
1 ½ cups sugar
1 tsp vanilla extract
Place in your mixer bowl and blend on medium speed until creamy.
3 egg whites
2 whole eggs
¾ cup milk
Add to the mixer and blend on low speed.
2 ¼ cups flour
1 tsp baking powered
1 tsp baking soda
⅛ tsp cinnamon
Add to the mixer and blend well.
Lightly oiled a 10" springform pan.
Pour the chocolate mixture in to the pan and bake in the preheated oven for 40 to 45 minutes.

Decorating

I wanted to create a style of design beyond the overdressed and the flamboyant approach. I envisioned simple lines and dramatic use of colors and forms—a classical simplicity of a design that is eye-catching. I want my displayed dessert to appear as exquisite jewels, as rare pieces of art. The shapes that I envisioned were to bring forth the images of a culinary artist with creative eyes and clever hands. My idea of dessert designing was really to please the mind and provoke the palette. I had no form in mind. It did not matter if it was classical or contemporary. I want each of my creations to make a statement of visual simplicity. The element of surprise is the taste, at that very first bite when one discovers that the substance is more remarkable than looks. My concept of designing desserts is about quality and simplicity. The same idea that has profoundly influenced my lifestyle.

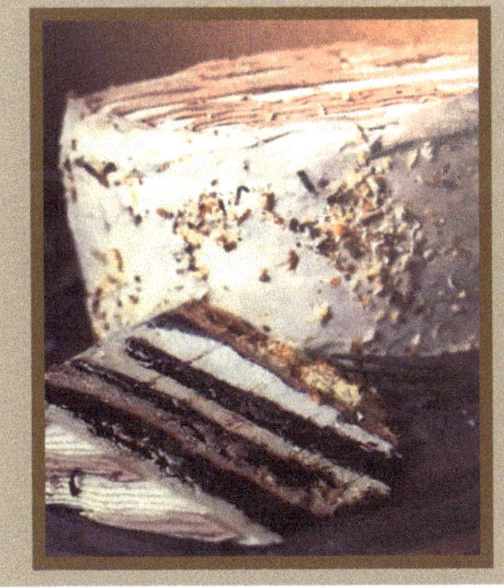

Most of the cake's moistness comes from the simple syrup you apply to the cake slices as you assemble the cake.

Sweet Chocolate Death

To make this cake start the day before serving

DAY 1

Chocolate Meringue

4 egg whites

¾ cup sugar

Run the outside of the mixing bowl through hot water. Eggs must be at room temperature.

Mix ingredients in your mixer at high speed until eggs are stiff, about 10 minutes.

2 tsp unsweetened cocoa

Add in, mix gently. Line the bottom of the springform pan with aluminum foil. Lightly butter the pan and spread the meringue evenly in it.

Bake at 175-degrees for approximately two hours or until meringue is hard. Turn off oven and let meringue set inside for a few more hours or leave in overnight.

Before assembling the cake, remove foil from the bottom of the meringue and place meringue back in the springform pan.

Prepare a 10" chocolate cake

DAY 2

Prepare the whipped cream

¾ cup heavy cream

½ tsp vanilla extract

½ tsp sugar

The colder the cream is, the easier it is to turn it to whipped cream. Using your mixer with a whisk attachment, whip on medium-high speed until medium peaks form, about 3 to 4 minutes. Set aside.

Chocolate Icing

12 oz semisweet chocolate

Melt in the double boil.

2 cups whipping cream

Pour cream into the bowl with the chocolate chips and mix well. With a large spoon, pour a thin layer of the icing on top of the meringue. Save the rest of the icing to be used later.

The prepared chocolate cake

Slice the cake horizontally into there equal slices. Place one of the slices on top of the icing.

Simple Syrup

2 cups of water

¼ cup sugar

Bring to a boil. Reduce heat. Simmer 5-6 minutes.

Brush the cake slice. Save the rest of the syrup for the other two slices.

Chocolate Mousse

24 oz semisweet chocolate

Melt on the double boil. Set aside.

¾ cup heavy cream

½ tsp vanilla extract

1 tsp sugar

Using your mixer with a whisk attachment, whip on medium-high speed until medium peaks form, about 3 to 4 minutes. Set aside.

8 pasteurize egg whites, save the egg yolks.

(How to pasteurize the eggs on page 55)

½ cup sugar

Beat on medium speed in a mixer for about four three minutes until soft peaks form.

"I know I will not have lived until I get a taste of Sweet Chocolate Death."

— Mesa Tribune

Applesauce adds sweetness to recipes with significantly fewer calories than sugar. It helps to replace some of the liquid fats, such as oils or melted butter. Using applesauce can be tricky and it should only be used in certain recipes to soften the texture, such as quick bread or some cakes. Avoid applying it in recipes with a crispy texture, such as cookies biscotti.

The melted semisweet chocolate

Add into the mixer and mix gently on low speed.

6 pasteurized egg yolks

Add in, one at a time, and mix well.

The whipped cream

Add to the mixer and mix gently. Pour half of the mousse on top of the first cake slice.

Lay the second slice of cake on top, brush with simple syrup.

Pour the rest of the mousse on the cake and cover with the third slice of cake.

Brush with the simple syrup.

Refrigerate until mousse is set, about 2 hours.

2 cups sliced almonds

Place on a baking sheet and toast the almonds in a 300-degree oven. About 4 to 5 minutes.

Remove from oven and set aside to cool.

Remove cake from the spring from pan and place it on a working surface.

The Chocolate Icing

Warm it gently and with a large spoon, pour a few spoonfuls at a time on the cake top. With a pastry spatula, cover the sides and top of the cake with the remaining icing.

The toasted almonds

Cover the sides of the cake.

Icing

6 oz semisweet chocolate – Melt on the double boil.

Use 2 tbsp melted chocolate to make chocolate shavings (page 46)

The rest of the melted chocolate

¾ cup whipping cream

Mix well while chocolate is warm.

Spread icing on the side of the cake.

Sprinkle sides of the cake with the chocolate shavings.

1 tsp cinnamon

1 tsp cocoa powder

Mix and sprinkle on the top of the cake.

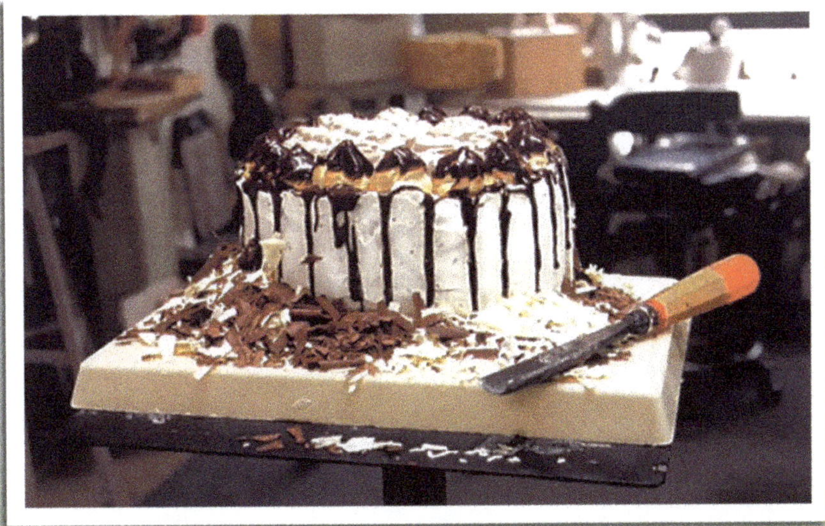

Chocolate Shavings

Cappuccino Mousse Cake

Prepare a 10" chocolate cake

Slice it horizontally to two equal slices. Use the bottom slice and save the top one for another use.

It is best to leave the bottom cake in the springform pan.

You could make truffles with the extra cake. *(See Easy Truffles with Leftover Cake on page 106)*

16 oz semisweet chocolate – Melt on the double boil.

Syrup

1 cup of water
⅛ cup sugar
1 tbsp coffee
1 tsp cocoa powder

Bring to a boil. Reduce heat. Simmer 5-6 minutes. Brush cake with the syrup mixture.

Cappuccino Mousse

2 cups whipped topping
1 tsp vanilla extract

Beat in your mixer on high speed for about three minutes, until topping is stiff.

The melted semisweet chocolate

⅛ cup coffee
1 tsp cocoa powder
¾ cup grated hazelnuts

Add into the mixer and mix gently on low speed.

Pour the mousse on top of the cake, refrigerate until mousse sets, about two hours.

Orange Cinnamon Topping

8 oz white chocolate – Melt on a double boil
¼ cup whipped topping

Beat in your mixer on high speed for about three minutes, until topping is stiff.
Set aside.

4 oz cream cheese
1 tbsp sugar

Place in your mixer and beat on medium speed until smooth and creamy.

⅛ cup sour cream
1 tsp orange peel
½ tsp cinnamon
1 tbsp Kahlua

Add in and blend well. Spread topping on the top of the mousse.

Refrigerate 2 to 3 hours. Remove from the springform pan.

Apple Cream Cake

Preheat oven to 350-degrees

Crust

¾ cup oats
½ cup graham cracker crumbs
½ cup melted unsalted butter

Mix well and press against the bottom of a 10" springform pan.

Apple Filling

6 apples, sliced
¾ cup brown sugar
¼ cup tapioca flour
½ cup raisins
½ cup Amaretto liqueur

Combine in a mixing bowl and mix well. Pour on top of the crust.

Cream Filling

1 ½ lb cream cheese
½ cup sugar

Place in your mixer and beat on medium speed until smooth and creamy.

4 eggs
¾ cup sour cream
Juice of ½ lemon
½ tsp vanilla
¼ cup whipping cream
¼ cup tapioca flour

Add to the mixer, reduce speed, and blend well. Pour mixture into the springform pan.

Bake in the preheated 350-degree oven for 1 ½ hour.

1 tsp cinnamon

Sprinkle on top of the cake. Refrigerate 8 to 10 hours before serving the cake.

Carrot Cake

Preheat oven to 350-degrees

Filling

1 cup of vegetable oil
1 cup of sugar
1 cup of coconut sugar

Place in your mixer and blend on medium speed for about two minutes.

3 eggs

Add to the mixer and blend well.

2 ½ cups shredded carrots
1 tsp vanilla extract
1 ½ cups fresh pineapple, cut in large pieces
½ cup raisins
¾ cup walnuts
1 tsp cinnamon
1 tsp baking soda
2 ½ cups flour

Add to the mixer and mix on medium speed for two to three minutes.

Lightly butter a 10" springform pan or a 10" x 10" baking pan and pour in the filling.

Bake in the 350-degree preheated oven for about 1 ¼ hours.

Let the cake cool.

Frosting

16 oz cream cheese
1 ½ cups powdered sugar

Place in your mixer and beat on medium speed until smooth and creamy.

2 oz unsalted butter, softened
1 tsp vanilla extract
1 cup shredded coconut
½ cup walnuts, grated
1 tsp honey

Add to the mixer and mix on low speed until all ingredients are blended well, about 3 minutes.

Spread the frosting on the entire cake.

NOTE: For gluten free,
substitute the 2 ½ cups flour with:
1 ½ cups gluten-free flour
½ cup brown rice flour
½ cup almond flour
1 tbsp arrowroot
1 tsp baking powder

Blackberry Fudge Cake

Preheat oven to 300-degrees

Cake

24 oz semisweet chocolate
24 oz white chocolate
12 oz unsalted butter

Melt together in the double boil. Set aside.

16 eggs
1 cup of coconut sugar
1 tsp. vanilla

Place in a mixer and beat on medium speed for 2 to 3 minutes.

Add the melted chocolates and mix on slow speed for about 1 minute.

2 cups blackberries

In your food processor, purée the blackberries and strain through a fine sieve to remove the seeds. You should end up with about 1 cup raspberry pure.

Add to the mixer and blend with the chocolate mixture.

Lightly butter a 10" springform pan and pour in the filling.

Place springform pan in a large baking sheet filled with ¼" of water.

Bake the fudge cake in the preheated 300-degree oven for 1 ¼ hours.

Turn the oven off and let the cake sit for 30 minutes.

Remove the cake from the oven and let cool for 6 to 8 hours before removing from the pan.

Icing

2 cups semisweet chocolate

Melt in a double boil

1 ½ cups whipping cream

Blend. Spread on the entire cake.

3 cups of shredded coconut

Place coconut on a baking pan and toast in a 350-degree oven, 5 to 6 minutes until golden brown.

Occasionally stir the coconut to be baked evenly.

Sprinkle the entire cake with the toasted coconut.

Cinnamon Stick Cake

Preheat oven to 350-degrees

Prepare crust (page 31)

Lightly buttered a 10" springform pan and line it with the crust.

Filling

2 lbs cream cheese
1 cup of sugar

Place in your mixer and beat on medium speed until smooth and creamy.

4 eggs
1 cup sour cream
Juice of ½ lemon
1 tbs vanilla extract
½ cup whipping cream
1 tsp cinnamon
1 tbsp tapioca flour

Add to the mixer, reduce speed, and blend well. Pour mixture into the springform pan.

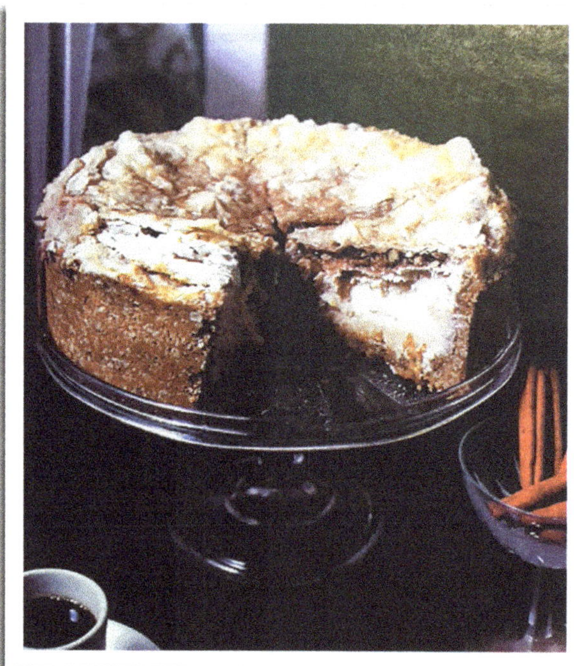

Cinnamon Stick Cake

Topping

3 cups pecan pieces
½ cup sugar
½ cup melted unsalted butter
1 tsp cinnamon
1 tsp ground cloves

Mix in a mixing bowl. Set aside.

16 sheets of the fillo dough

Place fillo on a working surface and cut into 10" circles. I use a 10" springform pan, and with a sharp knife, I slice the fillo around the pan.

¼ cup unsalted butter, melted

Place 8 fillo dough on top of the filling, one at a time, and brush each fillo with butter.

Spread topping evenly on top of the fillo.

Place the rest of the fillo on the topping, one at a time and brush each fillo with butter.

Bake in the preheated 350-degree oven for one hour and 15 minutes. Turn off the oven and let the cake sit in the oven for 30 minutes longer.

Syrup

2 cups of water
1 cinnamon stick
1 tsp cinnamon
3 whole cloves
½ cup sugar
2 tbs. Honey

Place in a small saucepan, bring to boil, simmer for 15 minutes.

Remove cake from oven and pour syrup over the top. Refrigerate overnight before moving from the springform pan.

Getting past the display cases of totally decadent and mouth-watering desserts takes a true showing of Herculean strength.

— Mesa Tribune

Sinful Act

Preheat over to 300-degrees

Crust

1 ½ cups rolled oats
1 ½ cups graham cracker crumbs
1 cup of sugar
8 oz unsalted butter, melted

Mix well in a mixing bowl.

Butter a 10" springform pan and press mixture against the sides and the bottom of the form.

Chocolate Chambord Cake

32 oz semisweet chocolate
12 oz unsalted butter

Melt together in the double boil. Place mixture into the bowl of your mixer.

9 eggs
½ cup sugar

Add to the mixer and blend well.

1 cup Raspberries

In your food processor, purée the raspberries and strain through a fine sieve to remove the seeds.

Add to the chocolate and mix well. Pour half of the chocolate mixture into the sprinform pan.

12 sheets of the fillo dough
2 oz unsalted butter

Cut fillo into 10" circles. I use a 10" springform pan, and with a sharp knife, I slice the fillo around the pan. Lay six fillo on top of chocolate Chambord, buttering each one.

White Chocolate cake

¾ cup cream cheese
¼ cup sugar

Cream together in your mixer.

16 oz white chocolate

Melt in a double boil.

1 cup sour cream
1 tsp vanilla extract
3 eggs

Add to the chocolate and blend well.

Pour batter on top of phyllo. Layer remainingsix phyllo on top of white chocolate cake.

Pour remaining dark chocolate cake batter across the phyllo top.

Place in a sheet pan fill with about 1/2-inch water .

Bake in the preheated oven for one hour. Turn oven off and let the cake rest in the oven for another 30 minutes.

Raspberry Syrup

½ cup frozen raspberries
2 tbsp sugar
½ cup hot water

Let raspberries in the water for a few minutes. Press through a sieve to discard the seeds. Pour over the top of the baked cake. Refrigerate for at least 12 hours before removing from the pan.

Cakes are associated with the most important moments in our life. How can it be a celebration without indulging in the sight and the taste of an enticing cake? The preparation and the decoration of a cake require love and imagination. It is the art that brings out both the powerful and sensitive side of our artistic self. The final result is fulfilling to the artist, awarded the satisfaction of watching the guests' ecstatic faces as they are enjoying the final creation.

Rated X Cake

Prepare one 10" chocolate cake

Slice it horizontally to four equal slices.

Melt 10 oz of semisweet chocolate on the double boil. Set aside

Melt 10 oz white chocolate on the double boil. Set aside.

Syrup

1 ½ cup of water
¼ cup sugar
1 tsp Kahlua
1 tbs coffee

Bring to a boil. Reduce heat. Simmer 5 to 6 minutes.

Place a slice of cake in the springform pan and brush it with part of the syrup.

Almond Mousse

4 pasteurized egg whites (save the egg yolks)
⅛ cup sugar

Beat on medium speed in a mixer for about three minutes until soft peaks form.

The melted semisweet chocolate

Add into the mixer and mix gently on low speed.

3 pasteurized egg yolks
⅛ cup coffee
½ cup sliced almonds, chopped

Add into the mixer and mix well. Spread on top of the first cake slice.

Place another slice of chocolate cake on top of the almond mousse.

Brush the cake with part of the simple syrup.

Banana Rum Filling

4 oz cream cheese
½ cup sugar

Place in your mixer and beat on medium speed until smooth and creamy.

½ cup sour cream
1 soft banana, chopped
1 tsp rum

Add to the mixer and blend on medium speed.

The melted white chocolate

Add to the mixer and blend well at slow speed.

Spread filling on top of the chocolate cake.

Place the third slice of cake on top of the banana rum filling.

Brush the cake with part of the simple syrup.

Grand Marnier Chocolate

1 cup whipping cream
1 tbsp Grand Marnier

Pour into a saucepan and heat gently on low speed.

8 oz semisweet chocolate

Add to the saucepan, a few at a time, and blend well. Turn heat off.

Let it cool for a few minutes

1 more cup whipping cream

Using your mixer with a whisk attachment, whip on medium-high speed until medium peaks form, about 3 to 4 minutes.

"It's Darn Difficult to stroll the dessert cases without eventually surrendering to a slice of one of Nick's celebrated desserts."
— Phoenix Downtown Magazine

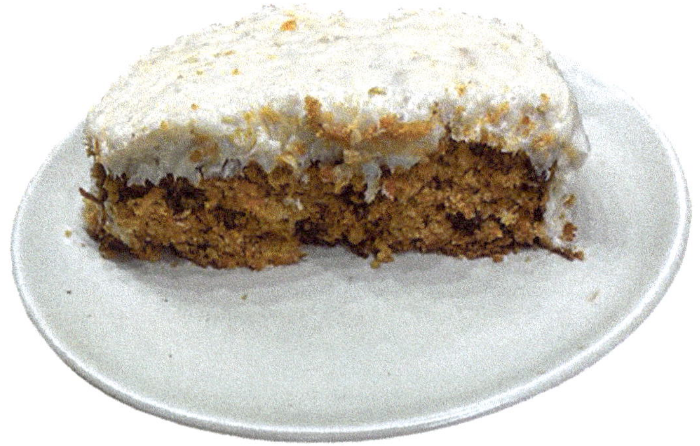

Fold the whipped cream into the semisweet chocolate, small amounts at a time, blending with a spatula, until the mixture is smooth.

Spread the Grand Marnier Chocolate on top of the genoise cake.

Top with the last slice of chocolate cake and brush the cake with syrup.

Refrigerate the cake for at least 3 to 4 hours before removing from the pan.

White chocolate shavings

4 oz of white chocolate,

Melt on a double boil. Make chocolate shavings (page 46)

12 amaretti cookies

(See recipe on page 130)

Arrange the amaretti cookies in a circle around the outer edge of the cake top.

Icing

12 oz semisweet chocolate

Melt on a double boil.

2 cups whipping cream

Add to the melded chocolate while on the double boil, and blend well. Spread icing over the cake, including cookies and sides. Refrigerate for 2 to 3 hours.

The white chocolate shavings

Sprinkle on top and sides of the cake.

The Rated X Cake is several chocolate cake layers spread with almond mousse, banana rum mousse and Grand Marnier chocolate surrounded by an amaretti cookie crust and balanced with chocolate ganache.

— Tribune papers

To make Vanilla Pastry Cream

2 cups milk

1 tsp. vanilla extract

Bring to boil, set aside.

6 egg yolks

⅔ cup sugar

Beat on medium speed, 4-5 minutes.

4 tbsp flour

Add in, mix well, remove from mixer.

Add the hot milk slowly, beating with a wire whip.

Bring mixture to boil, stirring, boil for one minute.

Remove, stir until smooth.

For Chocolate Pastry Cream add 6 oz semisweet chocolate, melted

Chestnut purée is made with fresh chestnuts, peeled, boiled and then pureed. Chestnut cream is made with chestnut puree mixed with milk, sugar, and a little vanilla. To easily peel the chestnut, boil in water for about 1 minute.

Use 2 ½ cups of chestnuts (about 1 lb) in 5 cups of milk, 1 tbsp sugar, ¼ tsp vanilla extract.

Chestnut puree and cream are sold canned in specialty shops.

White Passion Cake

Preheat your oven to 350-degrees

Prepare one 10" white cake

2 cups of shredded coconut

Place coconut on a baking pan and toast in a 350-degree oven, 5 to 6 minutes until golden brown. Occasionally stir the coconut to be baked evenly. Set aside.

24 oz white chocolate

Melt in a double boil over low heat. Set aside.

Chocolate shavings

2 large pieces of parchment paper.

4 tbsp of the melted chocolate

Make chocolate shavings *(page 46)*

Simple syrup

1 cup of water

¼ cup coconut sugar

1 tsp vanilla extract

Bring to a boil in a small pan reduce heat and simmer for 3 to 4 minutes. Set aside.

The prepared white cake

Slice it in three horizontal slices. Place one slice on a serving platter and brush it with part of the syrup.

Prepare the cream

3 cups whipped topping

½ tsp pure vanilla extract

With the wire whip of your mixer beat on high speed until it forms stiff peaks.

Set cream aside.

Macadamia Cream Filling

2 oz unsalted butter

¼ cup sugar

Place in your mixer and beat on medium speed until smooth and creamy.

½ cup Macadamia nuts, chopped

½ tsp vanilla

Juice of ½ orange

¼ cup heavy cream

1 cup of the melted white chocolate

Add to the mixer and blend gently for about two minutes.

Spread the macadamia cream filling on the first slice of the cake.

Mango mousse

4 oz cream cheese

½ cup of sugar

Place in your mixer and beat on medium speed until smooth and creamy.

½ cup sour cream

1 mango, peeled and chopped. Drain excess liquid.

Add to the mixer and blend gently.

1 ½ cup of the whipped topping

1 cup of the melted white chocolate

Add to the mixer and thoroughly blend at low speed. Pour filling on the first slice of the cake and top it with the second cake slice. Brush some of the simple syrup over the second cake slice.

Kiwi white chocolate

4 oz cream cheese

½ cup sugar

Place in your mixer and beat on medium speed until smooth and creamy.

¼ cup sour cream

3 kiwi, peeled and chopped

Add to the mixer and blend gently.

1 ½ cup of the whipped topping

1 cup of the melted white chocolate

Add to the mixer and thoroughly blend at low speed. Pour filling on the second slice of the cake and top it with the third cake slice. Brush some of the simple syrup over the second cake slice.

Refrigerate the cake for at least 2 to 3 hours.

Icing

8 oz cream cheese

¼ cup sour cream

Place in your mixer and beat on medium speed until smooth and creamy.

Remaining prepared cream

Remaining melted white chocolate

Add to the mixer and thoroughly blend at low speed.

Spread on the top and the sides of the cake.

The toasted coconut

Cover the sides of the cake with it.

White chocolate shavings

Take out the parchment paper from the freezer, remove the top paper, and break the thin chocolate into pieces. Cover the top of the cake with the white chocolate shavings.

Four Seasons Cake

Prepare one 10" chocolate cake.

Slice it horizontally in three slices.

Syrup

1 ½ cups of water
¼ cup sugar
⅛ cup frozen raspberries

Bring to a boil. Reduce heat. Simmer 5 to 6 minutes. Drain.

Place a slice of cake in the springform pan and brush it with syrup.

Pomegranate Mousse

6 oz semisweet chocolate
¼ cup heavy cream
2 oz unsalted butter

Melt in a double boil. Remove.

¼ cup pomegranate juice
2 tbsp coconut sugar

Add to the chocolate and blend.
Spread mousse on top of cake.

Kiwi Chocolate

4 oz cream cheese
½ cup sugar

Place in your mixer and beat on medium speed until smooth and creamy.

½ cup sour cream
2 kiwi, peeled and chopped

Add to the mixer and blend gently.

4 oz white chocolate

Melt in a double boil and add to the mixer.
Pour on top of the pomegranate mousse.
Top it with a slice of cake. Brush with syrup.

Strawberry Chocolate

6 oz semisweet chocolate
¼ cup heavy cream
2 oz unsalted butter

Melt in a double boil. Remove.

1 cup strawberries

Pulse 2 to 3 in the food processor and blend with the chocolate. Spread mousse on top of cake.

Cherry White Chocolate

4 oz cream cheese
1/2 cup sugar

Place in your mixer and beat on medium speed until smooth and creamy.

½ cup sour cream
½ cup frozen dark cherries, thawed and drained.
½ soft banana
1 tsp vanilla extract

Add to the mixer and blend gently.

4 oz white chocolate

Melt in a double boil and add to the mixer.
Pour on top of the strawberry chocolate.
Top it with a slice of cake. Brush with syrup.
Refrigerate for 5 to 6 hours.

Icing

2 cups whipped topping
½ tsp pure vanilla extract

With the wire whip of your mixer beat on high speed until it forms stiff peaks. Set aside.

4 oz cream cheese

Cream in your mixer.

4 oz white chocolate melted
¼ cup sour cream
The whipped cream

Add and mix well. Spread icing on top and sides of the cake.

Sprinkle the cake with Dark chocolate shavings..

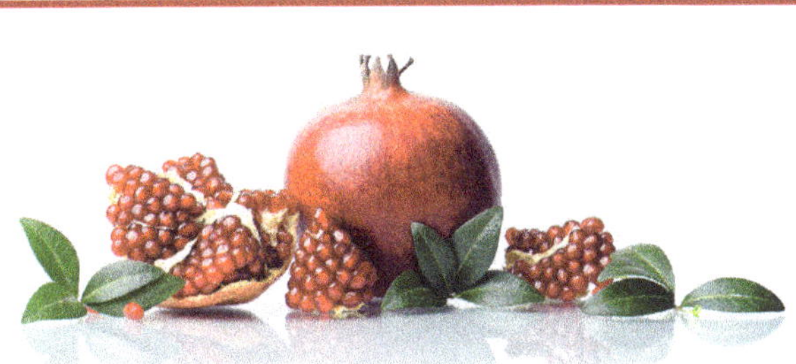

Pomegranate Juice

1 cup pomegranate seeds

Place ingredients in a food processor and pulse.

Pour the pulp into a mesh sieve placed over a bowl and squeeze the pulp through to strain out the juice.

½ cup water
1 tbsp sugar

Add to the pomegranate and mix.

After Death Cake

To make this cake start the day before serving.

DAY 1

Preheat oven to 175-degrees

Walnut Meringue

4 egg whites

¾ cup sugar

1 tsp vanilla extract

Run the outside of the mixing bowl through hot water. Eggs must be at room temperature.

Mix ingredients in your mixer at high speed until eggs are stiff, about 10 minutes.

Add in, mix gently. Line the bottom of the springform pan with aluminum foil. Lightly butter the aluminum foil and spread the meringue evenly on top of it.

Bake at 175-degrees for approximately two hours or until meringue is hard. Turn off the oven and let meringue set inside for a few more hours or leave overnight.

Before assembling the cake, remove foil from the bottom of the meringue and place meringue back in the springform pan.

Prepare a 10" white cake

DAY 2

24 oz white chocolate

Melt in a double boil over low heat. When chocolate melts, turn off the heat.

Prepare the cream

3 cups whipped topping

½ tsp pure vanilla extract

With the wire whip of your mixer beat on high speed until it forms stiff peaks.

Set cream aside.

Simple syrup

1 cup of water

¼ cup sugar

½ tsp almond extract

1 tbsp rum

Bring to a boil in a small pan, reduce heat and simmer for 3 to 4 minutes. Set aside.

The prepared white cake

Slice it in three horizontal slices. Place one slice on a serving platter and brush it with part of the syrup.

Cream Almond Filling

4 oz unsalted butter

½ cup sugar

Place in your mixer and beat on medium speed until smooth and creamy.

½ cup almonds, chopped

2 cups prepared whipped topping

2 tbsp orange juice

1 ½ cups melted white chocolate.

Add in and beat on slow speed about 2 to 3 minutes.

Spread cream almond filling on the meringue.

Place the first slice of cake on top of the walnut meringue.

Brush the cake slice with a part of simple syrup.

"Cakes and pies to Nick, they are like marble to Michaelangelo; just a starting point to White Passion Cake souped up with kiwi and wild mango mousse."

— Java Magazine, Dec. 1997

Banana Mousse

2 bananas

Place in your mixer and beat on medium speed until to a paste consistency.

2 cups prepared whipped topping

1 cup golden raisins

1 ½ cups of the melted white chocolate

Add to the mixer and mix on medium heat for another 2 to 3 minutes.

Spread banana mousse on top of the first slice of cake and with top banana mousse with the second cake slice. Brush the cake slice with a part of simple syrup.

White Chocolate Mousse

1½ cups prepared whipped topping

1 cup of the melted white chocolate

½ tsp vanilla extract

Add to the mixer and blend for about 1 to 2 minutes.

Spread white chocolate mousse on top of the second cake slice and top mousse with the last slice of cake. Refrigerate 2 to 3 hours.

White Chocolate Icing

4 oz cream cheese

¼ cup sugar

Place in your mixer and beat on medium speed until smooth and creamy.

The remaining prepared whipped topping

The remaining melted white chocolate

2 tbsp sour cream

Add to the mixer, blend on low speed until smooth, 2 to 3 minutes. Cover the entire cake with icing.

2 cups hazelnuts, grated

Sprinkle whole cake with the hazelnuts

White Chocolate Cake

16 oz white chocolate

Melt in a double boil.

12 oz cream cheese

½ cup sugar

Place cream cheese and sugar in your mixer and beat on medium speed until creamy.

1 cup sour cream

1 tsp. vanilla

3 eggs

Add to the mixer and blend on low speed for two to three minutes. Pour batter on top of fillo.

Layer remaining six fillo on top of white chocolate cake, buttering each fillo round.

Pour remaining dark cake batter across the top of the fillo rounds. Place springform pan in a large baking sheet filled with 1/4-inch of water.

Bake the cake in the 300-degree preheated oven for 1 ¼ hour.

Raspberry Sauce

1 cup raspberries

2 tbsp water

In your food processor, purée the raspberries and water and strain through a fine sieve.

⅛ cup Chambord

Blend with raspberries in a mixing bowl and pour the sauce over the cake.

Remove the cake from the oven and let cool for 6 to 8 hours before removing from the pan.

"In his legendary restaurant, Nick makes a dessert named Sinful Act. It is a diabolical, multi-layered chocolate creation."

— Best of Phoenix

Final Addiction

Preheat over to 325-degrees

Crust

¼ cup walnuts, grated
¼ cup oats
¼ cup graham cracker crumbs
⅛ cup unsalted butter, melted
⅛ cup sugar

Mix well in a mixing bowl.

Butter a 10" springform pan and press mixture against the sides and the bottom of the form.

Hazelnut Chestnut Filling

16 oz semisweet chocolate

Melt in the double boil.

8 oz cream cheese
1 cup of sugar

Place in your mixer and beat on medium speed until smooth and creamy.

½ cup chestnut purée
4 eggs

Add to the mixer and mix well on low speed, 2 to 3 minutes

The melted semisweet chocolate

1 cup whipping cream
¼ cup grated hazelnuts
2 tbsp Kahlua
1 tsp vanilla extract

Add in and mix well. Pour cake batter into the springform pan.

24 to 26 ladyfinger cookies (about 5" long)

Dip the ladyfingers against the inside of the springform pan to reach the bottom of the pan.

Continue until the inside of the pan covered with the ladyfingers.

White Chocolate Filling

12 oz white chocolate

Melt in the double boil.

8 oz cream cheese

½ cup sugar

Place in your mixer and beat on medium speed until smooth and creamy.

The melted white chocolate

1 cup sour cream

Add to the mixer and blend well.

Pour the white chocolate filling on top of hazelnut chestnut filling.

Stick a butter knife into the cake and swirl to mix both mixtures, creating a design of dark and white swirls on top of the cake.

Bake the cake in the 325-degree preheated oven for 1 ¼ hour.

Refrigerate 8 to 10 hours before removing from the springform pan.

After baking the cake, some of the ladyfingers may have risen. Press ladyfingers back down to reach the bottom of the pan again.

Icing

4 oz white chocolate

Melt in the double boil. Turn off the heat.

¼ cup sour cream

Add to the white chocolate and blend with a spatula.

Spread icing over sides of cake only.

½ cup hazelnuts, grated

Sprinkle the sides of the cake with the hazelnuts.

I've somehow survived the Final Addiction, a near-death blend of white and dark chocolates, hazelnut chocolate, chestnut purée and Kahlua."

— New Times

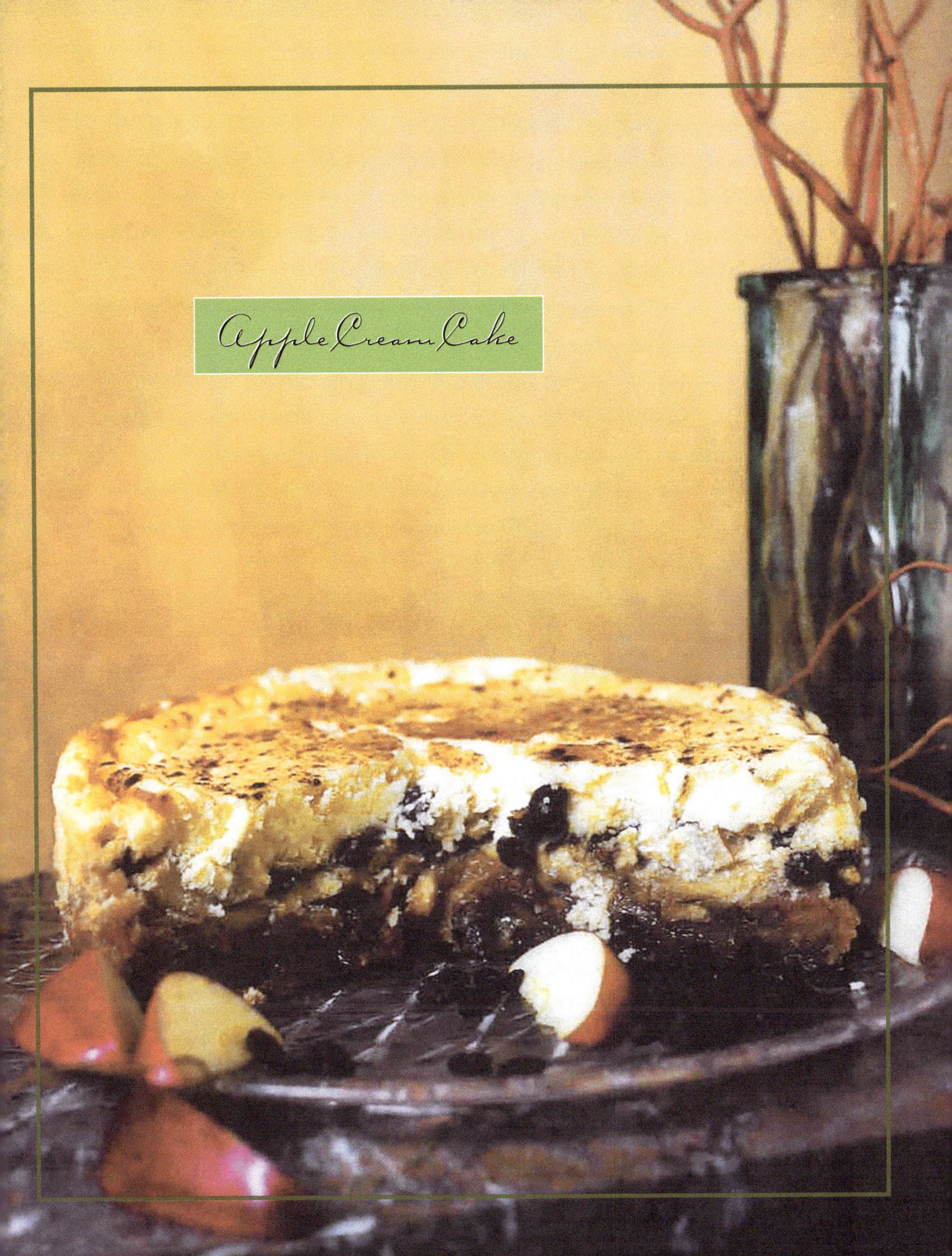
Apple Cream Cake

WHAT IS A DESSERT?

"To many, it is a daily luxury celebrating some of nature's finest culinary gifts. To unfortunate others, it is a sinful act of indulgence, guilty calories, and sadly untreasured pleasure.To me, dessert is a great challenge, with success measured only by a plate scraped clean. To combine flavors that create a smooth, pleasant taste finale to a perfect meal is great art."

How To Make Rosettes

Place a large star tip on the large pastry bag and fill it to about half or three quarters with the whipped topping. To pipe the whipped topping, place one hand on the top of the bag to push the topping down and your other hand towards the bottom of the bag to squeeze the topping.

To make rosettes placc the tip on the surface of the cake, squeeze and slowly lift the pastry bag.

For various designs, place the tip of the bag close to the surface of the cake and, with a continuous motion, move the tip while swirling or making up-and-down movements. You can be creative and pipe any design of your choice.

You could practice piping a few designs on parchment paper before icing directly onto the cake. The most common area to apply the topping is around the edges of the cake to make a border.

Chocolate

"Its exquisite aroma paralyzes the senses; it is like no other aroma that has ever fragranced the kitchen walls. When you first taste chocolate, it warms up your palette for an instant, pervading your mind for a while. Then suddenly, it awakens a mortal fever for its taste."

Learning to work with leftovers

Leftovers could be an inspiration for new recipes. Working in the restaurant, while preparing, especially desserts, sometimes we had some leftover melted chocolate or cake. Rather than refrigerating the leftover items we used them to create something new. Part of respecting food is that you do not waste it. Working with leftovers, it is an excellent chance to practice your skills on the preparation of your new recipe.

"I took a bite of Sweet Chocolate Death and suddenly I was floating above our table, moving irresistibly towards a brilliant light filled with warmth and love I'd never known."

— Java Magazine

"Baking is the most poetic of the culinary arts. Baking requires patience and daring instincts to express the mind on its fullest dimensions. The primary requirement for dessert making is imagination and the benefit is free time for the soul. To be exact, baking is not like poetry – it is poetry.

The pastry maker and the poet are committed to the task of nourishing the world with imaginary food for the soul. Anyone on this artistic level is capable of giving you a vision of paradise."

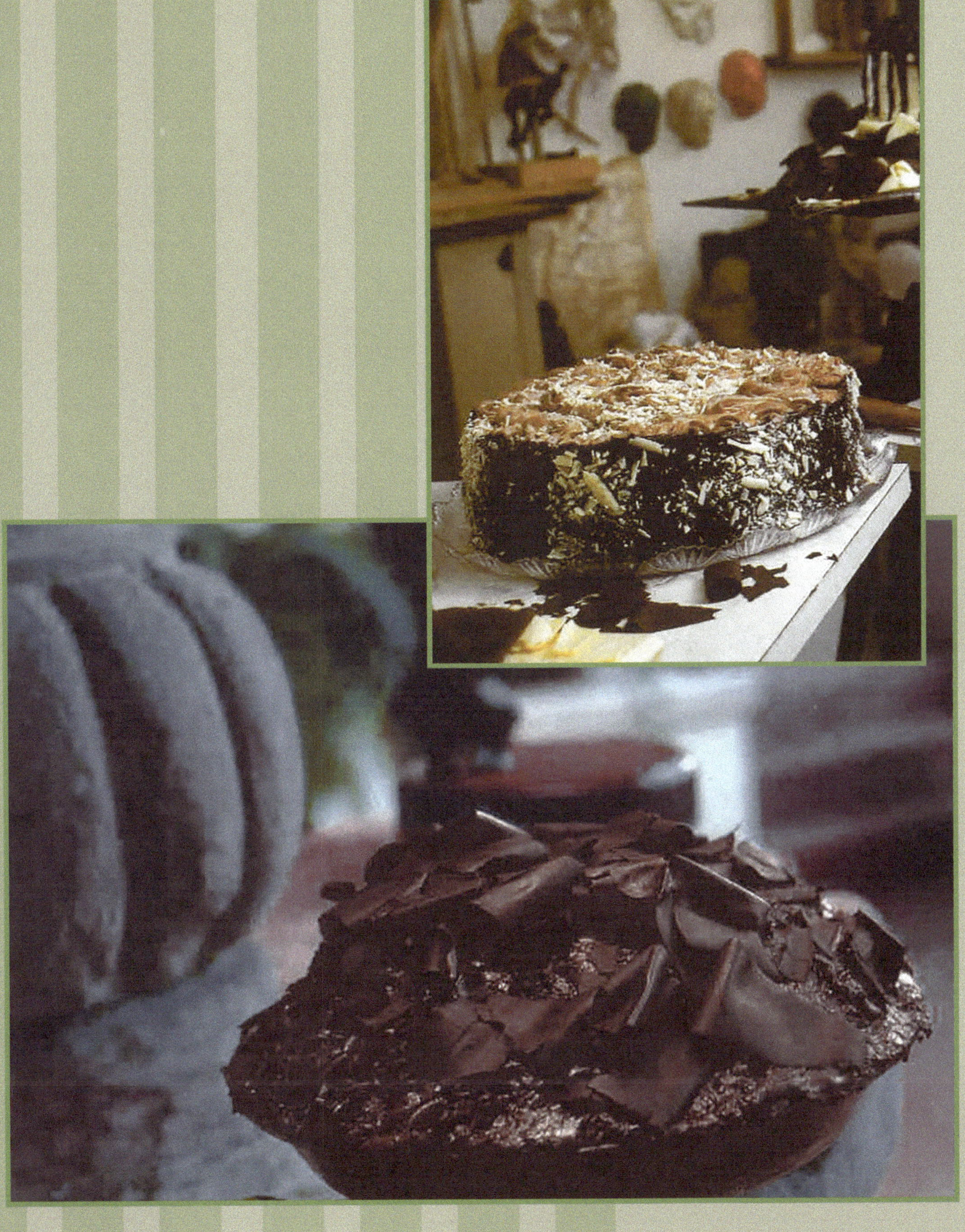

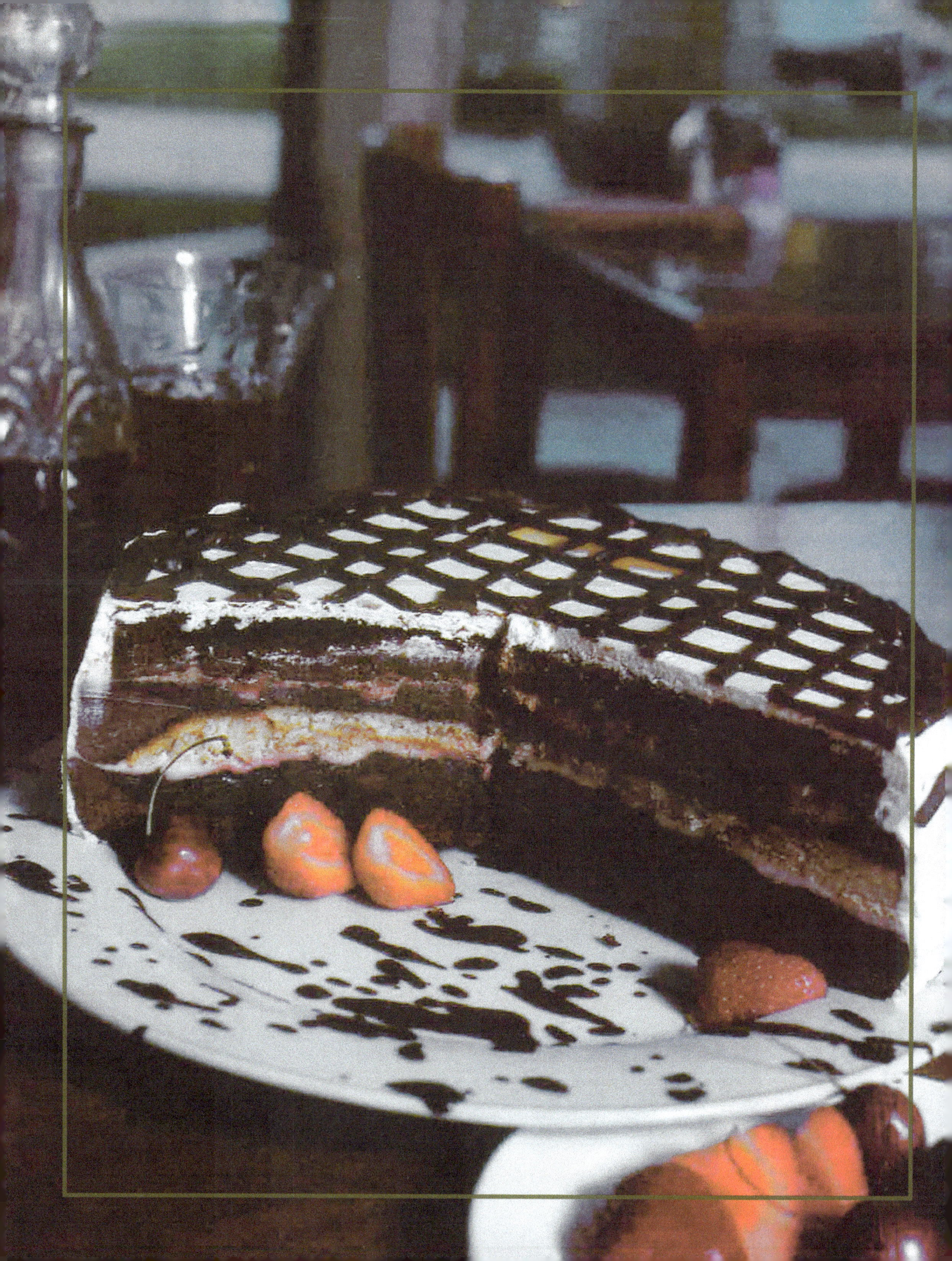

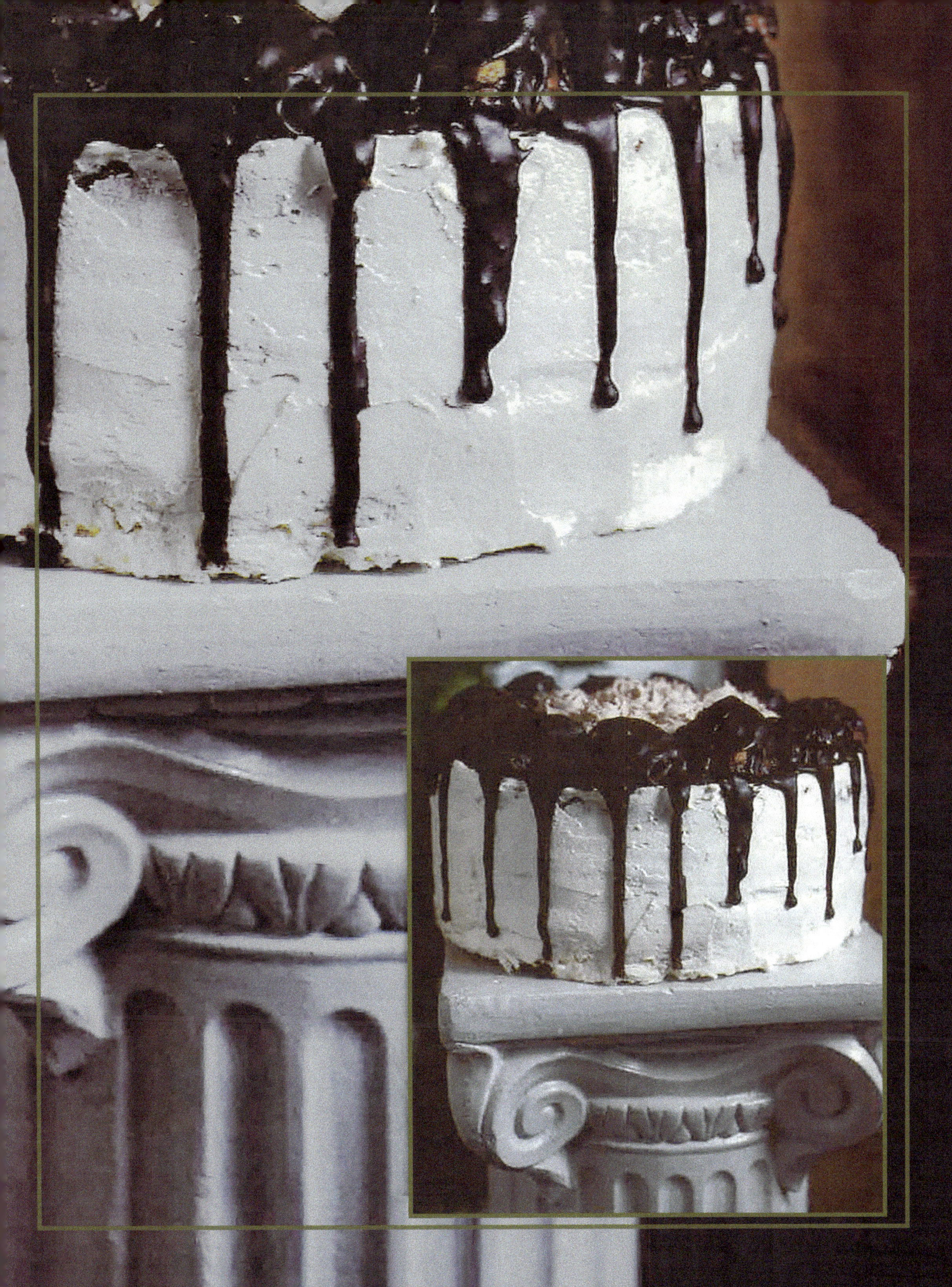

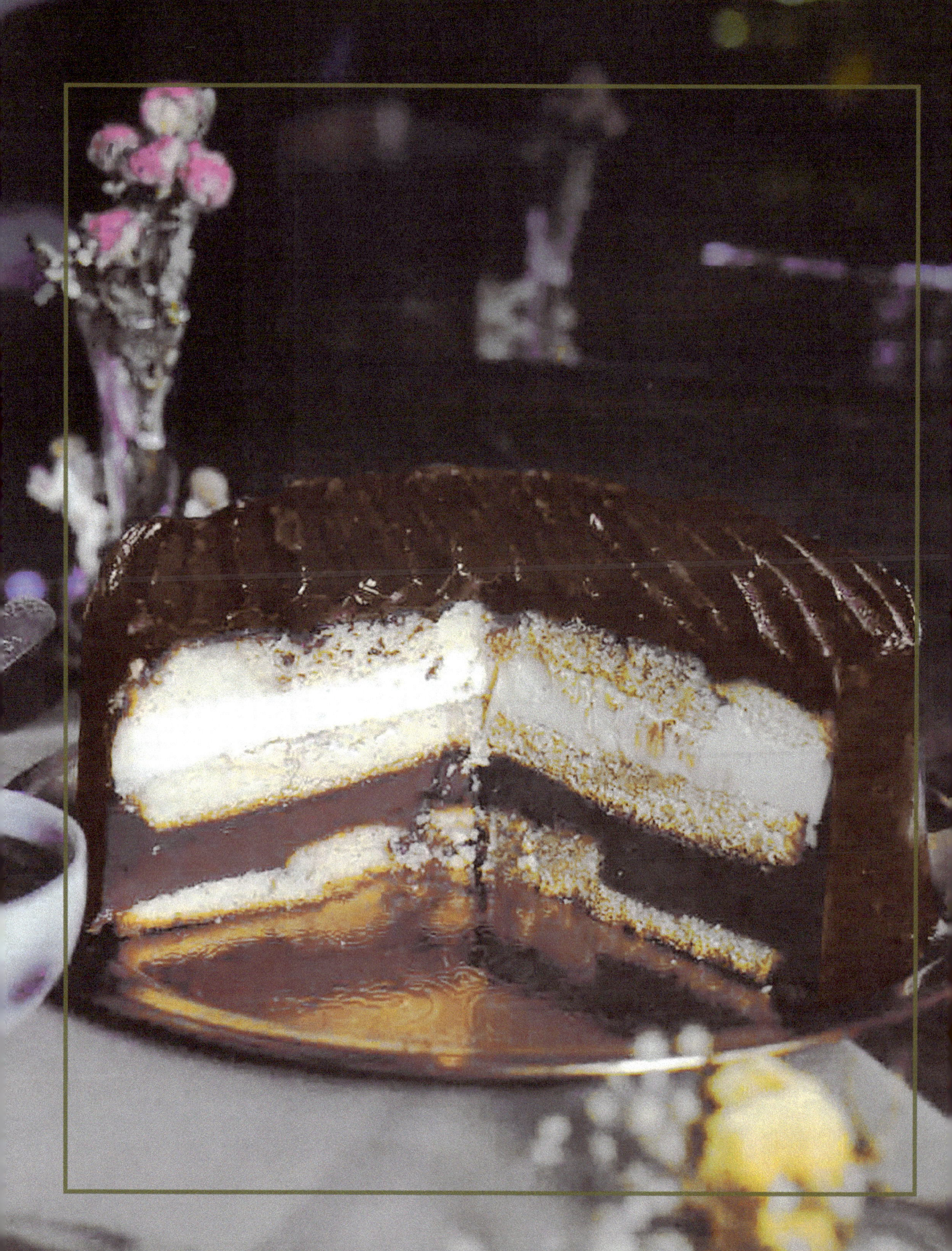

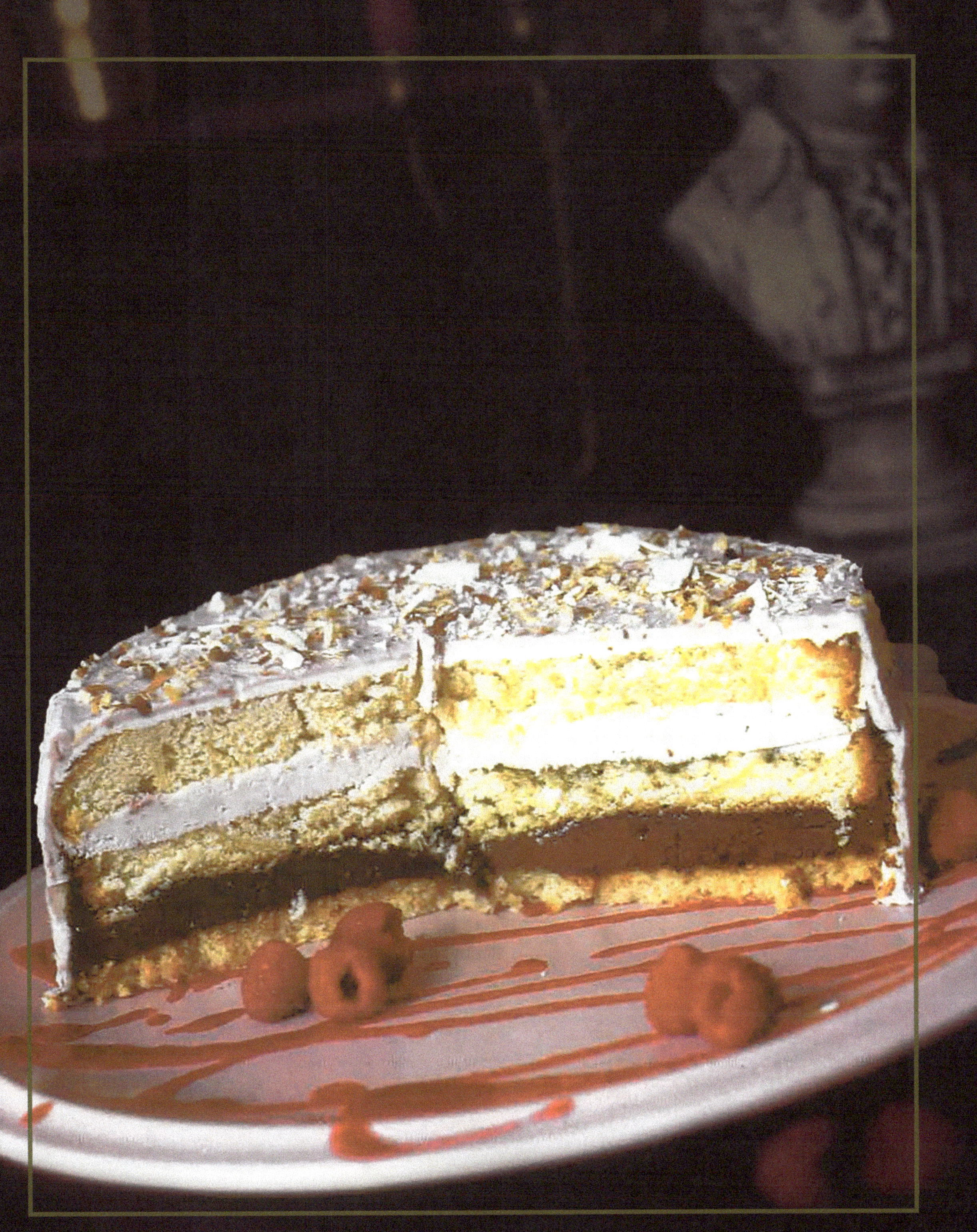

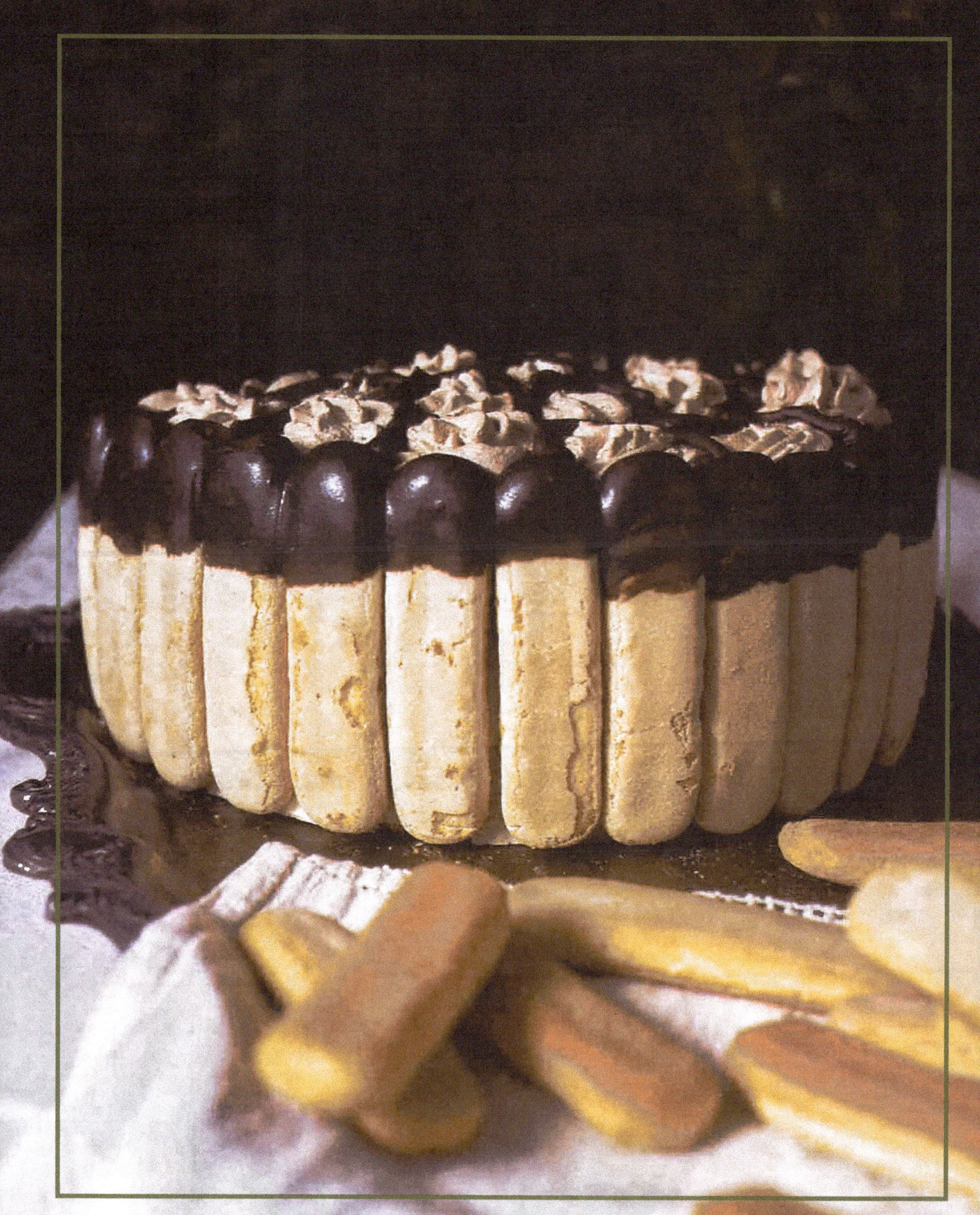

Lady Killer

Prepare one 10" white cake (page 59)

Slice the cake into 3 equal horizontal slices. Place the first slice on a service platter.

Rum simple syrup

1 cup of water
¼ cup sugar
1 tbsp rum

Bring to a boil in a small pan, reduce heat and simmer for 3 to 4 minutes.

Brush the first slice with part of the syrup.

Banana Peanut Chocolate

8 oz white chocolate

Melt in a double boil. Turn heat off.

4 oz sour cream
1 banana, chopped
2 oz. creamy peanut butter
½ cup whipping cream wormed in a small saucepan

Mix well on medium speed of your mixer.

Add the melted white chocolate and mix at slow speed for about two minutes.

Place the second slice on top and brush with part of the rum syrup.

Boysenberry Mousse

6 oz semisweet chocolate

Melt in a double boil.

1 ½ cups whipped topping
½ tsp pure vanilla extract

With the wire whip of your mixer beat on high speed until it forms stiff peaks.

Add the melted chocolate and blend for a few minutes until smooth.

1 cup boysenberries

In a food processor, purée the boysenberries and strain through a fine sieve to remove the seeds.

Add to the mixer and blend with the chocolate mixture.

Spread the boysenberry mousse on top of the cake.

Place the third slice on top of the mousse and brush with rum syrup.

White Chocolate Icing

12 oz white chocolate

Melt in a double boil.

4 oz unsalted butter
1 cups powder sugar

Place in your mixer and beat on medium speed until smooth and creamy.

4 oz sour cream

The melted white chocolate

Add to the mixer and blend well. Spread on top of the cake and a thin layer around the cake.

24 to 26 ladyfingers...or enough to cover the side of the cake (page 129)

Chocolate Icing

1 ¼ cup whipping cream

Gently heat in a small saucepan.

8 oz semisweet chocolate chips

Add to the saucepan and stir to melt the chocolate.

Dip the end of each ladyfinger in the chocolate and place it on the side of the cake with dipped chocolate end on top. Repeat the process until the ladyfingers have covered the sides of the cake.

Save the remaining icing.

Cocoa Cream

6 oz white chocolate

Melt in a double boil.

2 cups whipped topping
½ tsp vanilla extract

With the wire whip of your mixer beat on high speed until it forms stiff peaks.

1 tbsp cocoa powder

The melted chocolate

Add in and mix on low speed until smooth.

Place cocoa cream in a pastry bag with a large star tip and fill the top of the cake with rosettes.

The remaining icing

Place it in a pastry bag with a narrow straight tip and make chocolate lines around the rosettes.

Nineteen Twenty Eight

To make this cake start the day before serving.

DAY 1

Chocolate Meringue

8 egg whites

1 ½ cup sugar

Run the outside of the mixing bowl through hot water. Eggs must be at room temperature.

Mix ingredients in your mixer at high speed until eggs are stiff, about 10 minutes.

2 tsp. unsweetened cocoa

Add in, mix gently. Line the bottom of 2 springform pan with aluminum foil. Lightly butter the aluminum foil, separate the meringue in two parts, and spread the meringue evenly in the two springform pans.

Bake at 175-degrees for approximately 2 hours or until meringue is hard. Turn off the oven and let meringue set inside for a few more hours or leave overnight.

Before assembling the cake, remove foil from the bottom of the meringue and place meringue back in the springform pan.

Prepare a 10" chocolate cake.

DAY 2

Prepare the cream

4 cups whipped topping

1 tsp pure vanilla extract

With the wire whip of your mixer beat on high speed until it forms stiff peaks. Set aside.

First Cream Layer

Place one of the one meringue on a serving platter.

6 oz semisweet chocolate

Melt in a double boil. Remove from the heat.

2½ cups whipped topping

Add to the chocolate and stir with a spatula to blend well.

6 oz white chocolate

Melt in a double boil in a separate bowl. Remove from the heat.

2 ½ cups whipped topping

Add to the white chocolate and stir with a spatula to blend well.

Use two pastry bags with a wide straight tip.

Fill one bag with the dark chocolate cream.

Fill the other bag with the white chocolate cream.

Start with the dark cream and make a thick circle on the edges of the top of the meringue.

Then use the white cream and make a circle inside the dark circle.

Repeat the circles until half of the creams used.

One slice of chocolate cake

Approximately 2" thick. Place on top of the cream.

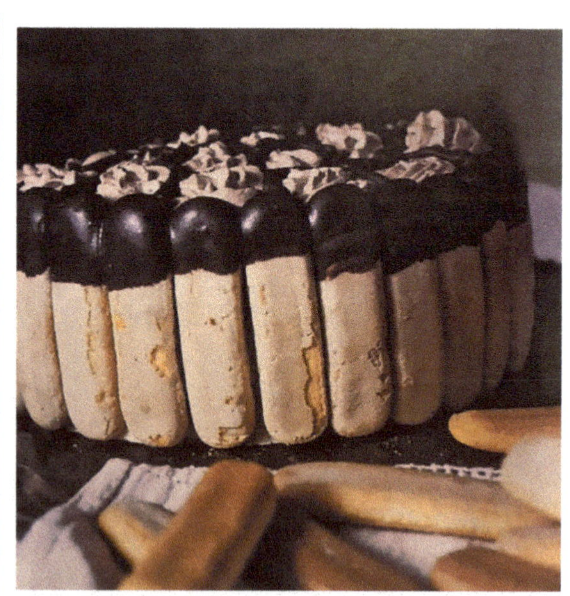

Lady Killer

Raspberry Sauce
2 cups raspberries
4 tbsp water
1 tsp sugar
In your food processor, purée the raspberries, water and sugar strain through a fine sieve to remove the seeds.
Brush the cake with part of the syrup. Reserve some syrup for later use.
Repeat the cream circles on the top of the cake with the remaining creams. This time start with the white cream. By doing this, when you slice the cake, you will have a black and white checkered effect.
Place the other meringue on top of the cream.

Dark Chocolate Icing
6 oz. semisweet chocolate
Melt in a double boil.
3 cups whipped topping
Add to the white chocolate and stir with a spatula to blend well.
Spread the icing on the entire cake.

White Chocolate Icing
½ cup heavy cream
Heat in a small saucepan.
4 oz. white chocolate
Add to the boiling pot and stir to melt.
Cover the sides of the cake with a thin layer of the white chocolate icing. Reserve the rest of the Icing. Run a brush gently on the sides of the cake over the white chocolate icing to give the cake an antique-like effect.

The reserved dark chocolate icing
Make rosettes on the edges of the top of the cake.

The reserved white chocolate icing
Spread in on the top of the cake.
1 tbsp of the remaining raspberry syrup
Pour on the white chocolate cream and swirl it with your finger to mix with the chocolate.
¼ cup heavy cream
Heat in a small saucepan.
2 oz white chocolate
Add to the boiling pot and stir to melt.
Place in a pastry bag with a narrow straight tip. Place the tip of the bag on the top edge of the cake. Squeeze the bag and let the chocolate run down to the side of the cake, making lines on the side of the cake. The lines should be approximately 2" apart.
¼ cup heavy cream
Heat in a small saucepan.
2 oz semisweet chocolate
Add to the boiling pot and stir to melt.
Mix well. Place in a pastry bag with a narrow straight tip.
Repeat the preceding process is making white lines now, between the dark lines.

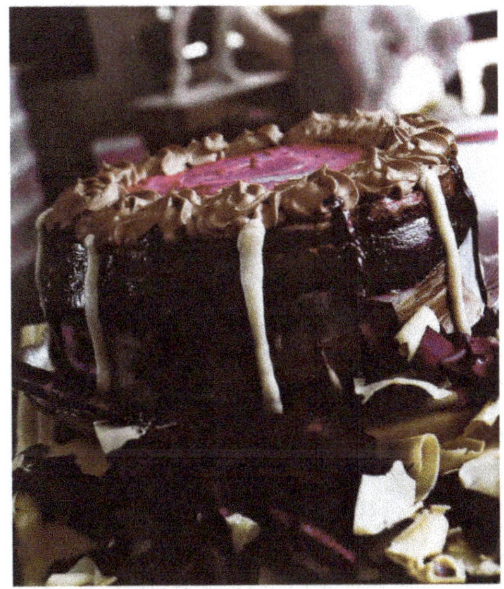

Nineteen Twenty Eight

"Some of us find reading Nick's dessert menu better than erotic poetry."
—Arizona Republic

Last Act

Preheat over to 325-degrees

Chocolate Coating

1 cup whipping cream

Heat in a small boiling pot over low heat.

6 oz semisweet chocolate

Add to the boiling pot and stir until chocolate melts.

Fruit Filling

8 strawberries

1 large banana, slice into about 1″ thick.

12 raspberries

Place a piece of parchment paper on a baking sheet.

Using a serving spoon with holes, dip strawberries and bananas, one at a time in the chocolate coating. Toss raspberries in the coating, not to break them if possible. Place all fruit on the parchment paper. Refrigerate for at least one hour until chocolate coating is firm.

White Chocolate Cake

32 oz white chocolate

Melt in the double boil. Set aside.

3 eggs, beaten with a fork

½ cup sugar

1 cup sour cream

1 tsp vanilla extract

¼ cup tapioca flour

8 oz unsalted butter, melted

Place in your mixer and beat on low speed for about two minutes.

The melted chocolate

Add to the mixer and beat on low speed for 2 to 3 minutes, until smooth and creamy.

Pour half of the batter in a lightly buttered 10-inch springform pan.

Place the coated fruit on top of the white chocolate cake.

Pour in the remaining white chocolate cake.

Bake the cake in the 325-degree preheated oven for 1 ¼ hour.

Refrigerate 8 to 10 hours before removing from the springform pan.

Icing

16 oz white chocolate

Melt in the double boil. Remove from the heat.

1 cup whipping cream

Beat in your mixer until stiff

½ cup sour cream

Add whipped cream and sour cream into the melted chocolate and blend well with a spatula.

Spread icing over the entire cake.

Using a thin spatula, run its tip across the top of the cake to create lines across the top.

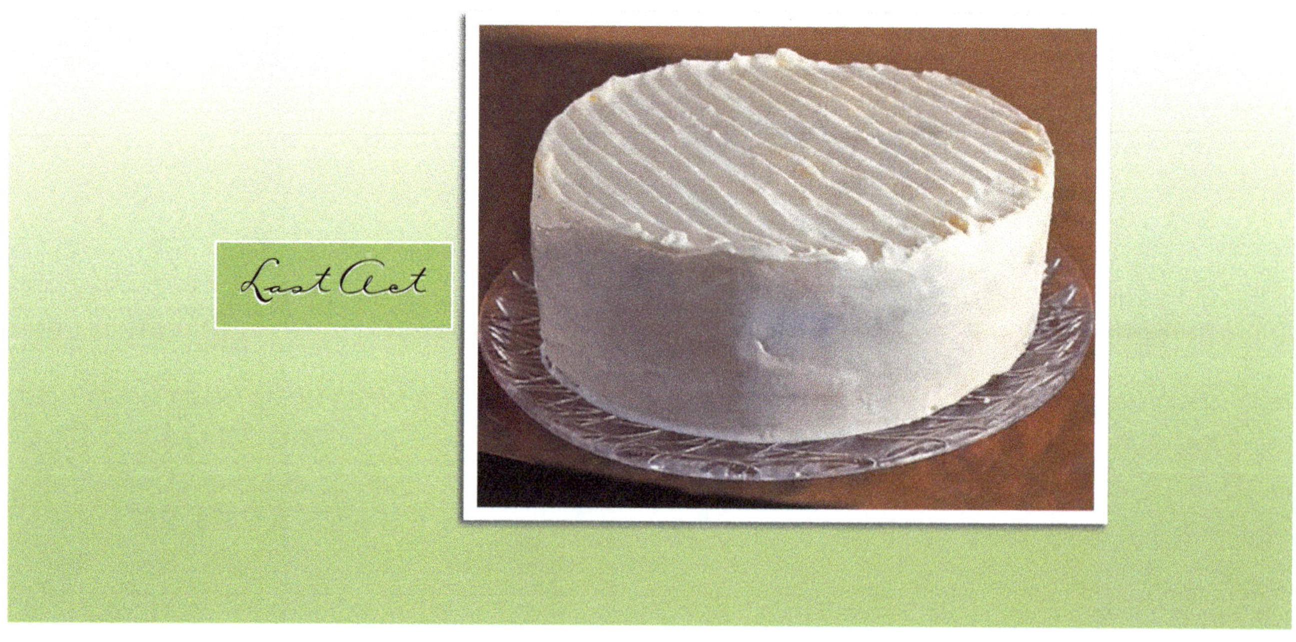
Last Act

Symphony of Chocolates

Prepare one 10" chocolate cake

Slice it horizontally to two equal slices.

Use the bottom slice and save the top one for another use. It is best to leave the bottom cake in the springform pan.

You could make truffles with the extra cake. See My Truffle recipe on Page

Chocolate shavings

2 large pieces of parchment paper.
4 tbsp of the melted chocolate

Make chocolate shavings (Page ?)

Prepare the cream

4 cups whipped topping
1 tsp pure vanilla extract

With the wire whip of your mixer beat on high speed until it forms stiff peaks. Set Aside.

Syrup

½ cup of water
⅛ cup sugar
1 tsp cocoa powder

Bring to a boil in a small pan, reduce heat and simmer for 3 to 4 minutes.

Brush the chocolate cake with the entire syrup.

White Chocolate

8 oz white chocolate

Melt in a double boil.

4 oz unsalted butter
½ cup sugar

Place in your mixer and beat on medium speed until smooth and creamy.

The melted white chocolate

2 cups whipped topping

Add to the mixer and blend well for about 2 minutes.

Spread on top of the cake.

Semisweet Chocolate

8 oz semisweet chocolate

Melt in a double boil.

½ cup unsalted butter
½ cup sugar

Place in your mixer and beat on medium speed until smooth and creamy.

The melted semisweet chocolate

2 cups whipped topping

Add in and mix well. Spread on top of white chocolate.

Chestnut Chocolate

8 oz. white chocolate

Melt in a double boil.

½ cup unsalted butter
½ cup sugar

Place in your mixer and mix on medium speed until creamy.

The melted White chocolate

2 cups whipped topping
1 tsp Kahlua
½ cup chestnut purée

Add to the mixer in and mix well on low speed.

Spread on top of semisweet chocolate. Refrigerate for 2 to 3 hours, remove from pan.

Chocolate Orange Icing

8 oz white chocolate

Melt in a double boil.

6 oz cream cheese,
1 tbsp sugar

Place in your mixer and beat on medium speed until smooth and creamy.

The melted white chocolate

The remaining whipped topping
¼ cup sour cream
1 tbsp orange peel
¼ tsp cinnamon
1 tbsp Kahlua

Add in and mix well. Spread on the entire cake.

The chocolate shavings, crumbled into small pieces.

¼ cup chocolate vermicelli

Sprinkle all over the top and sides of the cake.

Kiwi Mango Barcake

Preheat oven to 350-degrees

White Cake (page 59)

Lightly butter an approximately 11" x 4" x 3" pan to make the cake. I use a glass or ceramic baking pan.

Set cake aside and let it cool. Remove and slice into three horizontal slices.

Simple Syrup

1 cup of water

2 tbsp coconut sugar

Bring to a boil in a small saucepan. Reduce heat and simmer for 5-6 minutes. Place the first slice of the white cake on a serving tray. Brush the cake with part of the simple syrup.

Prepare the whipped topping

3 cups whipped topping

1 tsp vanilla extract

Using your mixer with a whisk attachment, whip on medium-high speed until medium peaks form, about 3 to 4 minutes. Set aside.

Mango mousse

4 oz cream cheese

½ cup of sugar

Place in your mixer and beat on medium speed until smooth and creamy.

½ cup sour cream

1 mango, peeled and chopped. Drain excess liquid.

Add to the mixer and blend gently.

1 ½ cup of the whipped topping

1 cup of the melted white chocolate

Add to the mixer and thoroughly blend at low speed. Pour filling on the first slice of the cake and top it with the second cake slice. Brush some of the simple syrup over the second cake slice.

Kiwi white chocolate

4 oz cream cheese

½ cup sugar

Place in your mixer and beat on medium speed until smooth and creamy.

¼ cup sour cream

3 kiwi, peeled and chopped

Add to the mixer and blend gently.

1 ½ cup of the whipped topping

1 cup of the melted white chocolate

Add to the mixer and thoroughly blend at low speed. Pour filling on the second slice of the cake and top it with the third cake slice. Brush some of the simple syrup over the second cake slice.

Refrigerate the cake for at least 2 to 3 hours.

Icing

8 oz cream cheese

¼ cup sour cream

Place in your mixer and beat on medium speed until smooth and creamy.

Remaining prepared cream

Remaining melted white chocolate

Add to the mixer and thoroughly blend at low speed.

Spread on the top and the sides of the cake.

2 cups of shredded coconut

Place on a baking pan and toast in a 350-degree oven, 5 to 6 minutes until golden brown.

Occasionally stir the coconut to be baked evenly. Set aside.

When the cake is ready for the icing, cover the sides of the cake with the toasted coconut and arrange the white chocolate shaving on the top of the cake.

"In this tiny hole-in-the-wall, dynamic chef-owner Nick Ligidakis single-handedly bakes luscious desserts."
— Zagat Restaurant Survey

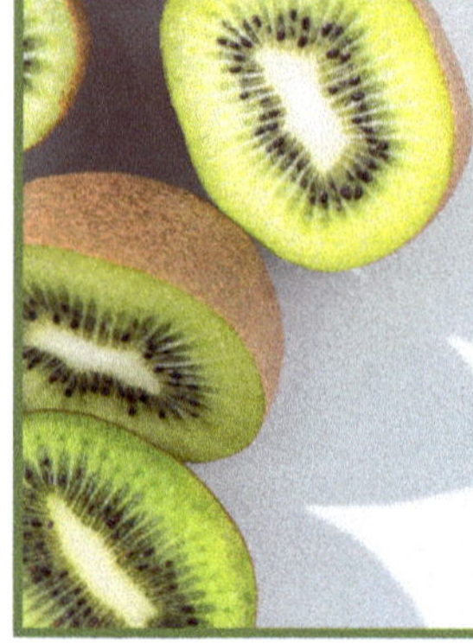

Commercial kiwi fruit cultivation began in New Zealand in 1906. The berry is a woody vine native of China's Yanzi Valley. Kiwi grew from plants collected by a British botanist and brought to the west at the turn of the century.

Amaretto Cream Barcake

Preheat oven to 350-degrees

White Cake (recipe on page 59)

Lightly butter an approximately 11" x 4" x 3" pan to make the cake. I use a glass or ceramic baking pan. Set cake aside and let it cool. Remove and slice into three horizontal slices.

Prepare the whipped topping

3 cups whipped topping
1 tsp vanilla extract

Using your mixer with a whisk attachment, whip on medium-high speed until medium peaks form, about 3 to 4 minutes. Set aside.

12 oz white chocolate

Melt in a double boiler. Use 3 tbsp to make white chocolate shavings (page 46)

Amaretto Syrup

1 cup of water
2 tbsp coconut sugar
1 tbsp amaretto liqueur

Bring to a boil in a small saucepan. Reduce heat and simmer for 5-6 minutes. Place the first slice of the white cake on a serving tray. Brush the cake with part of the simple syrup.

The white cake

Slice it horizontally in three equal slices. Place the first slice of the chocolate cake on a serving tray. Brush the bottom slice of the cake with part of the amaretto syrup.

Almond cream filling

3 cups of whipped topping
1 cup of the melted white chocolate
½ cup of sliced almonds

Blend well in a mixing bowl with a spatula and spread on the first cake slice.

Cover it with the second slice, brush with part of the amaretto syrup.

Amaretto cream filling

3 cups of whipped topping
The remaining melted white chocolate
2 tbsp amaretto liqueur

Blend well in a mixing bowl with a spatula and spread on the cake slice.

Cover it with the third cake slice, brush with part of the amaretto syrup.

Icing

2 cups of whipped topping

Spread on the sides and top of the cake.

Decoration

Place the remaining whipped topping in a pastry bag with a star tip and pipe it around the edges of the cake top.

Decorate sides with the white chocolate shavings.

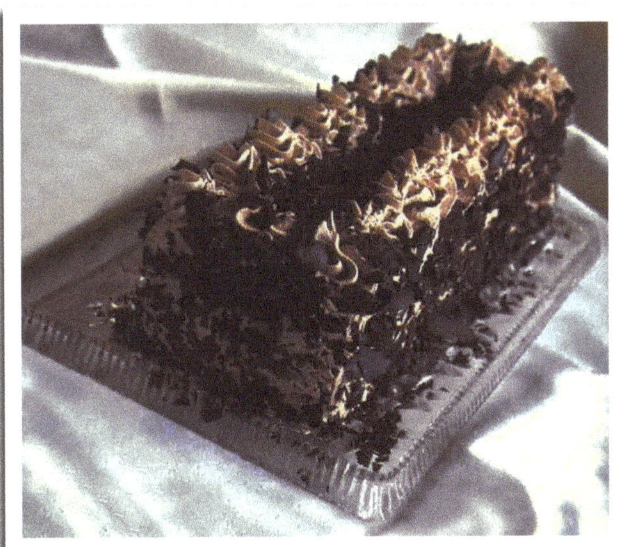

The best flavorings come from extracting the essential flavors of the plant. The natural liquid is the best ingredient to use, but they are costly to produce. Now the market is full of synthetic flavors. Fruits like raspberries and strawberries are ideal for syrups to use for cake flavoring, ice cream, tarts, and so much more. Nut essences are an excellent way to flavor cakes and cookies. Vanilla extract is probably the most widely used essence. It is used to flavor just about anything in baking. Licorice, with its distinctive flavor, is used for candy. Grenadine is a liquid made from pomegranate essence.

Dark Cherry Barcake

Preheat oven to 350-degrees

Chocolate Cake (recipe on page 59)

Lightly butter an approximately 11" x 4" x 3" pan to make the cake. I use a glass or ceramic baking pan. Set cake aside and let it cool. Remove and slice into three horizontal slices.

Prepare the whipped topping

4 cups whipped topping
1 tsp vanilla extract

Whip in your mixer on medium speed until medium peaks form, about 3 to 4 minutes. Set aside.

12 oz semisweet chocolate

Melt in a double boiler. Set aside. Use 3 tbsp to make chocolate shavings (page 46)

Simple Syrup

1 cup of water
2 tbsp sugar

Bring to a boil in a small saucepan. Reduce heat and simmer for 5 to 6 minutes.

The chocolate cake

Place the first slice of the chocolate cake on a serving tray. Brush with part of the simple syrup.

Cherry Chocolate

6 oz semisweet chocolate

Melt in a double boiler

2 ½ cups of the whipped topping
1 cup dark cherries

Add to the melted chocolate and blend with a spatula. Spread on the top of the first cake slice.

Place second slice on top and brush with simple syrup.

Cream Filling

4 oz white chocolate

Melt in a double boiler.

4 oz cream cheese
2 tbsp sugar

Place in your mixer and beat on medium speed until smooth and creamy.

2 cups of the whipped topping

Add the whipped topping and the melted white chocolate and blend well 2 to 3 minutes.

Add in, mix well, and spread on top of the second slice of the cake.

Cover it with the third white cake slice, brush with part of the simple syrup.

Icing

2 cups of the whipped topping
2 tbsp cocoa powder

Blend well with a spatula. Spread on the entire cake.

Decoration

Use the remaining whipped topping to make rosettes around the top edges of the cake.

2 cups cherry pie filling
1 tbsp orange peel

Mix well and spread the pie cherry filling between the rosettes.

Sprinkle the dark chocolate shaving on the sides of the cake.

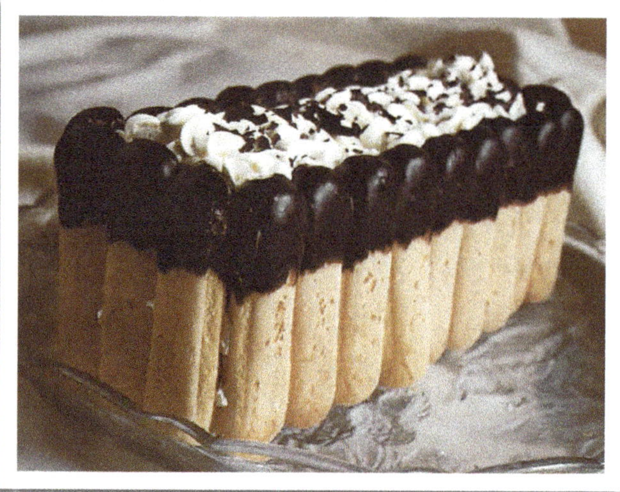

Special Occasion Cakes

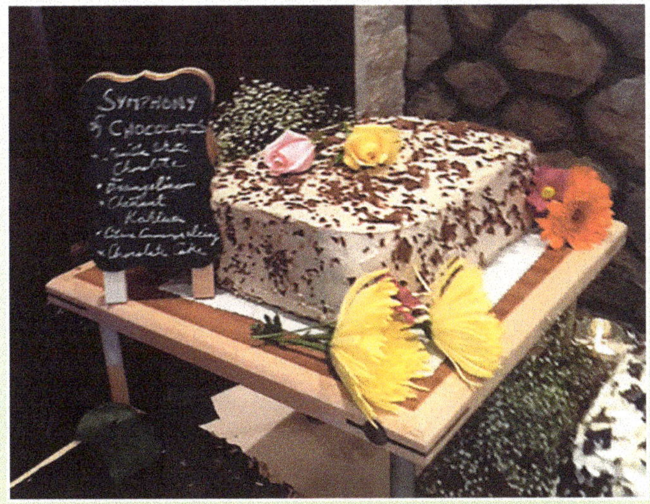

Symphony of Chocolate

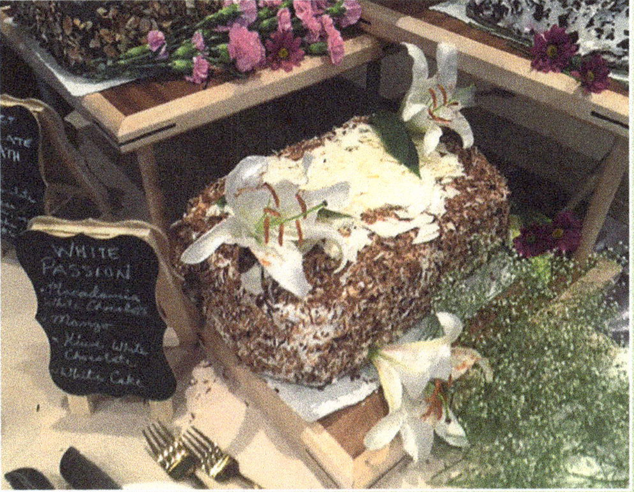

White Passion Cake

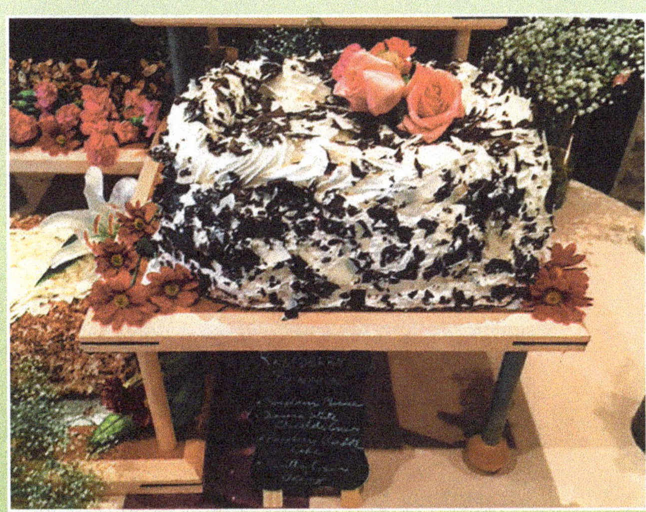

Raspberry Banana Cake

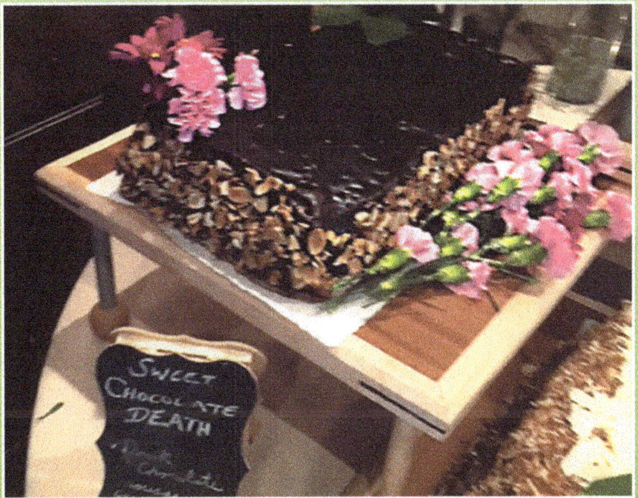

Sweet Chocolate Death

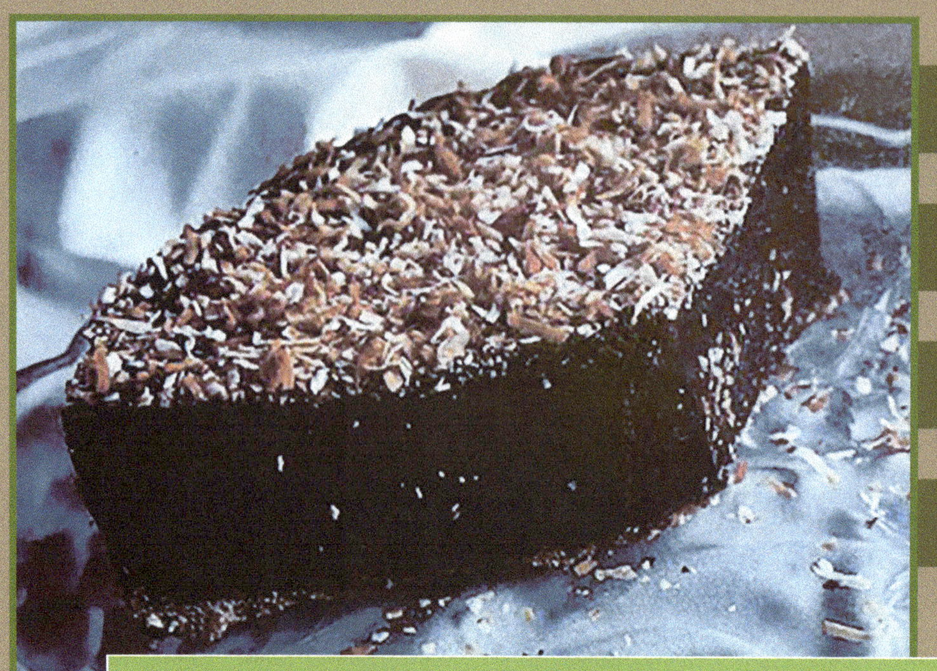

Blackberry Fudge Cake

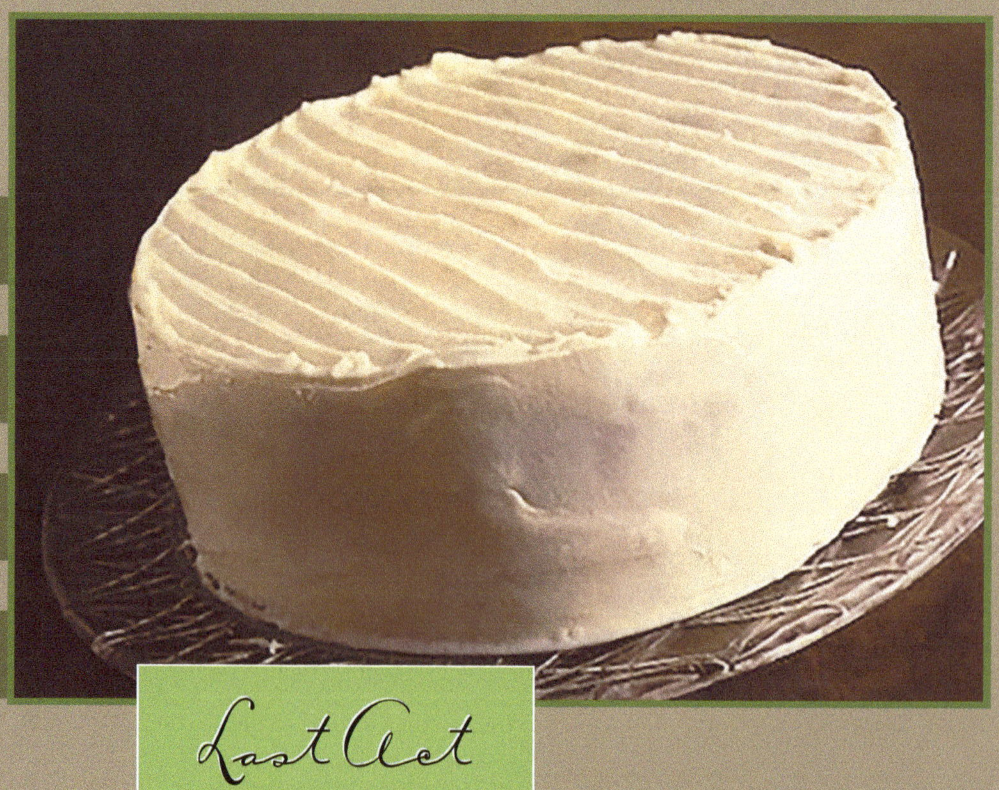

Last Act

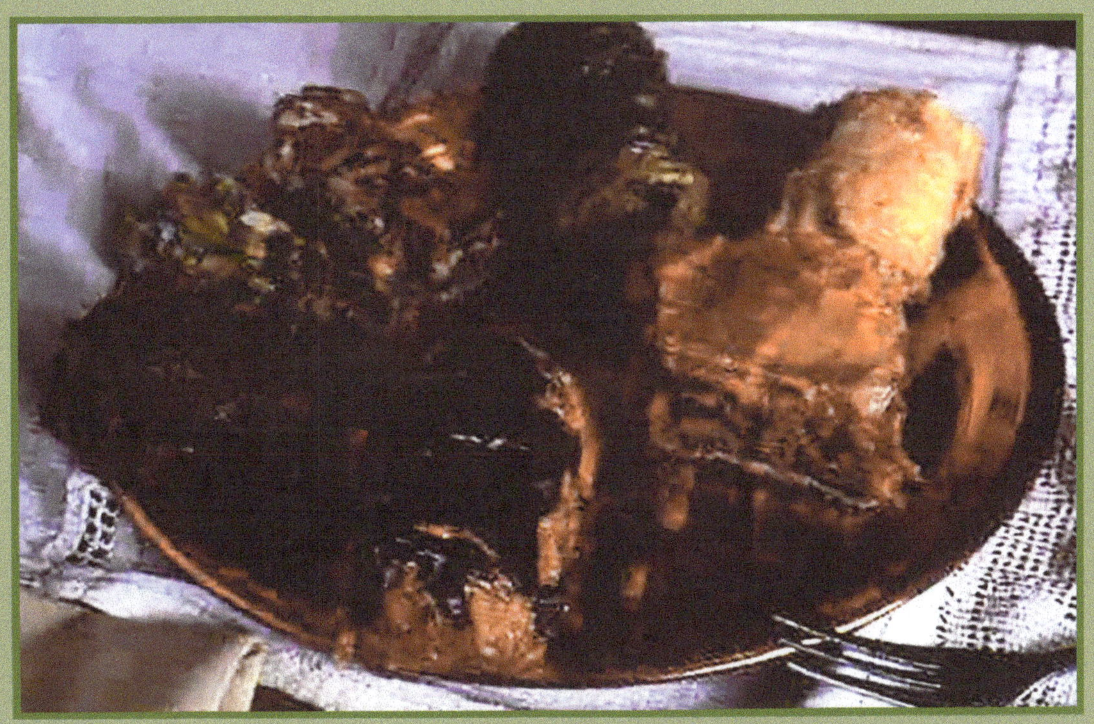

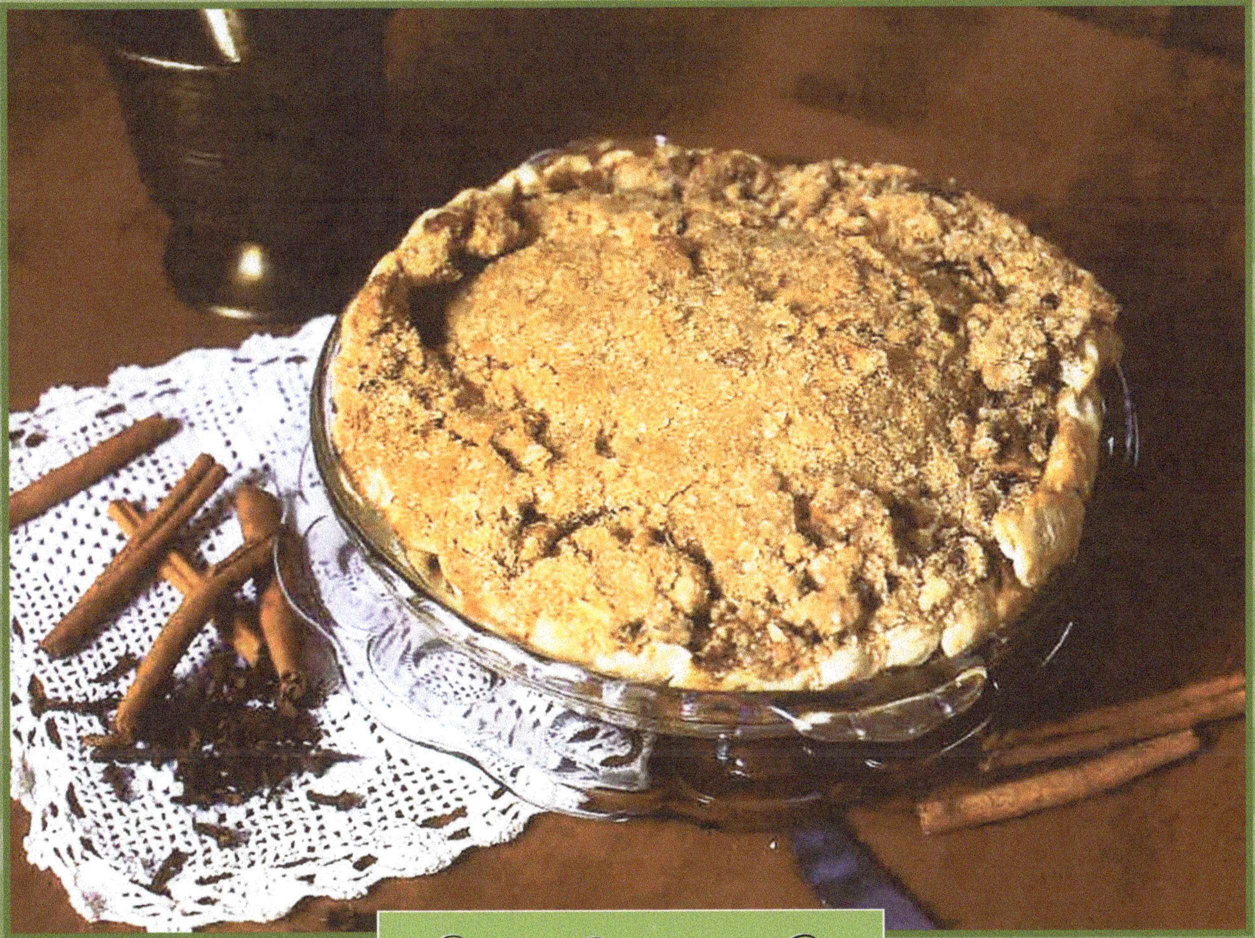

Rum Apple Pie

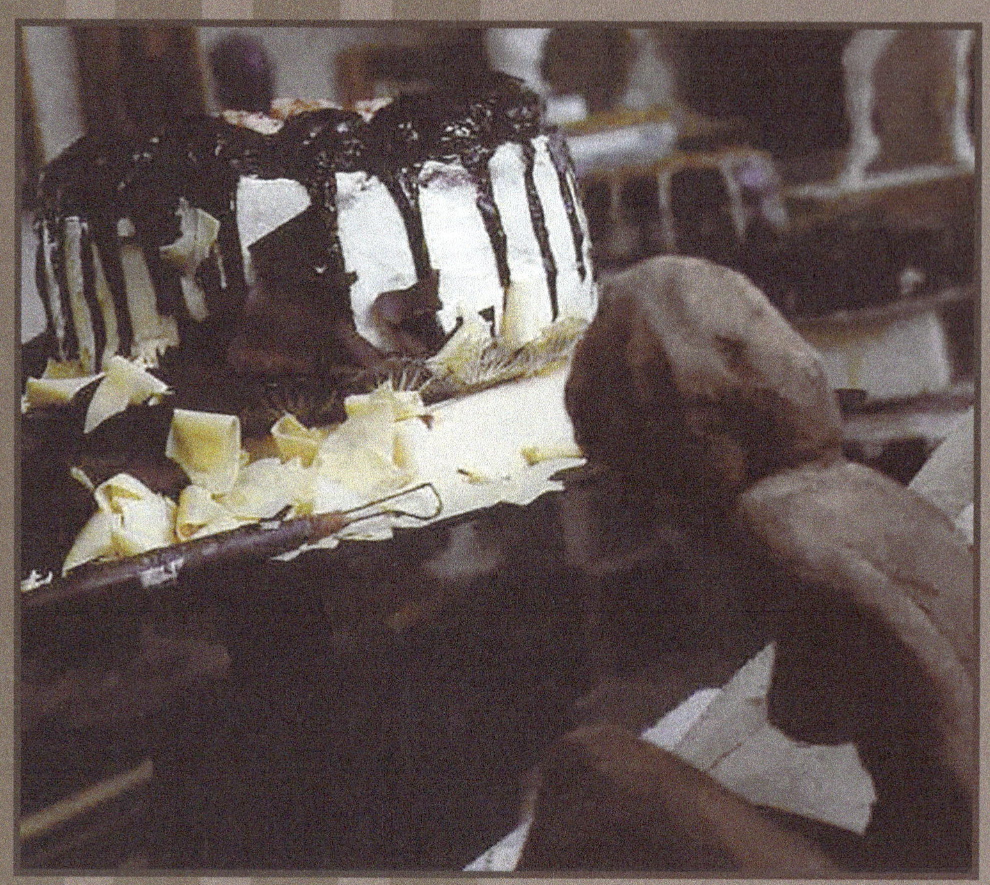

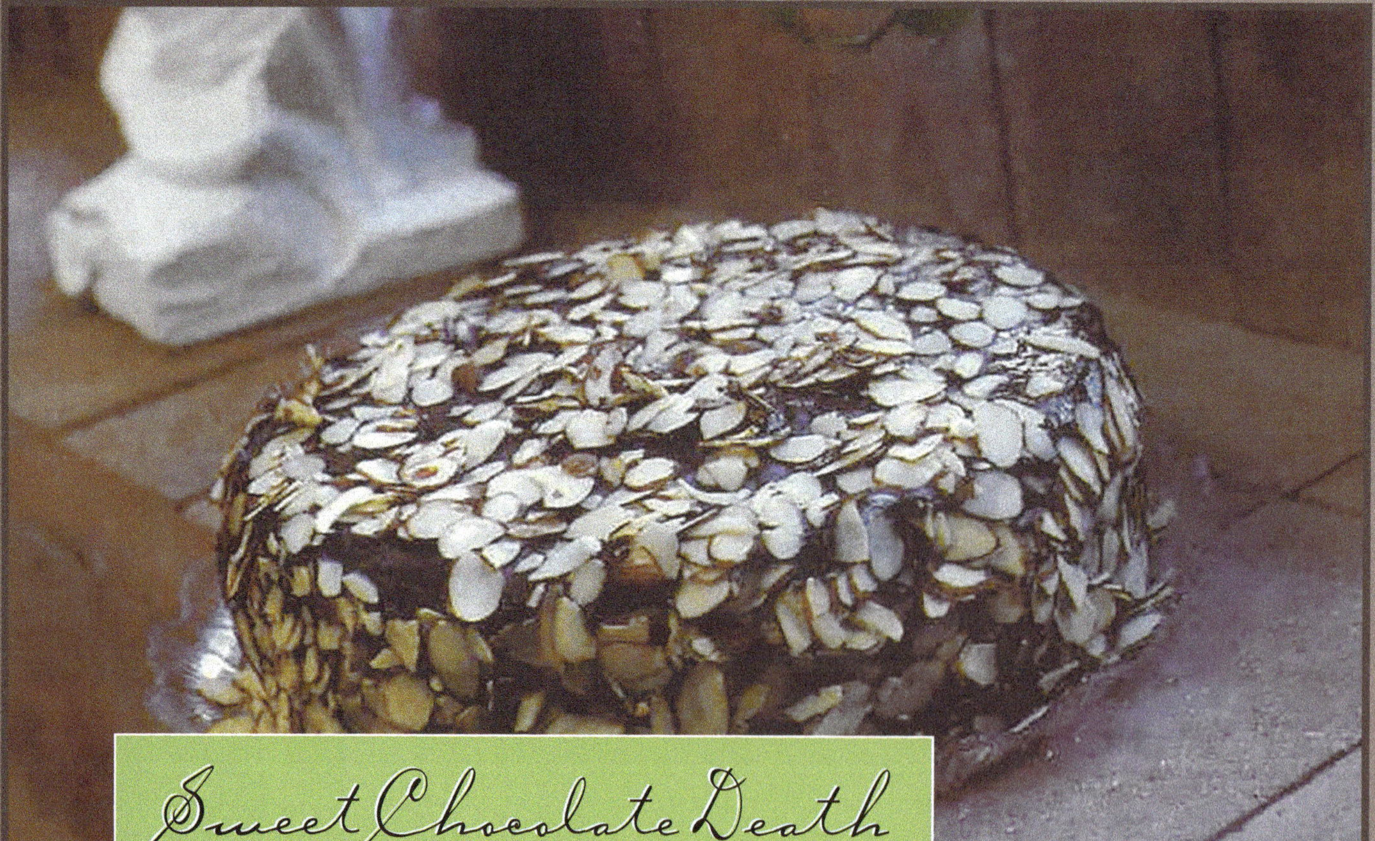

Sweet Chocolate Death

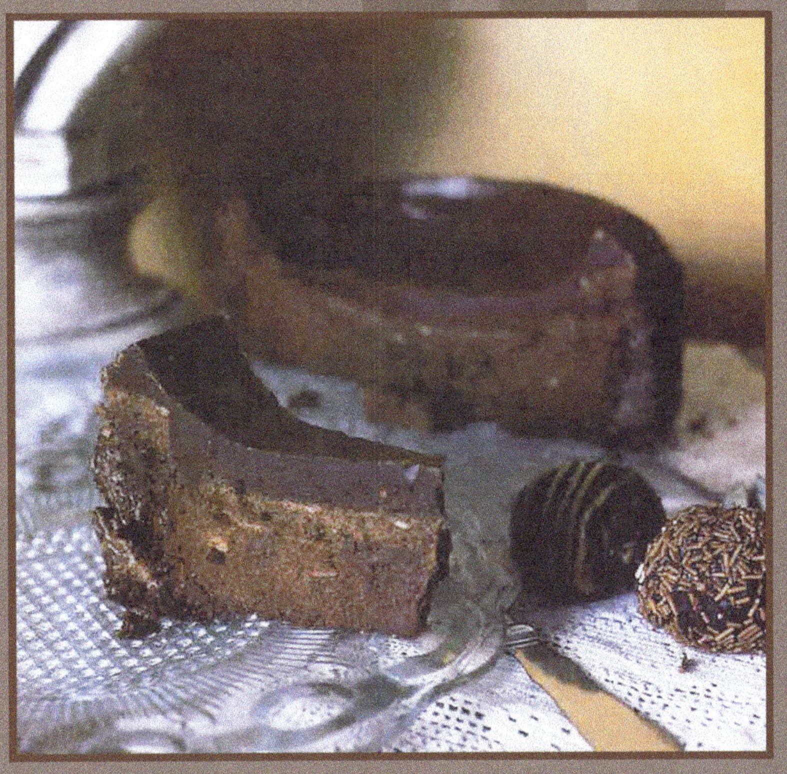

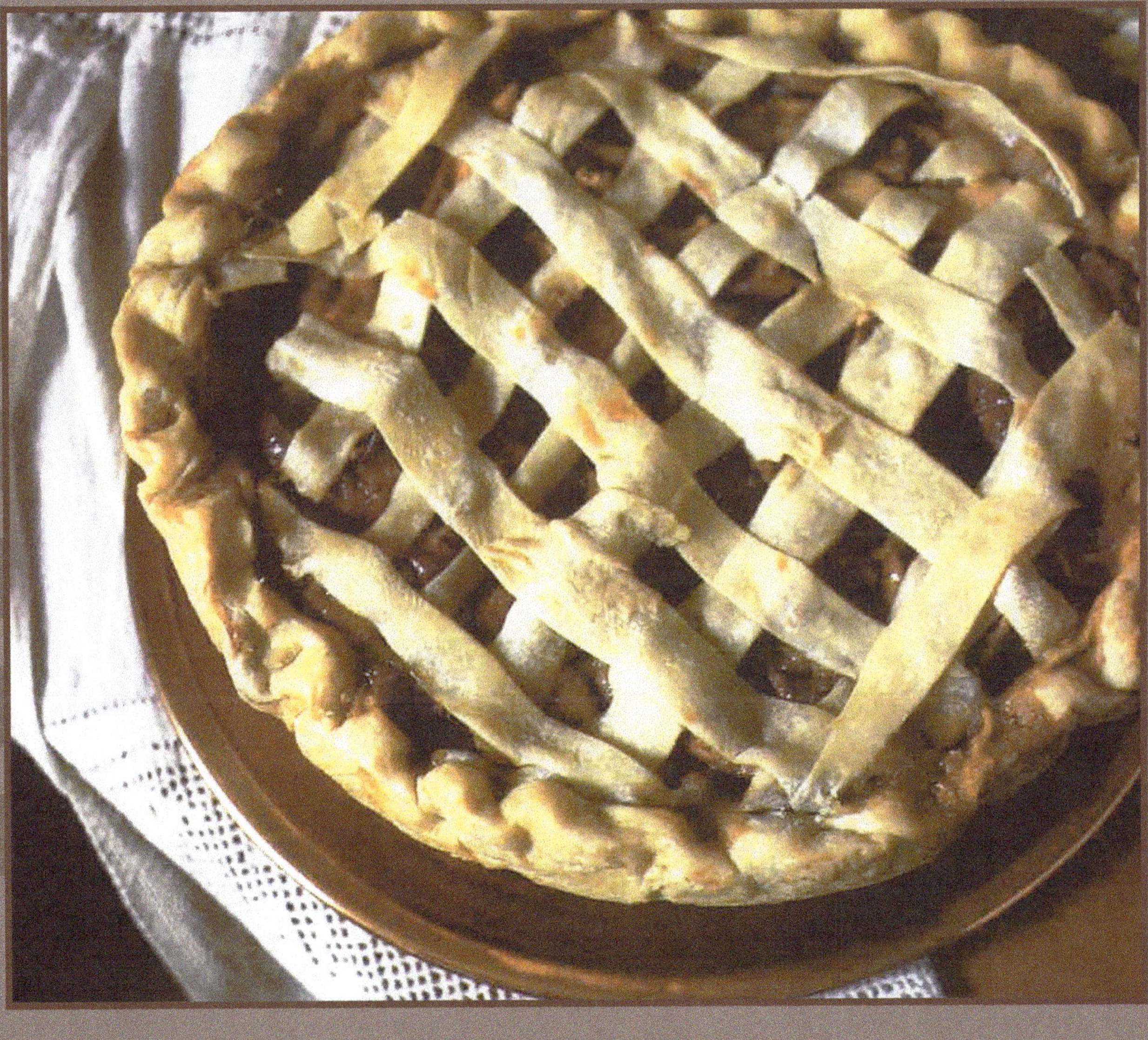

Nineteen Twenty Eight

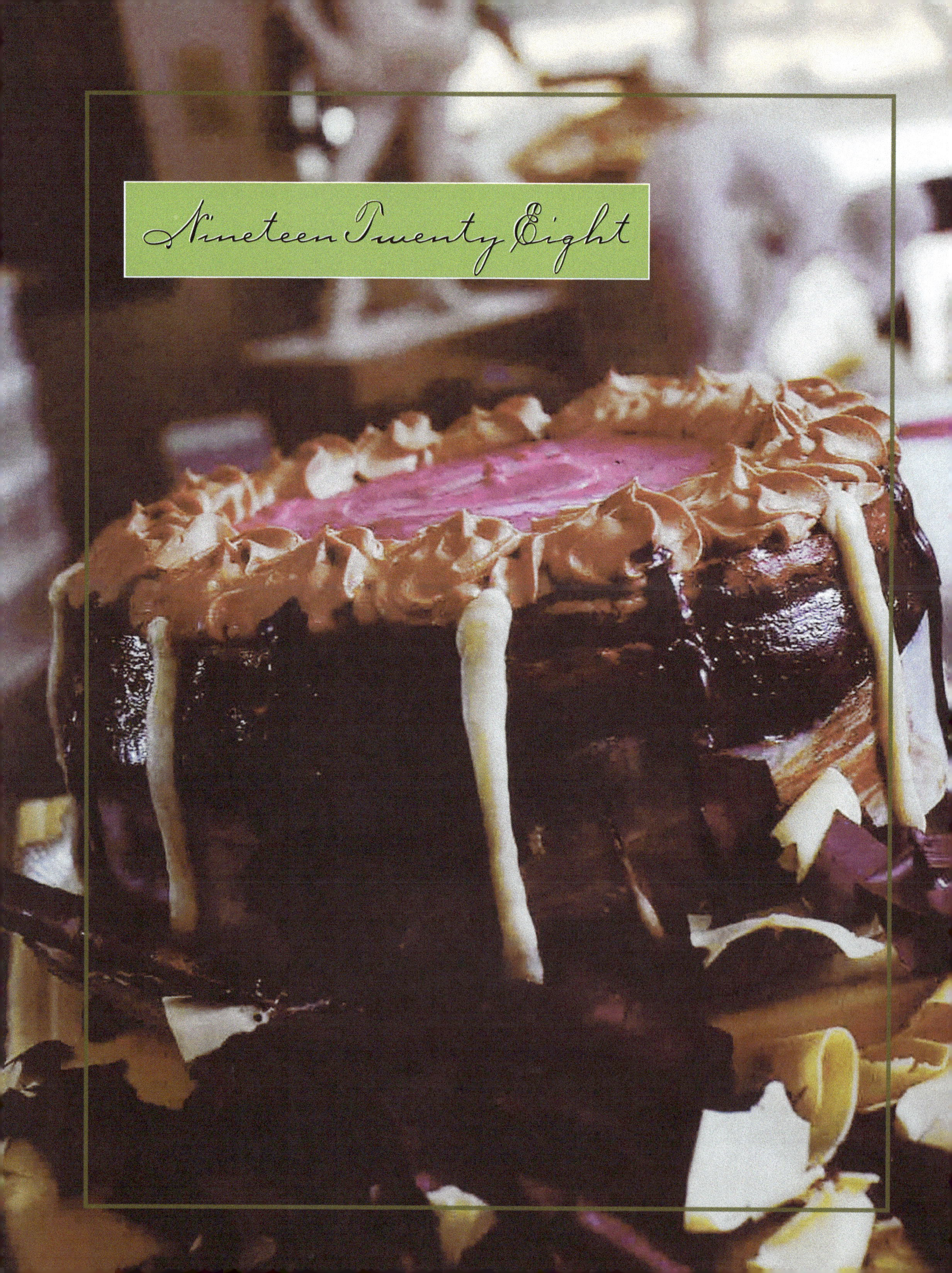

Raspberry Banana Barcake

Preheat oven to 350-degrees

Chocolate cake (page 59)

Lightly butter an approximately 11" x 4" x 3" pan to make the cake. I use a glass or ceramic baking pan. Set cake aside and let it cool. Remove and slice bake into three horizontal slices.

Prepare the whipped topping

4 cups whipped topping

1 tsp vanilla extract

Using your mixer with a whisk attachment, whip on medium-high speed until medium peaks form, about 3 to 4 minutes. Set aside. You should have about 10 cups of cream.

8 oz semisweet chocolate – Melt in a double boiler

Use 3 tbsp of the melted chocolate to make dark chocolate shavings (Page 46)

8 oz white chocolate – Melt in a double boiler

Use 3 tbsp to make white chocolate shavings (Page 46)

Raspberry Syrup

½ cup raspberries

1 cup of water

1 tbsp sugar

In a small boiling pot, bring to a boil. Reduce heat and simmer for 5-6 minutes.

Strain through a fine sieve to remove the raspberry seeds. Place the first slice of the chocolate cake on a serving tray. Brush the bottom slice of the cake with part of the raspberry syrup.

Raspberry Chocolate

2 ½ cups of the prepared whipped topping

The melted semisweet chocolate

Blend well in a mixing bowl with a spatula and spread on the first cake slice.

1 cup raspberries (if fresh is not available, use frozen)

Arrange on top of chocolate cream. Place the second cake slice on top of the chocolate cream. Brush with part of raspberry syrup.

Banana White Chocolate

2 ½ cups of cream filling

The melted white chocolate

Mix well and spread on the second cake slice.

2 bananas, peeled and thinly sliced

Arrange on top of the chocolate cream. Cover with the third slice. Brush with raspberry syrup.

Icing

6 oz of white chocolate, melted in a double boil.

2 ½ cups of the prepared whipped topping

Mix well and ice the entire cake.

Decoration

Fill a pastry bag with a star tip with the remaining cream filling and make rosettes on the edges of the top of the cake.

Decorate the sides of the cake with dark chocolate shavings.

Sprinkle dark and white chocolate shavings on top of the cake.

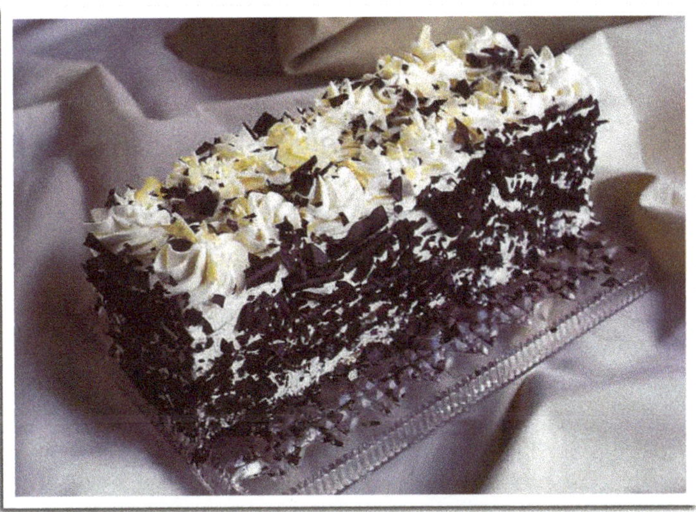

Rasberry Banana Barcakes

White Pistachio Brownies

Preheat your oven to 350-degrees
Lightly butter an approximately
12" x 16" x 2" glass or ceramic baking pan.

White Chocolate Layer

16 oz white chocolate
Melt in a double boil.

16 oz unsalted butter
1½ cups sugar
Place in your mixer and beat on medium speed until smooth.

1 tbsp vanilla extract
8 eggs
Add to the mixer and blend for about 1 minute.

2 cups flour
1 cup whipping cream
Add to your mixer and blend well for about 2 to 3 minutes.

The melted chocolate

Turn the speed of the mixer to slow and fold in the melted chocolate.

Pour the mixture into the pan.

Pistachio Cream Layer

24 oz cream cheese
1 cup of sugar
Place in your mixer and beat on medium speed until smooth and creamy.

6 eggs
Add to the mixer and blend for about 1 minute.

1 tsp vanilla
¼ cup tapioca flour
2 cups pistachios
Place pistachios in your food processor and pulse 1 to 2 times.

Add all ingredients into your mixer and blend 1 to 2 minutes.

Pour pistachio cream on top of the first layer.

Bake in the preheated 350-degree oven for 45 to 50 minutes.

Makes 24 brownies

Peanut Butter Brownies

Preheat your oven to 350-degrees
Lightly butter an approximately
12" x 16" x 2" glass or ceramic baking pan

Brownies

1 ½ cups unsalted butter
1 cup of sugar
½ cup brown sugar
Place in your mixer and beat on medium speed until smooth.

8 eggs
Add to the mixer and blend for about 1 minute.

1 ½ cups creamy peanut butter
2 ½ cups flour
1 ½ cups oats
1 ½ cups walnut pieces
2 tsp baking soda
Add to the mixer and blend for about 2 to 3 minutes.

Pour the mixture into the pan.

Bake in the preheated 350-degree oven for 45 to 50 minutes.

Let the brownies cool for 10 to 15 minutes before using the icing.

Icing

4 cups powdered sugar
2 cups creamy peanut butter
1 cup milk
¾ cup cocoa powder
Place in your mixer and beat on low speed until smooth.

Top brownies with icing.

Makes 24 brownies

"The Cheesecake Brownie was creamy beyond belief."
— Western Express

Cheesecake Brownies

Preheat your oven to 350-degrees
Lightly butter an approximately
12" x 16" x 2" glass or ceramic baking pan

Coconut Pecan Layer

8 oz semisweet chocolate
Melt in a double boil.

12 oz unsalted butter
1 cup of coconut sugar
Place in your mixer and beat on medium speed until smooth.

6 eggs
1 tsp vanilla extract
1 ½ cups pecan pieces
1 ½ cups flour
Add to your mixer and blend well for about 2 to 3 minutes.

The melted chocolate

Turn the speed of the mixer to slow and fold in the melted chocolate.

Pour the mixture into the pan.

Almond Cream Layer

24 oz cream cheese
1 cup of sugar
Place in your mixer and beat on medium speed until smooth and creamy.

6 eggs
Add to the mixer and blend for about 1 to 2 minutes.

¼ cup unsweetened cocoa
1 tsp vanilla extract
¼ cup flour
1 cup slivered almonds
Place almonds in your food processor and pulse 2 to 3 times.

Add all ingredients into your mixer and blend 1 to 2 minutes.

Pour almond cream on top of the first layer.

Starting from one comer of the pan, run a butter knife in a zig-zag pattern through the pan to partly incorporate the two layers.

Bake in the preheated 350-degree oven for 45 to 50 minutes.

Makes 24 brownies

Fig Date Raspberry Brownie, Gluten-Free

Preheat over to 350-degrees

Brownies

½ cup unsalted butter, low-fat, organic
¼ cup coconut sugar
Place in the mixer's bowl and cream together on low speed.

3 eggs
Add and blend on slow speed.

1 banana, mashed
1 cup dried figs, California
1 cup pitted dates, chopped
Pulse above ingredients 2 to 3 times in the food processor.

Add to the mixer.

½ cup gluten-free flour
½ cup coconut flour
1 tbsp arrowroot
1 tbsp flaxseed
½ tsp baking powder
Add to the mixer and blend on low speed.

½ cup fresh raspberries
½ cup pecans, chopped
½ cup white chocolate, melted
Add to the mixer and mix gently.

Pour mixture in an 8" x 8" inch lightly butter class baking pan and bake in the preheated oven for 55 to 60 minutes.

Topping

1 cup semisweet chocolate
Melt chocolate in a double boil

¼ cup almond milk, heated
Add to the chocolate and stir well and remove from the heat.

When brownies are done, remove from oven and pour the chocolate mixture on top.

Refrigerate for at least 1 hour before serving.

Makes 20 small brownies

Caramel Brownies, Gluten-Free

Preheat over to 350-degrees

Caramel sauce

¾ cups unsweetened coconut milk
½ cup coconut sugar
1 tbsp low-fat, unsalted butter
⅛ tsp vanilla extract
1 tsp honey

Combine ingredients in a saucepan and simmer for about 30 minutes, until liquid thickens.

Brownies

½ cup unsalted butter, low-fat, organic
¼ cup coconut sugar

Place in the mixer's bowl and cream together on low speed.

3 eggs

Add and blend on slow speed.

½ cup coconut flour
¼ cup brown rice flour

Add to the mixer and blend on low speed

1 cup semisweet chocolate,

Melt in a double boil.

2 tbsp caramel sauce.

Save the rest of the sauce.

½ cup pecans, chopped

Add to the mixer and mix gently.

Pour mixture in an 8" x 8" inch lightly butter class baking pan and bake in the preheated oven for 55 to 60 minutes.

Topping

½ cup white chocolate chips

Place caramel sauce in a saucepan.

Add to the white chocolate and stir on low heat until melted. When brownies are done, remove from oven and pour the chocolate mixture on top.

Refrigerate for at least 1 hour before serving.

Makes 20 small brownies

Peanut Butter Brownies, Gluten-Free

Preheat over to 350-degrees

Brownies

½ cup unsalted butter, low-fat, organic
½ cup coconut sugar

Place in the mixer's bowl and cream together on low speed.

2 eggs

Add and blend on slow speed.

1 banana, mashed
¾ cup low-fat peanut, unsalted butter

Add to the mixer

1 cup brown rice flour
½ cup almond flour
1 tbsp cocoa powder
1 tbsp flaxseed
1 tsp baking powder

Add to the mixer and blend on low speed

¼ cup almond milk

Add to the mixer and mix gently. Turn mixer off.

½ cup pitted dates
2 tsp water

Place in a food processor and pulse 3 to 4 times. Add date paste to the mixer and blend well on low speed.

Pour mixture in an 8" x 8" lightly butter class baking pan and cook in the preheated oven for 55 to 60 minutes.

Topping

1 cup semisweet chocolate

Melt in a double boil.

¼ cup low-fat peanut, unsalted butter
½ cup almond milk

When chocolate is melted, add the above ingredients to the melted chocolate, stir well and remove from the heat.

When brownies are done, remove from oven and pour the chocolate mixture on top.

Refrigerate for at least 1 hour before serving.

Makes 20 small brownies

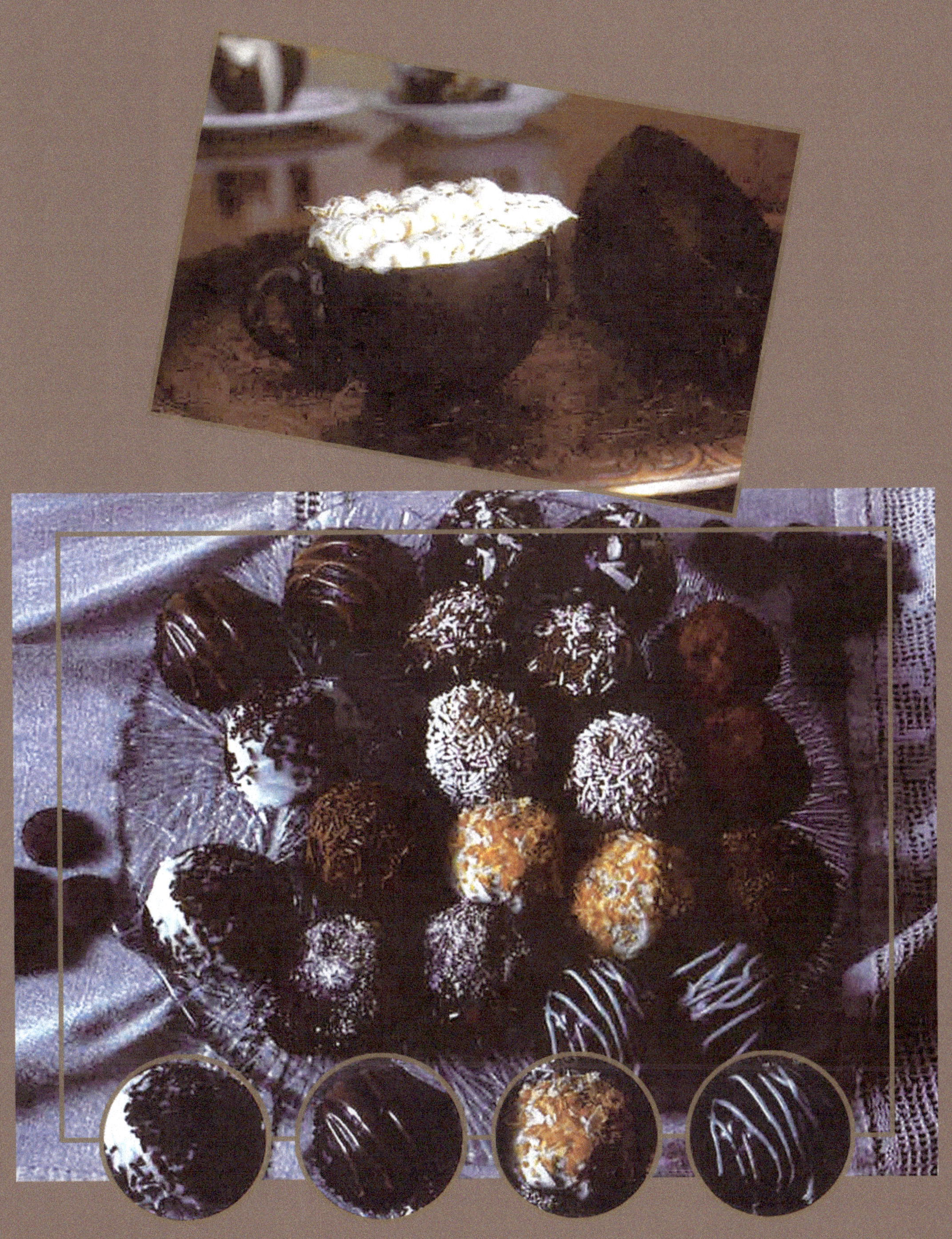

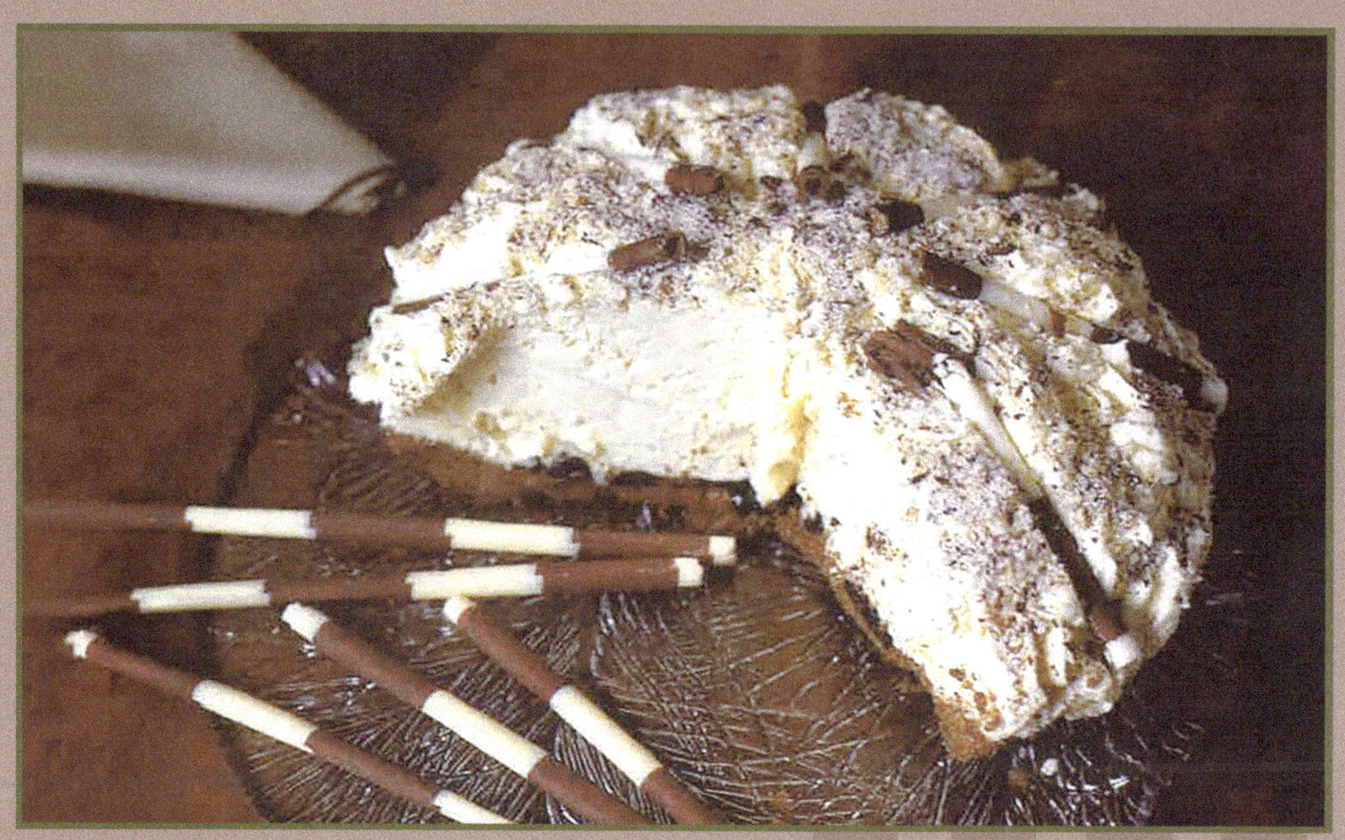

White Chocolate Pie

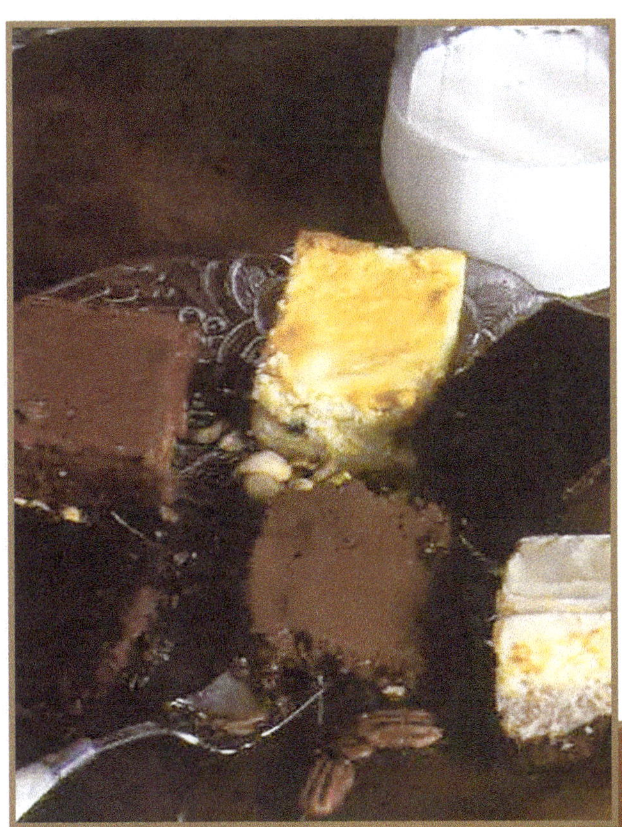

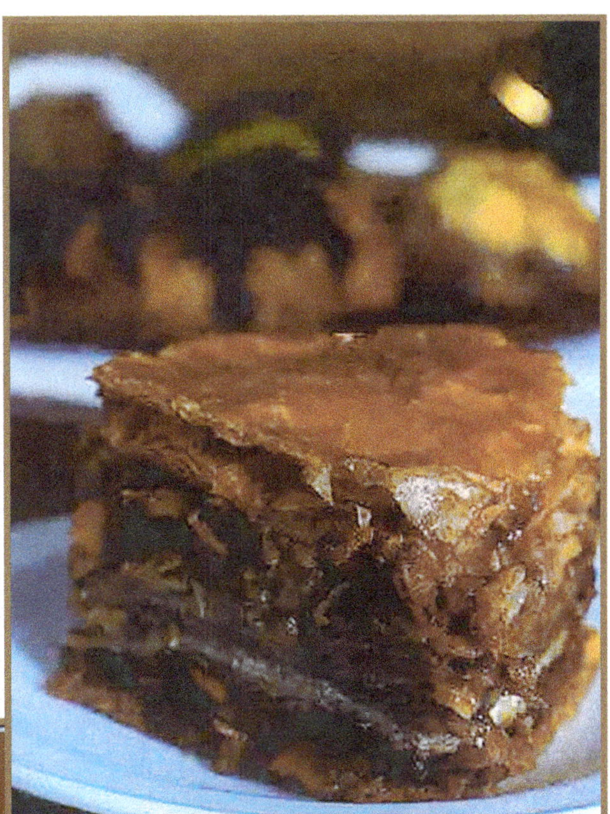

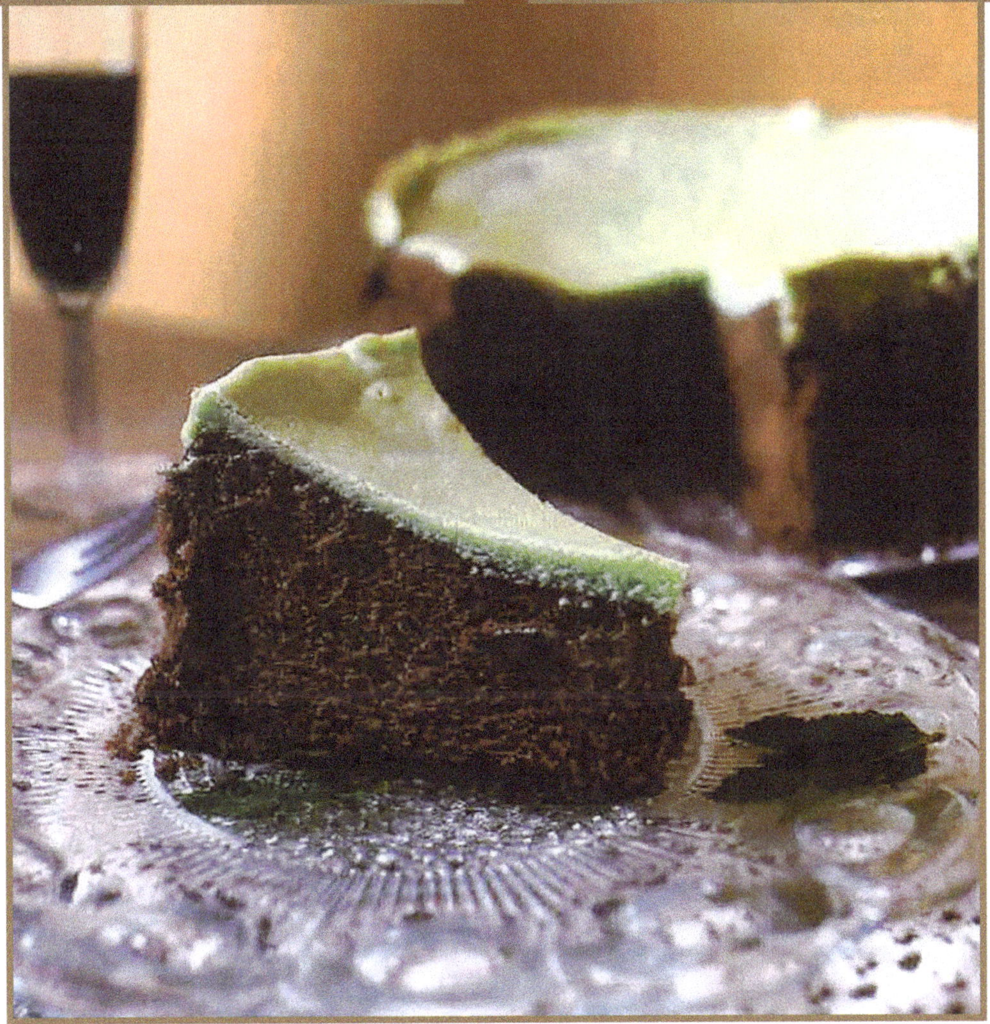

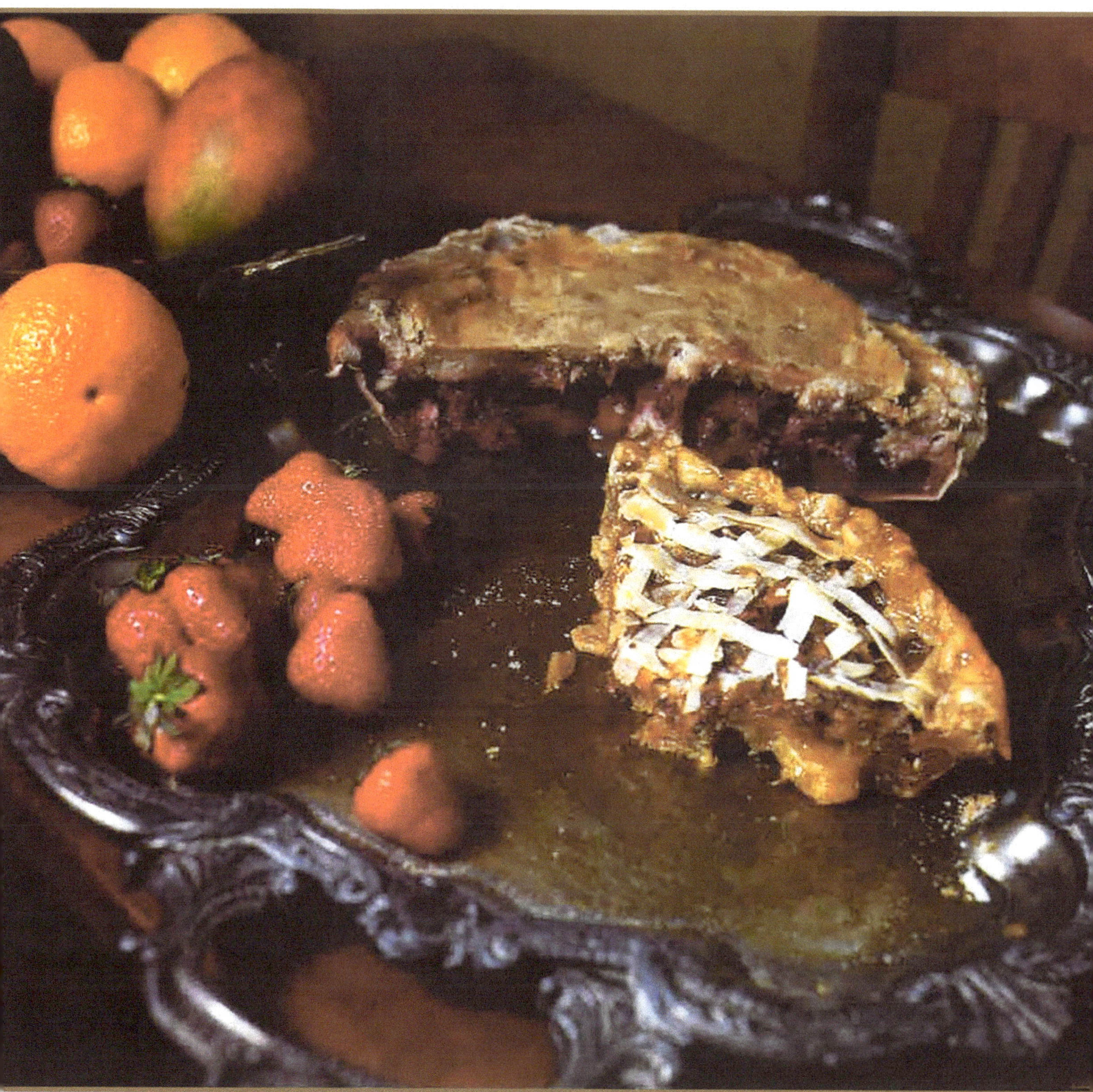

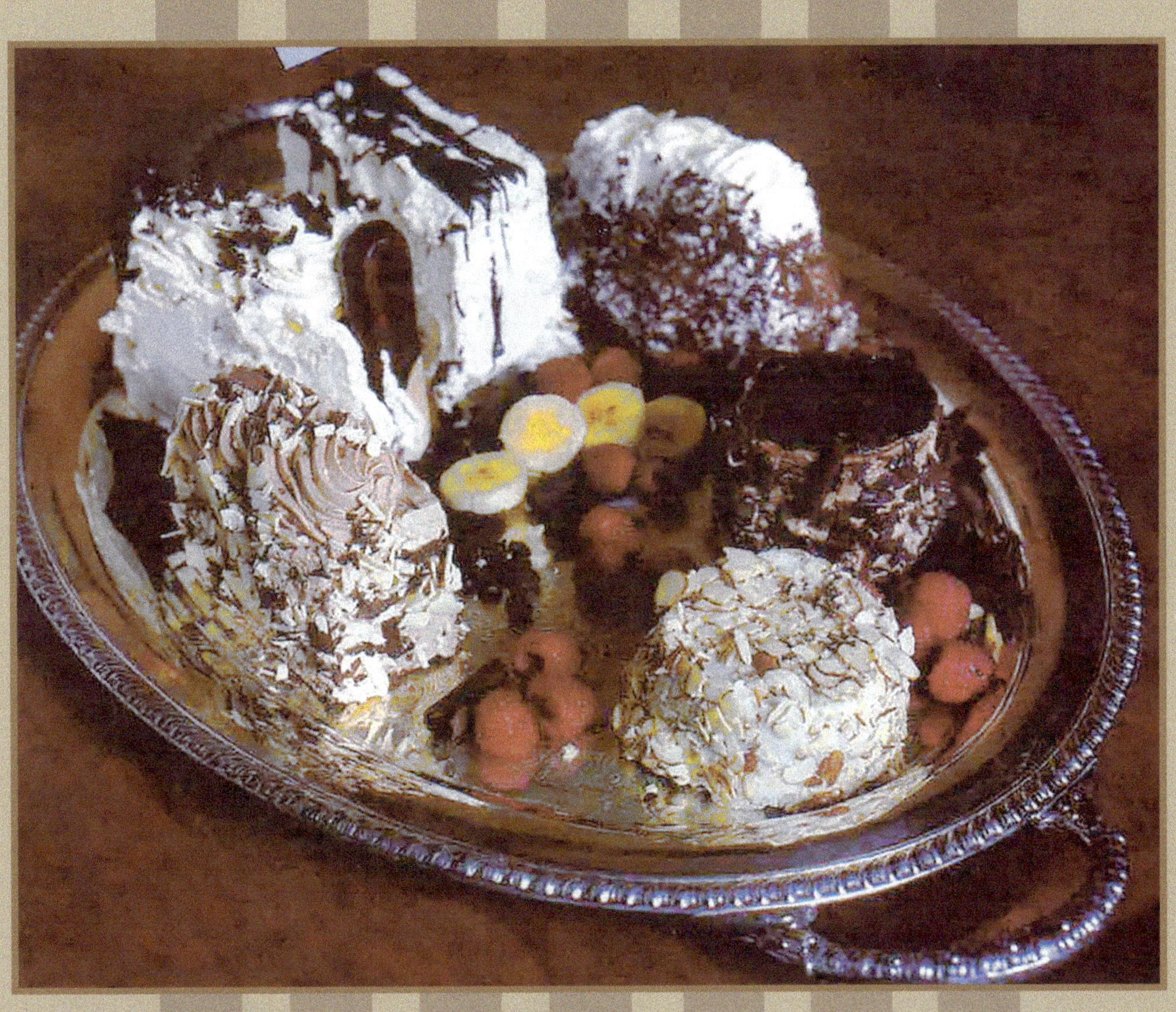

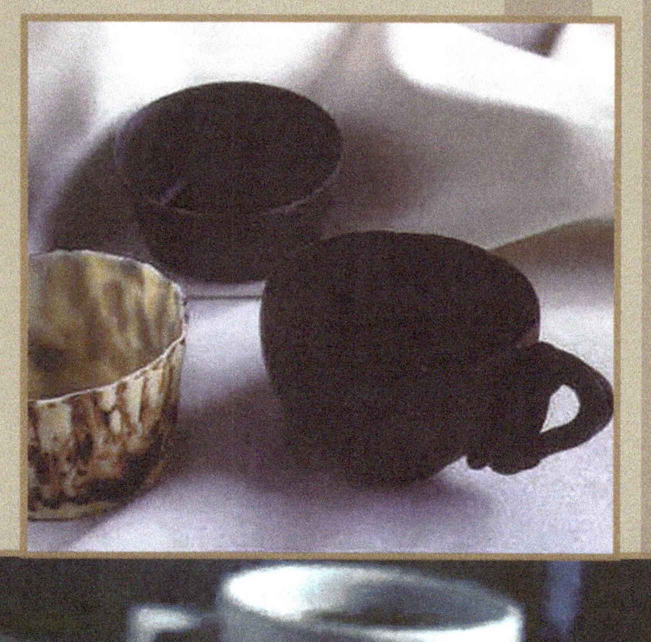

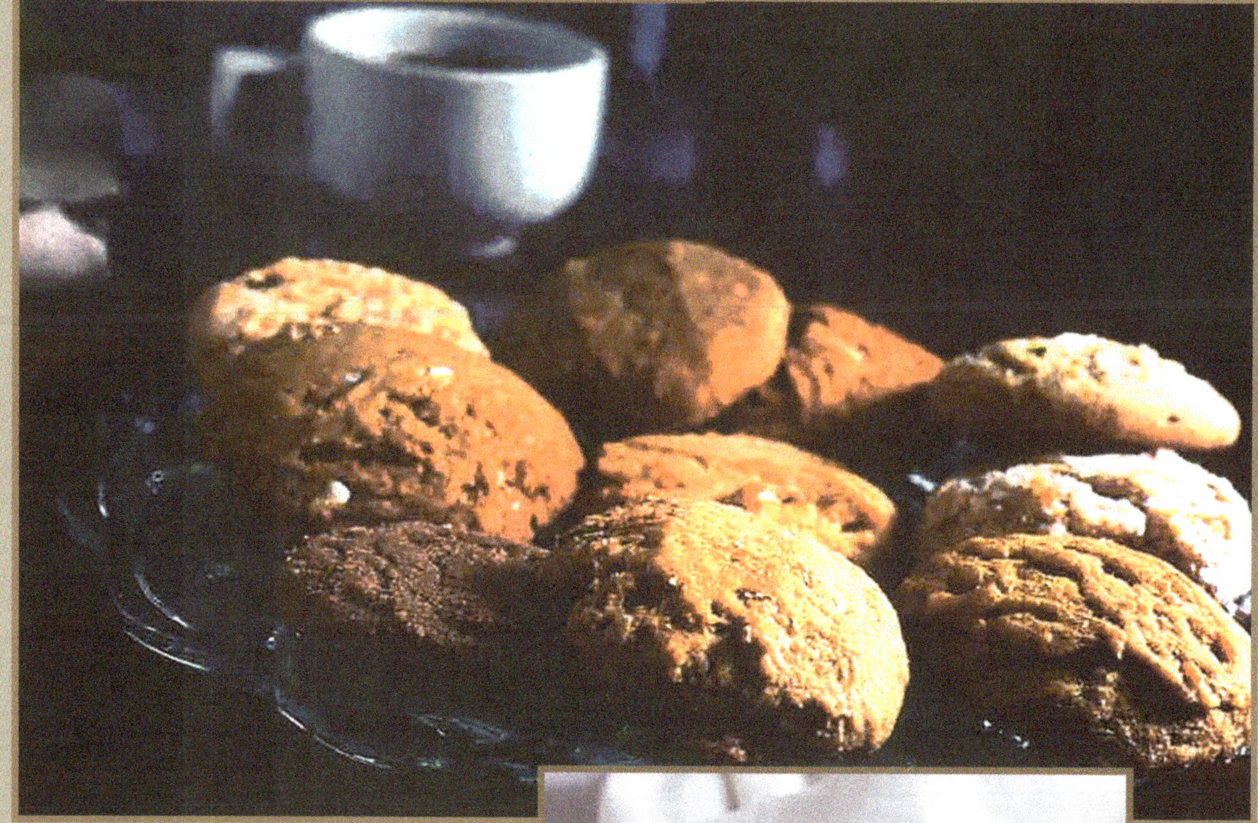

Gluten-free Brownies

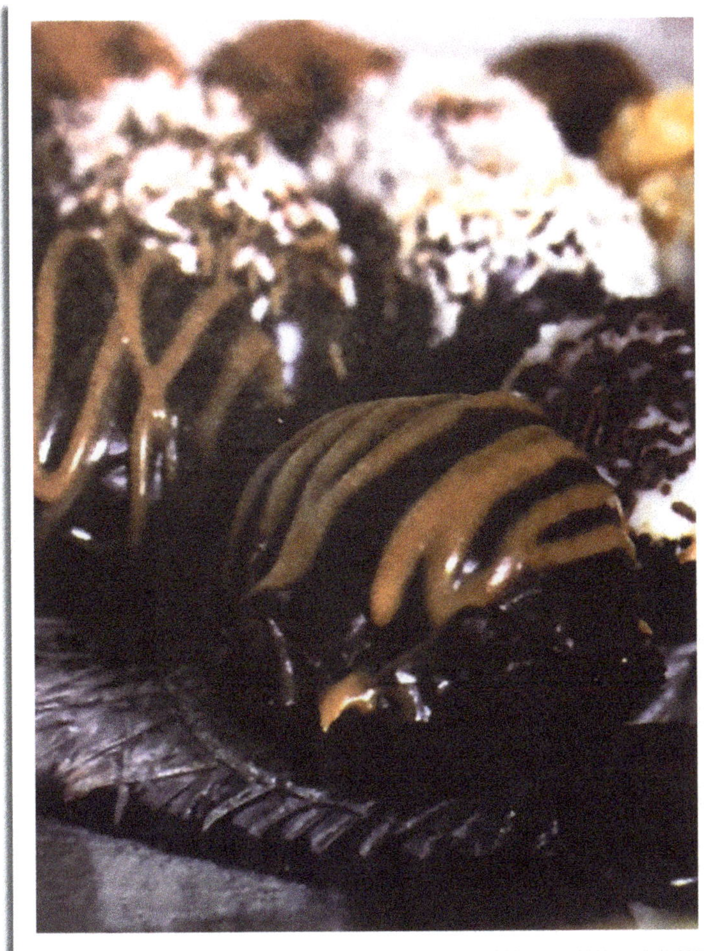

Truffles

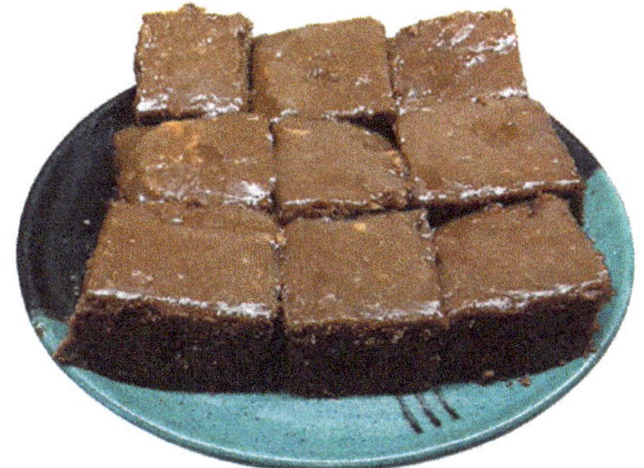

Caramel Brownies

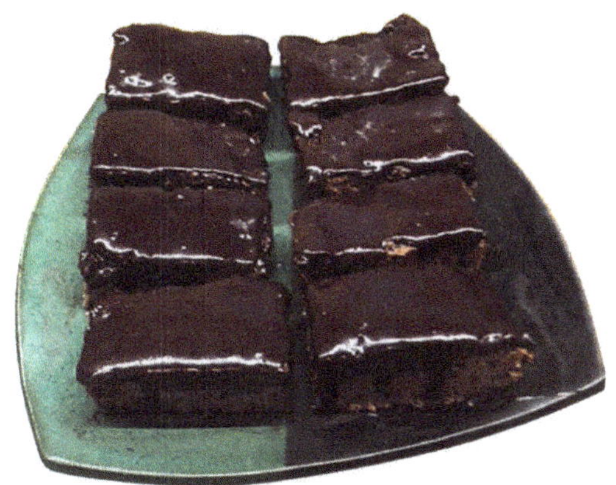

Fig Date Raspberry Brownie

"A larger-than-life force of nature known as Nick Ligidakis, he is a restaurateur legend in Phoenix."
— New Times

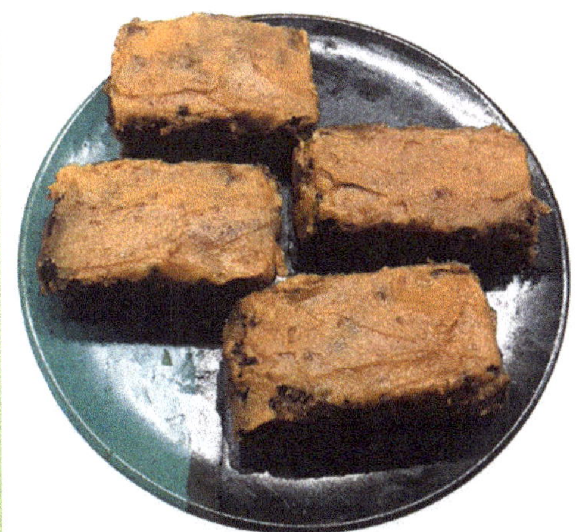

Peanut Butter Brownies

Caramel is sugar cooked with water until it turns light brown. Use 1 ½ cups sugar and ⅔ cup water. Place in a saucepan over medium heat. Shake pan in a circular motion until the sugar boils and turns light brown. It takes about 4 minutes. Use immediately. It makes about 1 cup of caramel.

Flavoring the Truffles

Prepare the truffle mixture and add your desire flavor.

Flavor Suggestions

Raspberry, Caramel, Hazelnut Mocha
Grand Marnier, Chestnut, Dark Cherry

Icing the Truffles

½ cup heavy cream
Heat in a saucepan on low heat.
8 oz semisweet chocolate
Add and stir until chocolate melts.
Place icing on a flat tray and let cool.
Scoop out the truffle mixture with a medium size ice cream scoop.
Roll the truffle ball between the palms of your hands to smooth it out.
Place parchment paper in another tray.
Roll the truffles, one at a time in the icing and place it on the parchment paper.
Refrigerate the tray for about 1 hour or so until the chocolate icing is firm.
Decorate the truffles.

Truffle decoration

The primary decoration for truffles is either cocoa powder or chocolate sprinkles.
Roll the truffles in either or the cocoa or the sprinkles and serve.
Other decorations: Chocolate vermicelli, toasted coconut, grated hazelnuts, white chocolate sprinkles.

Easy Truffles with Leftover Cake

16 oz semisweet chocolate
Melt in a double boil.
12 oz unsalted butter
¼ cup of coconut sugar
Place in your mixer and beat on medium speed until smooth and creamy.
½ cup whipping cream
6 cups of chocolate cake,
Use leftover cake or make half of the recipe of chocolate cake (page 59)

The melted chocolate

½ cup of desire add-on flavors
Add and mix well.

Makes 35 to 40 truffles

A chocolate truffle is a ganache. Ganache is simply a mixture of chocolate and cream, melted in a double boil and firmed up in the refrigerator. I use a small amount of butter for a firm mixture.

Basic Truffles

16 oz semisweet chocolate
¾ cup heavy cream
2 oz unsalted butter
Heat in a double boil until chocolate is melted.
Stir ingredients to smooth.
Refrigerate for about 2 hours.

Makes 40 to 45 truffles

Warm water reactivates the yeast to feed the sugars found in flour. The release of sweetness provides the flavor molecules into the baking product. Using a little sugar while dissolving the yeast helps to speed up the flavor distribution process. The use of salt with yeast regulates the yeast activity to a slow and steady rise. Salt also slows down enzyme activity in the dough, helping to strengthens the gluten structure. When using hot water rather than warm water, the extreme heat kills the yeast, and the entire activity comes to a stop.

Basic Truffles

16 oz semisweet chocolate
1 cup heavy cream
4 oz unsweetened butter
1 tsp vanilla extract

Melt in double boil under gentle heat until chocolate is melted. Stir to blend well. Pour in a shallow dish and refrigerate for at least 3 hours.

For a flavor truffle add your favor filling before refrigerating.

Truffle Variations

Add ½ cup raspberries to every 2 cups truffle mixture and blend.
Suggested decorating; cocoa powder.

Caramel
Add 3 tbsp of caramel sauce to every 2 cups truffle mixture and blend.
Suggested decorating; Ground hazelnuts.

Rum
Add 1 tbsp dark rum to every 2 cups truffle mixture and blend.
Suggested decorating; White chocolate sprinkles.

Orange Cappuccino
Add 1 tbsp orange zest, finely chopped and 1 tsp espresso coffee to every 2 cups truffle mixture and blend.
Suggested decorating – Chocolate vermicelli.

Raspberry
Add ½ cup raspberries to every 2 cups truffle mixture and blend.
Suggested decorating; cocoa powder.

Other truffle flavors

Dark Cherry
Add ½ cup chopped dark cherries to every 2 cups truffle mixture and blend. Decorate with chocolate vermicelli.

Peanut
Add 1 tbsp peanut butter to every 2 cups truffle mixture and blend. Decorate with white chocolate vermicelli.

How many of you would say you were introduced to cooking by beating a pan of fudge, by licking a spoon and overwhelmed by sweetness? Dessert making at home is a child's fondest memories. It is an event that sometimes involves entire families and believe me; a time of precious memories. The satisfaction that comes out of making your pastry is immeasurable.

Here is a simple fudge recipe. Start with this one, and who knows, someday you too may write a book of your own experiences.

To Make Fudge

18 oz semisweet chocolate
3 tbsp unsalted butter
14 oz sweetened condensed milk
1 tsp vanilla extract

Place in a double boiler and mix until chocolate melts.

Let cool a bit.

Lightly buttered a 8" square class pan. Pour mixture in and refrigerate for at least 4 hours.

Cut into squares and serve.

Variations: Before cooling the fudge, add 1 cup chopped walnuts. Or 8 oz chopped dried dates. Or use your favorite nuts, dried fruit or combination of both.

"I've always wanted to impart a distinctive touch to every one of my recipes, even simple things like brownies. If done correctly, simplicity can be inspiring and more impressive than complicated dishes."

Pecan Bars

Preheat oven to 350-degrees

Lightly butter an approximately 9" x 13" glass baking dish.

Crust

¾ cups sugar

6 oz soft unsalted butter

1 ½ cups flour

Mix gently in a mixing bowl and spread in the glass dish.

Filling

6 oz unsalted butter, melted

½ cup brown sugar

¾ cup honey

¼ cup heavy cream

2 lbs pecan pieces

Blend well with a spatula in a mixing bowl. Spread filling over crust.

Bake in the preheated 350-degree over for 20 minutes.

Refrigerate 3 to 4 hours.

Cut into desired size bars.

To Make Butter Cream

1 ⅓ cups sugar

⅓ cup water

Bring to a boil, reduce heat. Simmer for about 5-6 minutes. Set aside.

12 egg yolks

Whip at medium speed, add the sugar-water a little at a time, let cool.

1 ½ lbs unsalted butter, softened

Cut in to small pieces and add in. Beat at low speed for about 5 minutes. At this point, you can add the desired flavoring.

Coffee Butter Cream: Add 2 ½ tbsp instant coffee

Chocolate Butter Cream: Add 10 oz melted chocolate

Mini Mousse Cake

Preheat oven to 350-degrees

Prepare a 10" chocolate cake (page 59)

Pour chocolate cake mixture in lightly oil a 12-cup muffin pan.

Bake in the preheated 350-degree oven for approx. 30 minutes.

Remove and let mini chocolate cakes cool.

Chocolate Mousse

4 oz semisweet chocolate

Melt in a double boiler

2 cups of whipped topping

1 tsp vanilla extract

Using your mixer with a whisk attachment, whip on medium-high speed until medium peaks form, about 3 to 4 minutes.

Fold the melted chocolate into the whipped topping. Blend well with a spatula.

Place the first slice of the chocolate cake on a working surface. Using an ice cream scoop, place a scoop of mousse on the bottom cake.

Cover with the top part of the cake.

Chocolate Icing

6 oz semisweet chocolate

Melt in a double boil.

1 cup whipping cream

Add to the melted chocolate and mix well

Place mini mousse cakes on a screen with a pan on the bottom. Spoon some of the icing on the top of the cake, so it rolls all over the cake.

Smooth the icing with a small spatula.

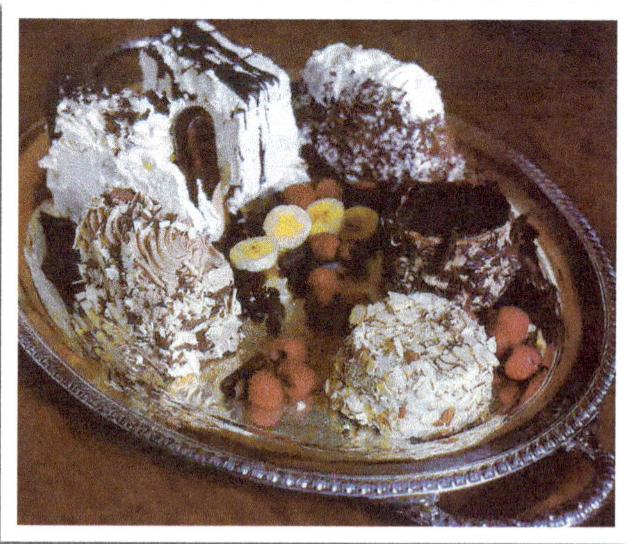

Mini Carrot Cake

Preheat oven to 350-degrees

Filling

½ cup of vegetable oil
1 cup of sugar

Place in your mixer and blend on medium speed for about two minutes.

2 eggs

Add to the mixer and blend well.

1 ½ cups shredded carrots
½ tsp vanilla extract
½ cup pineapple pieces
¼ cup pineapple juice
½ cup raisins
½ cup walnuts
½ tsp. cinnamon
1 tsp. baking soda
1 ¼ cups flour

Add to the mixer and mix on medium speed for two to three minutes.

Lightly oil 12-cup muffin pan.

Scoop mixture into the muffin pan.

Bake at in the 350-degree preheated oven for about 1 hour. Let the cake cool.

Frosting

10 oz cream cheese
1 cup powdered sugar

Place in your mixer and beat on medium speed until smooth and creamy.

1 tbsp cup unsalted butter, softened
½ tsp vanilla extract
½ cup shredded coconut
¼ cup grated walnuts
⅛ tsp honey

Add to the mixer and mix on low speed until all ingredients are blended well, about 3 minutes.

Spread the frosting on the mini cakes.

"Ligidakis stresses quality. Because of this, he refuses to compromise when it comes to ingredients he uses."
—Arizona Republic

Grand Marnier Pudding

12 oz white chocolate

Melt in a double boil.

16 oz cream cheese
½ cup of sugar

Place in your mixer and beat on medium speed until smooth and creamy.

The melted white chocolate

Add and blend well on low speed.

Turn mixer off.

1 ½ cups Amaretto cookies (Recipe on page 130)
¼ cup strong coffee, preferably espresso

Soak the cookies in the coffee.

2 tbs dark rum
2 tbsp Grand Marnier

Add soaked cookies, rum, and Grand Marnier into the mixer and blend gently until the the mixture is smooth.

6 dessert stem classes, approximately 5 to 6 oz

Fill the glasses halfway with pudding.

1 pint blackberries

Place a layer of blackberries on top of the pudding and divide the rest of the pudding into the glasses.

Decorate with an Amaretto cookie on top of each pudding.

Refrigerate 1 to 2 hours before serving.

How many of you would say you were introduced to cooking by beating a pan of fudge, by licking a spoon and overwhelmed by sweetness? Dessert making is one of a child's fondest memories. It is an event that sometimes involves entire families and believe me, a time of precious memories. The satisfaction that comes from making your pastry is immeasurable. Start with this simple fudge recipe and who knows, someday you may write a book from your own experiences.

Papaya Fruit Pudding

Cream Filling
16 oz cream cheese
1 cup coconut sugar
Beat in high speed of your mixer until creamy.
1 cup coconut milk
1 tsp ginger
1 tbsp arrowroot
1 tbsp grated orange peel
Add to the mixer and blend on low speed.
1 tsp orange juice
2 papayas, peeled
1 tsp lemon juice
Reserve eight thin slices of papaya. Chop remaining fruit into small cubes, and add to the blender. Mix well
Divide filling in to tall glass. Decorate with papaya slices.
2 cups ginger snap cookie crumbs
Sprinkle on top of the puddings. Refrigerate for about 2 hours before serving.

Rice Pudding

½ cup rice, long grain
2 cup of water
In a saucepan bring water and rice to a boil. Reduce heat to medium. Simmer, stirring occasionally, for about 30 minutes, until the water has been absorbed and rice is soft.
2 ½ cups milk
4 tbsp sugar
1 tsp vanilla extract
Add in, let simmer for about 1 to 2 minutes minutes, stirring to blend well.
3 tbsp arrowroot
Add in, remove from heat and blend well.
Ladle pudding into individual serving dishes.
Cinnamon
Sprinkle on top of the pudding. Refrigerate for at least three hours before serving.
Makes 6 servings

Peach Bread Pudding

Preheat oven to 350-degrees
3 eggs, beaten
4 oz unsalted butter, melted
1 cup yogurt
1 cup milk
1 tsp vanilla extract
Mix well in a mixing bowl
8 cups cubed bread
10 peaches, pilled and cut and diced
1 cup pecan pieces
Add to the bowl
Let sit for 30 minutes
Oil a 9" x 13" class baking dish.
Pour mixture in the dish.
3 tbsp coconut sugar
½ tsp cinnamon
Mix and pour over the mixture.
Bake in the preheated oven for 20 to 22 minutes.
Caramel sauce (page 98) pour over.

Cooking is a responsibility

"Never serve food you wouldn't eat yourself." This is what I used to say to my cooks and to potential chefs. When I was conducting cooking classes or training interns out of culinary schools, my goal was always to educate potential chefs about the chemistry of foods, encouraging them to create their own style of cooking and to respect the quality and wholesomeness of the food they serve. Furthermore, simplify the cooking process and not be intimidated about the fancy terminology some chefs use. In this book my goal remains the same, to learn how to create new tastes and above all recognize the paramount step to every chef's success is to use quality ingredients.

Kahlua and Cream Pudding

12 oz white chocolate

Melt in a double boil.

1 cup whipped topping

Using your mixer with a whisk attachment, beat on medium-high speed until peaks form, about 3 to 4 minutes. Set aside

6 oz unsalted butter

½ cup of sugar

Place in your mixer and beat on medium speed until smooth and creamy.

The whipped topping

The melted white chocolate

Add to the mixer and blend on low speed.

3 tbsp Kahlua

Add into the mixer and blend gently until the mixture is smooth.

6 dessert stem classes, approximately 5 to 6 oz

Fill the glasses halfway with pudding.

2 bananas, thinly sliced

Place a couple of layers of bananas on top of the pudding and divide the rest of the pudding into the glasses.

Refrigerate 1 to 2 hours before serving.

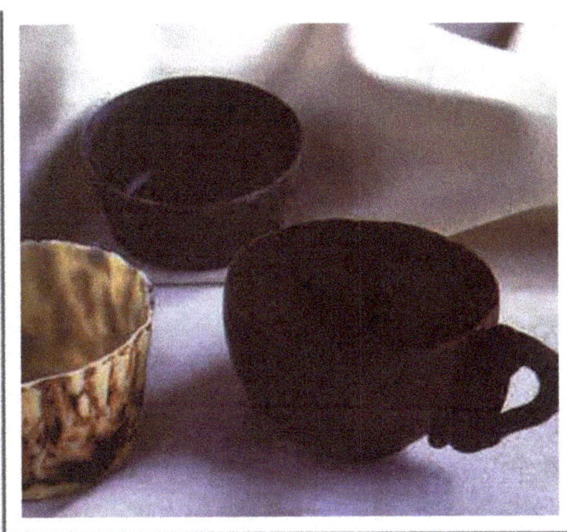

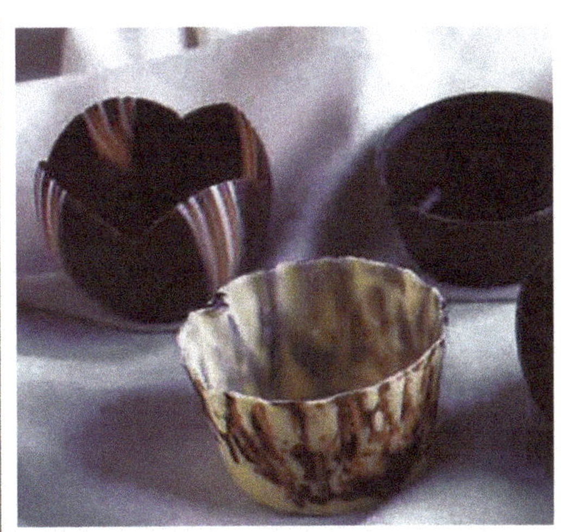

"Forget everything you ever thought about puddings and try Nick's Jack Daniel's Pudding, with bittersweet, semisweet chocolates, whipped cream and Jack Daniels whiskey combined into one heavenly mixture."

— The Western Express

The Complicated World of Baking Methods

As I mentioned in an earlier section, cooking and baking must be handled with a different approach. The two fundamental principles of baking are the proportion of flour and the method used to merge the dry and wet ingredients. If these steps are not done correctly, it will result in a disastrous outcome that cannot be corrected, unlike in cooking when you can "fix" the texture and taste by adding more spices or thickeners along the way. If you are looking for information in various books or online for baking at home, most likely you will be confused and sometimes discouraged to do what otherwise it should be a fun experience. There are methods of Rubbing-in, which is similar to Cutting-in. There is the Melting method, the Whisking method, which is similar to the Whipping method. And there is the Roll-in method, the Creaming method, the All-in method, which is like the Quick method, also called the Muffin method, and so on. Ultimately all these methods are various techniques to, mainly, produce different textures in cakes and rarely used in home cooking. If you are new to baking or you are trying to further educate yourself about the amazing world of baking, these various baking methods will make your head spin for days. If you follow a recipe, it should explain how to mix and bake your ingredients. The two common methods, especially with gluten-free baking, are the creaming and quick methods. The quick method is beneficial in gluten-free baking because you are working with "naked" flours, stripped of the protection gluten provides for safe baking. Simply put, the creaming method is one that blends fats, like butter, with sugar until creamy and then beaten eggs are slowly added to the mixture. This is the traditional method and the basis for cookie and cake making. A soft cake or chewy cookie is the product of the creaming method. The creaming method incorporates air into the dough while mixing. The air, with the help of baking soda or baking powder, is what helps the cake or cookies rise. The quick method, also called the muffin method, is one of the simplest of all other methods. It is a technique where the dry ingredients, such as flour and the liquid ingredients, like beaten eggs and milk, are mixed in different bowls, and then quickly combined. Once the two are combined and stirred together very briefly, the finished batter is ready to be baked. The advantage of the correctly done quick method in gluten-free baking is that it produces a light and airy product since the gentle blending protects your defenseless gluten-free flours. The batter will be somewhat lumpy and much thinner than it would be when using the creaming method. The quick baking method is mainly used for muffins, pancakes, quick breads, and waffles. Since muffins are defined by their "peak-top," they must be baked in higher temperatures. The high heat cooks the edges of the muffin quickly and forces the batter to rise. If you over-mix the batter in the quick method, then you will, most likely, end up with rubbery muffins and quick breads, dense pancakes, or doughy waffles. Quick method: Place the flour and other dry ingredients in a large bowl and mix them with a wire whisk until thoroughly blended. Combine beaten eggs with the rest of the wet ingredients in a separate bowl, pour the mixture slowly in the center of the dry ingredients and stir with a wooden spoon until all ingredients are combined. This step should take a few seconds. For muffins and quick breads, a thick and lumpy muffin batter is good. The lumps will go away when they bake, for pancakes and waffles stir a bit longer to a little smoother mixture.

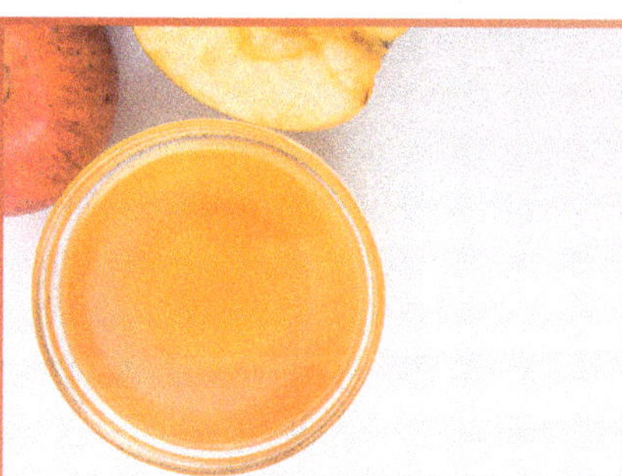

Cider vinegar is made from apples and it has a mild fruity flavor. Most other vinegar, especially balsamic vinegar, comes with a sharp flavor. However, vinegar loses its sharpness when used in batters with multiple ingredients. Vinegar is used in baking as an acidity agent to start a chemical reaction needed to lift the batter. It is best used in recipes that do not include much acidity. Furthermore, vinegar helps to balance the sweetness of your baking good.

Multi-Grain Bread

2 cups whole wheat flour
2 cups white flour
1 tbsp dry yeast
1 tsp salt

Mix in your mixer with a dough hook.

¼ cups rolled oats
⅛ cup chia seeds
¼ cup raw sunflower seeds
⅛ cup poppy seeds
¼ cup flax seeds
¼ cup sesame seeds
¼ cup almonds, chopped
1 ¼ cups warm water
⅓ cup olive oil
¼ cup honey

Add to the mixer and mix until well, combined.

Place dough in a lightly coated mixing bowl with olive oil.

Cover with a towel and let it rise until double in size, about 2 hours.

Preheat oven to 375-degrees

Remove and knead the dough on

9" x 5" x 2 ½" inches glass or ceramic loaf pans and bake in the preheated oven for 30 to 35 minutes.

Kalamata Olive Bread

4 cups flour plus
2 tbsp yeast
½ teaspoon salt

Mix in your mixer with a dough hook.

1 garlic clove, minced
3 tablespoons olive
1 tsp rosemary
1 ½ cup of warm water

Add to the mixer and mix until well combined.

Remove and knead the dough on a lightly floured counter.

Place dough in a lightly coated mixing bowl with olive oil.

Cover with a towel and let it rise until double in size, about 2 hours.

Preheat oven to 375-degrees

Place dough in a lightly floured counter, flatten out.

1 ½ cup Kalamata olives, chopped

Add to the dough and mix by hand.

Divide dough it into two parts and shape into loaves.

Place on a lightly oiled baking sheet, gently brush loaves with olive oil.

Bake bread for 30 to 35 minutes.

Baking powder vs. Baking soda

Both baking powder and baking soda are leavening agents. While they bear similarities in texture, they differ in how they interact with other ingredients. Baking soda requires acid and a liquid to become activated and help baked goods rise. Conversely, baking powder only needs a liquid to become activated. Substituting one for the other is possible with careful adjustments. Because baking soda lacks the acid that baking powder would generally add to the recipe, you have to make sure when using baking soda is in a recipe that includes acidity ingredients, such as sour cream, yogurt, lemon or vinegar. Baking powder contains baking soda and powdered acid, and it works best with non-acid ingredients. However, the most significant difference is that the double-acting (there is a single-acting) baking powder reacts twice, once exposed to moisture and then again when exposed to heat. At the same time, baking soda reacts once when exposed to moisture. Both baking soda and baking power produce small amounts of carbon dioxide. Because of the double-acting effect, the baking power release it twice and most of it during the baking process while baking soda release it when mixed with acidity ingredients. The bottom line, the baking powder adds flavor to your baking product, contrary to baking soda that leaves a bitter aftertaste. I tend to use more baking powder than baking soda.

Focaccia with Rosemary and Garlic

Oil Mixture:
½ cup olive oil
3 garlic cloves, chopped
1 tbsp fresh rosemary
1 tbsp fresh or dried thyme
Place in a saute pan and cook on low heat for about 10 minutes.
Set aside.
1 ½ cups warm water
Water should be warm.
Hot water will kill the yeast.
¼ oz active yeast
1 tsp sugar
Stir and place in the bowl of your mixer. Let sit for about 5 minutes
½ tsp salt
¼ cup of the oil mixture
3 ¾ cups flour
Add to the mixing bowl, turn the speed of your mixer to low and blend well, 3 to 4 minutes.
Transfer dough to a lightly flour surface and knead for 2 to 3 minutes.

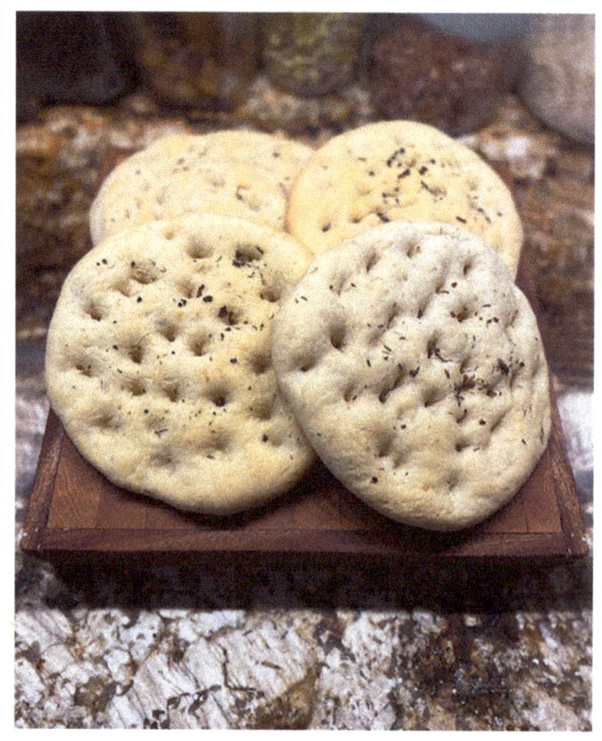

Use part of the oil mixture to lightly oil the mixing bowl used to blend your dough.
Return dough to the mixing bowl.
Cover with plastic and let set in a warm place for 1 hour.
Remove the dough and place on a lightly floured working surface. Deflate the dough and cut in to four equal pieces.
Knead each peace into a shape of a ball.
Place ball on a lightly floured surface, press to flatten and use a rolling pin to open the dough into, about, 8-inch round
Using some of the oil mixture, lightly oiled two large baking sheets (Approximately 17" x 11") place two round on each baking sheet, cover and let rise for about 1 hour.
Half an hour in to the rising of the dough, preheat your oven to 450-degrees.
After the second rising, brush the four focaccia rounds with the remaining oil mixture.
Using your fingers dimple the entire surface of the focaccia rounds.
Bake in the preheated oven for 30 to 35 minutes, until focaccia tops are light brown.

Various Toppings:
Tomatoes; Feta; Sliced Tomatoes; Crumbled Feta Cheese; Kalamata Olives – sliced; Basil; Pesto; Romano cheese; Sun-dried Tomatoes; capers.
Focaccia makes an excellent bread for panini and great bread for olive oil and balsamic vinegar dip.
NOTE: The dimples on focaccia reduce the air in the dough and prevent the bread from rising too quickly. Also, if using extra flavoring, dimples help the bread to soak the flavor as it bakes.

Focaccia with Rosemary and Garlic

Mango Bread, Gluten-Free

Preheat oven to 350-degrees

Dry Mix

½ cup brown rice flour
¾ cup coconut flour
1 cup gluten-free muffin mix flour
¼ cup arrowroot
1 tbsp flaxseed
2 tsp baking powder
¼ tsp nutmeg

Place in a mixing bowl and blend well.

Wet Ingredients

2 eggs, beaten
1 cup unsweetened coconut milk
4 tbsp olive oil
3 tbsp Greek yogurt

Mix in a separate bowl.

Pour slowly into the dry ingredients and thoroughly mix.

½ cup walnuts, chopped
1 ripe banana, mashed
½ mango, peeled and chopped

Add to the batter and mix.

Lightly grease with olive oil an 8" x 4" x 2 ½" glass or ceramic bread baking pan.

Pour in the mixture and bake in the preheated oven for 60 to 65 minutes.

Remove from oven and let cool before removing the bread.

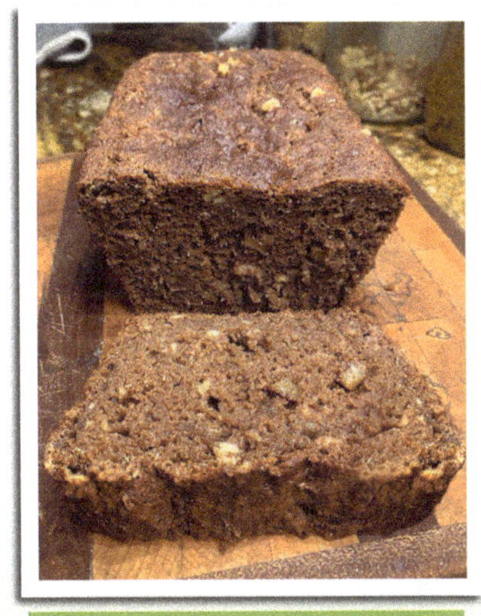

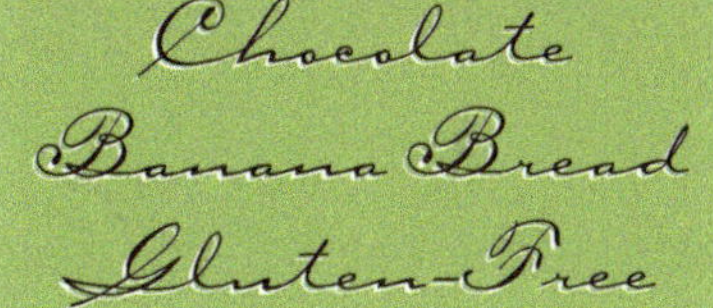

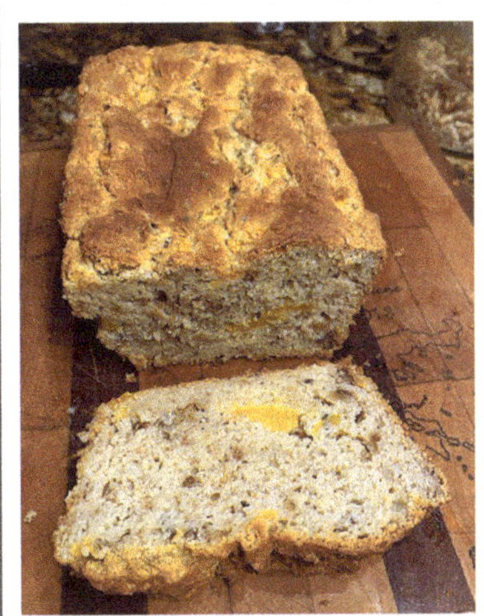

Mango Bread
Gluten-Free

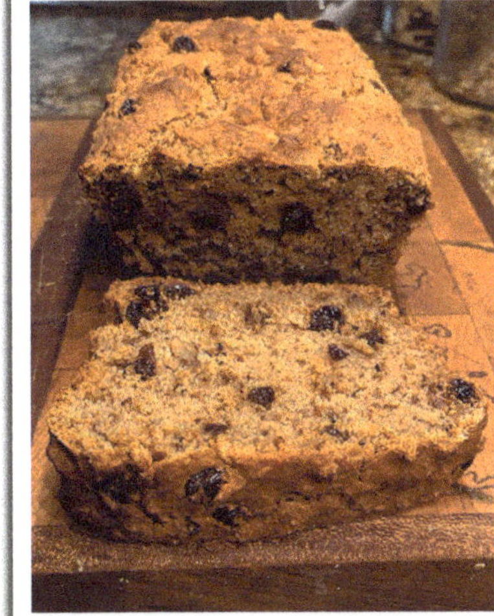

Cinnamon
Raisin Bread
Gluten-Free

Blueberry Quick Bread, Gluten-Free

Preheat oven to 350-degrees

Dry mix

1 cup brown rice flour
1cup gluten-free muffin mix
¼ cup tapioca flour
2 tbsp arrowroot
1 tbsp flaxseed
2 tsp baking power
½ cup coconut sugar

Place in a mixing bowl and blend well.

Wet Ingredients

2 eggs, beaten
1 cup almond milk
2 tbsp olive oil
½ cup Greek yogurt
1 tsp vanilla extract
2 tbsp lemon juice
2 tbsp lemon zest

Mix in a separate bowl.

Pour slowly into the dry ingredients and thoroughly mix

1 ½ cups blueberries

Add to the batter and mix.

Lightly grease with olive oil an 8" x 4" x 2 ½" glass or ceramic bread baking pan.

Pour in the mixture and bake in the preheated oven for for 60 to 65 minutes

Remove from oven and let cool before removing the bread.

Cinnamon Banana Quick Bread

Preheat oven to 350-degree

½ cup unsalted butter
1 cup of sugar

Place in your mixer bowl and blend on medium speed for about two minutes.

2 eggs
½ cup milk

Add to the mixer and mix well.

2 cups flour
1 tbsp baking soda
1 tsp baking powder

Add to the mixer and blend until smooth.

1 large banana, chopped
1 tsp cinnamon
1 cup walnut pieces
1 tsp lemon juice

Add in and blend well.

Add to the batter and mix.

Lightly grease with olive oil an 8" x 4" x 2 ½" glass or ceramic bread baking pan.

Pour in the mixture and bake in the preheated oven for for 60 to 65 minutes.

Remove from oven and let cool before removing the bread.

Gluten-free Flour Chemistry

When at first made the Walnut Banana Mango bread, the center was undercooked. I increased the coconut flour measurement, decreased the measurement of olive oil, and added Greek yogurt. Also, I chopped the mango rather than pulse it in the food processor. It worked.

Also, the Cinnamon Raisin Bread was dry at first. I replaced the almond flour and added brown rice flour. I added Greek yogurt and applesauce – much improved.

The primary reason your bread turns out undercooked in the center is that the oven is too hot and improper dry ingredients measurements. However, with gluten-free flour, the flours used and the amount of liquid can also make a difference.

The apparent reason that your bread is not moist is that there is not enough liquid. But, with gluten-free flour, which lacks gluten strength to make the dough elastic, the problem is the flour. Some gluten-free flours, mostly the nut flours, absolve more moistness than others. Knowing the behavior of your gluten-free flours is an essential part of successful gluten-free baking.

Cinnamon Raisin Bread, Gluten-Free

Preheat oven to 350-degrees

Dry Mix

½ cup rolled oats
1 cup brown rice flour
½ cup walnuts, chopped
1 cup gluten-free muffin mix
1 tbsp arrowroot
1 tbsp flaxseed
2 tsp baking powder
1 cup raisins
1 tbsp coconut sugar
1 tsp cinnamon

Place in a mixing bowl and blend well.

Wet Ingredients

2 large eggs, beaten
1 cup unsweetened almond milk
2 tbsp olive oil
½ tsp pure vanilla extract
4 tbsp Greek yogurt
3 tbsp applesauce

Mix in a separate bowl.

Pour slowly into the dry ingredients and thoroughly mix.

½ cup walnut pieces

Add to the batter and mix.

Lightly grease with olive oil an 8" x 4" x 2 ½" glass or ceramic bread baking pan.

Pour in the mixture and bake in the preheated oven for for 60 to 65 minutes.

Remove from oven and let cool before removing the bread.

Chocolate Banana Quick Bread, Gluten-Free

Preheat oven to 350-degrees

Dry Mix

1 cup brown rice flour
¼ cup coconut flour
1 cup muffin mix
2 tbsp arrowroot
2 tsp baking powder
½ cup coconut sugar
½ cup unsweetened cocoa and chocolate powder

Place in a mixing bowl and blend well.

Wet Ingredients

2 eggs, beaten
1 tsp vanilla
1 cup almond milk
2 tbsp olive oil

Mix in a separate bowl.

Pour slowly into the dry ingredients and thoroughly mix.

¼ cup unsweetened applesauce
½ cup walnut pieces
2 large bananas, mashed
2 tbsp Greek yogurt

Add to the batter and mix.

Lightly grease with olive oil an 8" x 4" x 2 ½" glass or ceramic bread baking pan.

Pour in the mixture and bake in the preheated oven for for 60 to 65 minutes.

Remove from oven and let cool before removing the bread.

Quick Breads

A toasted quick bread slice is enjoyable for breakfast or a snack, especially the banana walnut mango bread. The cinnamon raisin bread makes a flavorful French toast. The lemon date bread is a delicious light summer dessert.

NOTE: If you bake your quick bread at too hot temperature will cause the outer portion of your bread to cook too quickly and be undercook in the middle. If you use too much liquid or fruit the bread will be wet in the center if you use too many dry ingredients your bread will be dense – this is true especially when working with gluten-free flours.

Date Lemon Bread Bread, Gluten-Free

Preheat oven to 350-degrees
1 cup dried dates
2 tsp water
Using soft dates is important to limit the water usage to pulse the dates.
Too much liquid will make your bread mushy.
Place in the food processor and pulse 2 or 3 times. Set aside.

Dry Mix
½ cup brown rice flour
½ cup almond flour
1 cup gluten-free muffin mix flour
¼ cup tapioca flour
2 tbsp arrowroot 1 tbsp flaxseed
2 tsp baking powder
¼ tsp ground ginger
½ tsp cinnamon
Place in a mixing bowl and blend well.

Wet Ingredients
2 eggs, beaten
1 tbsp juice from a lemon
1 tbsp lemon peel, chopped
1 cup unsweetened almond milk
2 tbsp olive oil
Mix in a separate bowl.
Pour slowly into the dry ingredients and thoroughly mix.
½ cup pecans, chopped

The date paste
Add to the batter and mix.
Lightly grease with olive oil an 8" x 4" x 2 ½" glass or ceramic bread baking pan.
Pour in the mixture and bake in the preheated oven for for 60 to 65 minutes.
Remove from oven and let cool before removing the bread.
4 eggs
Add to the mixing bowl and continue mixing on slow speed.
Once eggs are blended with butter and oil, turn off the mixer.
2 cups gluten-free flour
1 ½ cups white rice flour
1 cup brown rice flour
1 cup almond flour
¼ cup tapioca
¼ cup arrowroot
2 tsp baking powder
1 tsp baking soda
1 tsp nutmeg
Add and continue mixing until all ingredients are blended well.

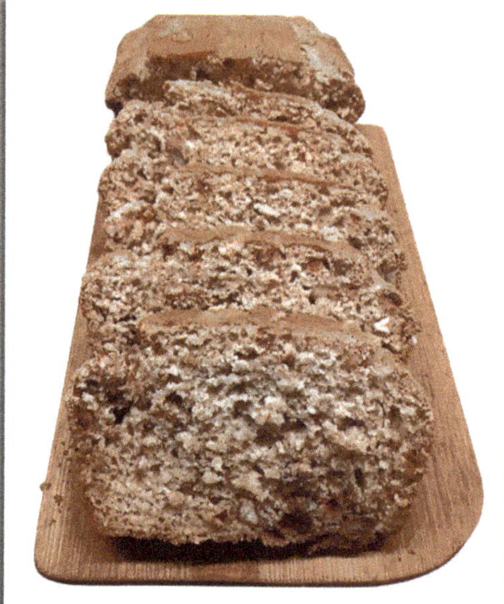

Date Lemon Bread, Gluten-Free

MUFFIN MIX

For muffins, use the quick mixing method, also known as the muffin mixing method. The Gluten-free muffin recipes in this book are made with two different batters: One is simple with muffin mix flour, the other with a combination of flours. If you are like me and you do not make muffins often, the muffin mix is more practical. Muffin mix flours are much improved, and with a little "doctoring-up," they make a good muffin.

Blueberry Muffins

Preheat oven to 400-degrees
2 cups flour
1 cup of sugar
2 tsp baking powder

Place ingredients in a large mixing bowl and stir with a wooden spoon to blend well.

2 eggs beaten
½ cup of vegetable oil
½ cup milk
1 tsp vanilla extract

Add slowly to the bowl, mixing with a wooden spoon until the dough is smooth.

2 cups blueberries

Add to the mixing bowl and stir to incorporate in the batter.

Using an ice cream scoop, pour the batter into paper-lined 12-muffin pan cups.

Fill the cups to about ¼ inch from the top.

Bake in the preheated oven for about 22 to 25 minutes.

Let muffins cool before removing from the cups.

Cranberry Orange Muffins

Preheat oven to 400-degrees
2 cups flour
1 cup of sugar
2 tsp baking powder
1 tsp cinnamon

Place ingredients in a large mixing bowl and stir with a wooden spoon to blend well.

2 eggs beaten
½ cup of vegetable oil
½ cup milk
1 tsp vanilla extract
2 tbsp orange juice

Add slowly to the bowl, mixing with a wooden spoon until the dough is smooth.

2 cups raspberries
2 tbsp orange zest

Add to the mixing bowl and stir to incorporate in the batter.

Using an ice cream scoop, pour the batter into paper-lined 12-muffin pan cups.

Fill the cups to about ¼" from the top.

Bake in the preheated oven for about 22 to 25 minutes.

Let muffins cool before removing from the cups.

"Awaiting us were Nick's specialty desserts. Mere words cannot describe. With names like Last Act, Fatal Obsession, they should allbe Rated X and considered a Sinful Act. Need we say more?"

— Echo Magazine

"Nick Ligidakis is a cult favorite among locals."

— Zagat Survey

Lemon Muffins

Preheat oven to 400-degrees
2 cups flour
1 cup of sugar
2 tsp baking powder
Place ingredients in a large mixing bowl and stir with a wooden spoon to blend well.
2 eggs beaten
½ cup of vegetable oil
½ cup milk
1 tsp vanilla extract
1 tbsp lemon juice
2 tbsp lemon zest
Add slowly to the bowl, mixing with a wooden spoon until the dough is smooth.
Add to the mixing bowl and stir to incorporate in the batter.
Using an ice cream scoop, fill halfway the paper-lined 12-muffin pan cups.
Add a spoonful of lemon filling and continue to fill the muffin cup,about ¼" from the top.
Bake in the preheated oven for about 22 to 25 minutes.
Let muffins cool before removing from the cups.

Lemon Filling
¼ cup coconut sugar
3 tbsp arrowroot
¾ cup almond milk
Whisk in a saucepan.
1 egg yolk
1 tbsp finely chopped lemon zest
Add and mix with the whisk.
Place saucepan over medium heat and cook until the mixture thickens 3 to 4 minutes.
Remove from the heat.
¼ cup juice of a lemon
1 tbsp low-fat organic, unsalted butter
Add to the pan and stir well.

Blueberry, Mango and Walnut Muffins, Gluten-Free

Preheat oven to 400-degrees
3 cups gluten-free muffin mix
¼ tsp nutmeg
1 tsp flaxseed
Place ingredients in a large mixing bowl and stir with a wooden spoon to blend well.
½ low-fat milk
½ cup unsweetened coconut milk
½ cup olive oil
2 eggs, beaten
Add slowly to the bowl, mixing with a wooden spoon until dough is smooth.
½ mango, peeled and chopped
1 cup fresh blueberries
2 tbsp low-fat Greek yogurt
½ cup walnuts, chopped
Add to the mixing bowl and stir to incorporate in the batter.
Using an ice cream scoop, pour the batter into paper-lined 12-muffin pan cups.
Fill the cups to about ¼" from the top.
Bake in the preheated oven for about 22 to 25 minutes.
Let muffins cool before removing from the cups.

"A larger-than-life force of nature known as Nick Ligidakis, he is a restaurateur legend in Phoenix."
— New Times

Pumpkin, White Chocolate Muffins, Gluten-Free

Preheat oven to 400-degrees
3 cups gluten-free muffin mix
¼ tsp nutmeg
Place ingredients in a large mixing bowl and stir with a wooden spoon to blend well.
½ cup low-fat milk
½ cup unsweetened almond milk
½ cup olive oil
2 eggs, beaten
Pour in the center of the flour mixture and stir until all ingredients are just combined.
½ cup pumpkin purée
1 cup white chocolate chips
Add to the mixing bowl and stir to incorporate in the batter.
Using an ice cream scoop, pour the batter into paper lined
12-muffin pan cups.
Fill the cups to about ¼" from the top.
Bake in the preheated oven for about 22 to 25 minutes. Let muffins cool before removing from the cups.

Cherry Almond and Blueberry Muffins, Gluten-Free

Preheat oven to 400-degrees
3 cups gluten-free muffin mix
2 tsp flaxseed
Place ingredients in a large mixing bowl and stir with a wooden spoon to blend well.
½ unsweetened almond milk
½ cup low-fat milk
½ cup olive oil
2 eggs, beaten
¼ tsp vanilla extract
Pour in the center of the flour mixture and stir until all ingredients are just combined.
1 cup fresh blueberries
1 cup frozen dark cherries, defrosted and cut in halves
½ cup sliced almonds
Add to the mixing bowl and stir to incorporate in the batter.
Using an ice cream scoop, pour the batter into paper lined 12-muffin pan cups. Fill the cups to about ¼" from the top.
Bake in the preheated oven for about 22 to 25 minutes.
Let muffins cool before removing from the cups.

To Make Custard

6 cups milk
1 cup sugar
Bring to boil in a large saucepan.
1 tbsp flour
Add in, stir to melt, remove from heat.
6 eggs
½ cup sugar
1 tsp vanilla extract
Beat in a mixer at medium speed until frothy, fold slowly in to hot milk, stirring with a wire whisk.
1 cup semolina flour
6 tbsp cake flour
Add in, mix well. Place in a bowl to set.
Lemon Custard: Follow the custard recipe Add ¾ cup lemon pie filling.
Strawberry Custard: Pulse 1 cup strawberries in the food processor and add to the custard recipe.
You can flavor the custard recipe with the flavor of your choice.

Cream Puffs

To make the pastry

Preheat oven to 375-degrees

Line a baking sheet with parchment paper.

1 cup of water

½ cup unsalted Butter

In a saucepan, heat water and butter, over medium-high heat until mixture comes to a boil.

1 cup flour

Remove saucepan from heat, add flour and stir quickly with a wooden spoon.

Once all of the flour is incorporated, place the saucepan back over medium-high heat.

Stir continuously for about 2 minutes until the dough is smooth.

3 Eggs

Place mixture into the bowl of your mixer and let cool for a few minutes. Add the eggs one at a time until egg is fully incorporated.

Place batter in a pastry bag fitted with a medium round tip. Pipe the batter into 12 rounds on the prepared baking sheet.

Bake for 20 to 25 minutes in the preheated oven, until golden brown.

Filling

2 oz white chocolate

Melt in a double boil.

2 cups whipped topping

1 tbsp sugar

½ tsp teaspoon vanilla

Beat in your mixer until soft peaks form

Fold in the melted white chocolate

When the pastry is cool, use a pastry bag with a small round tip, poke a hole in the bottom of each puff, and pipe the filling into the shells.

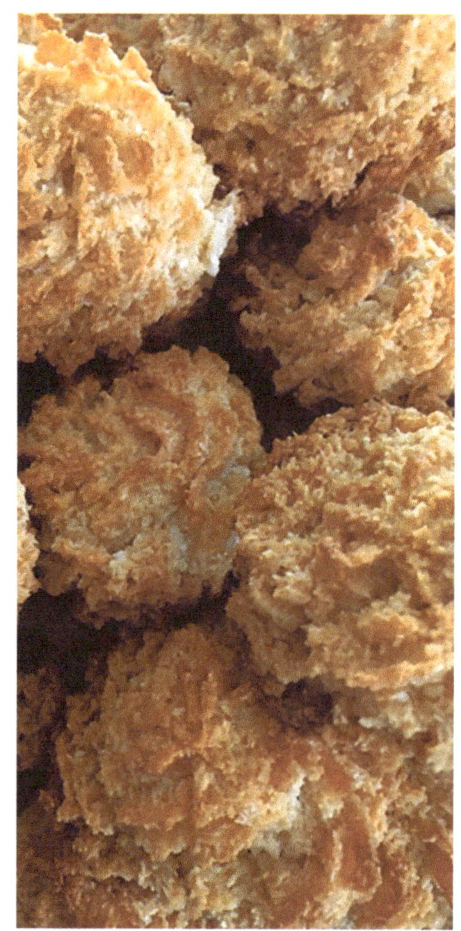

Coconut Macaroons

Preheat oven to 350-degrees

Line up 2 baking sheets with parchment paper

4 large egg whites, at room temperature

½ cup granulated sugar

Beat on medium speed in your mixer until soft peaks form. About 3 minutes.

1 tsp pure vanilla extract

4 cups sweetened shredded coconut

2 tbsp coconut flour

Add to your mixer, turn speed to low and blend well.

Fill a pastry bag with a large star tip and pipe macaroon on the baking sheets, about two inches apart.

If you don't have a pastry bag, use a small scoop.

Bake for about 15 to 18 minutes, until golden brown.

Chocolate Macaroons

6 oz semisweet chocolate

⅛ cup heavy cream

Melt in a double boil. Cool the macaroons.

Deep them, holding from the bottom into the chocolate. Place them back on the sheets. Let cool.

Makes about 24 macaroons.

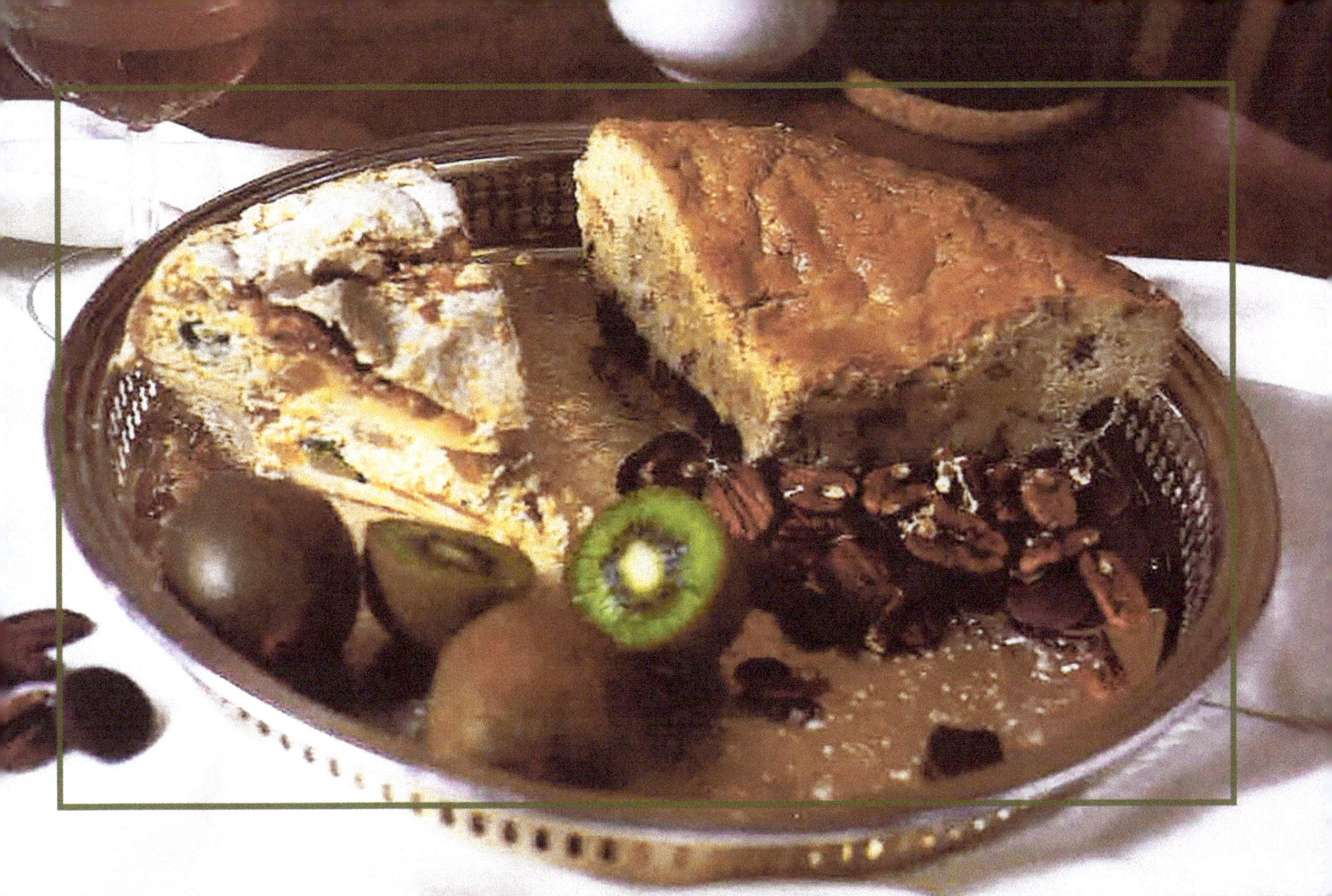

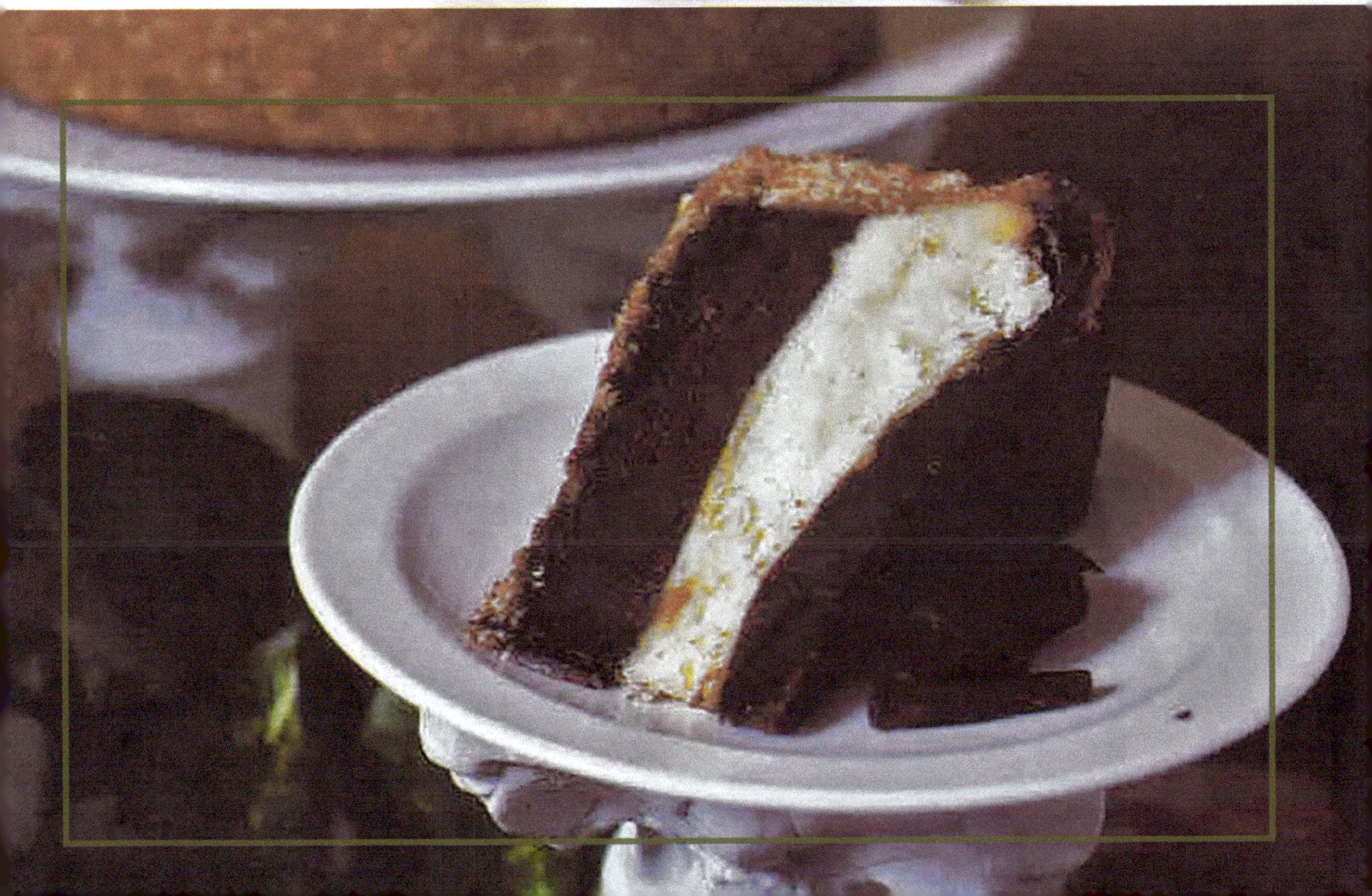

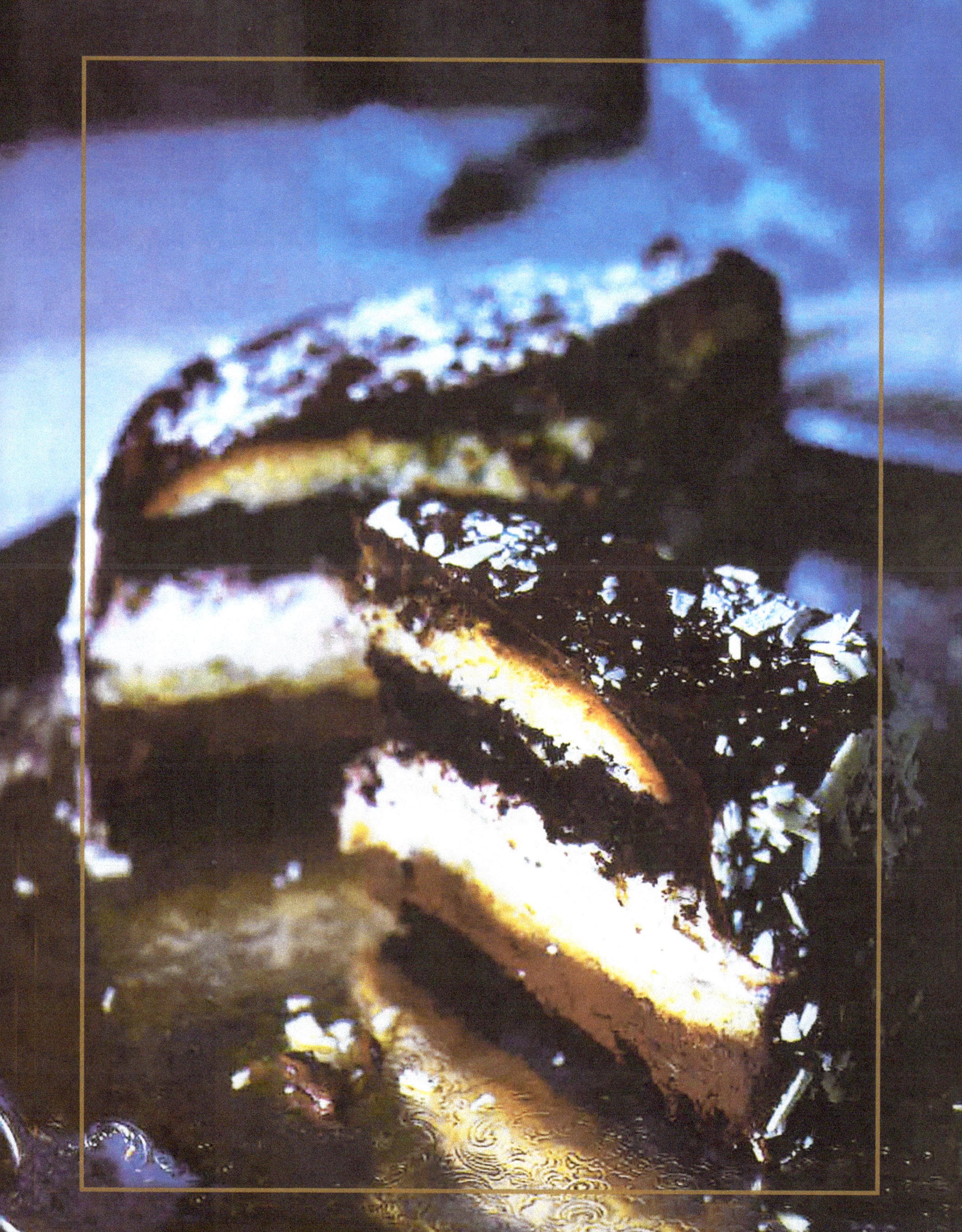

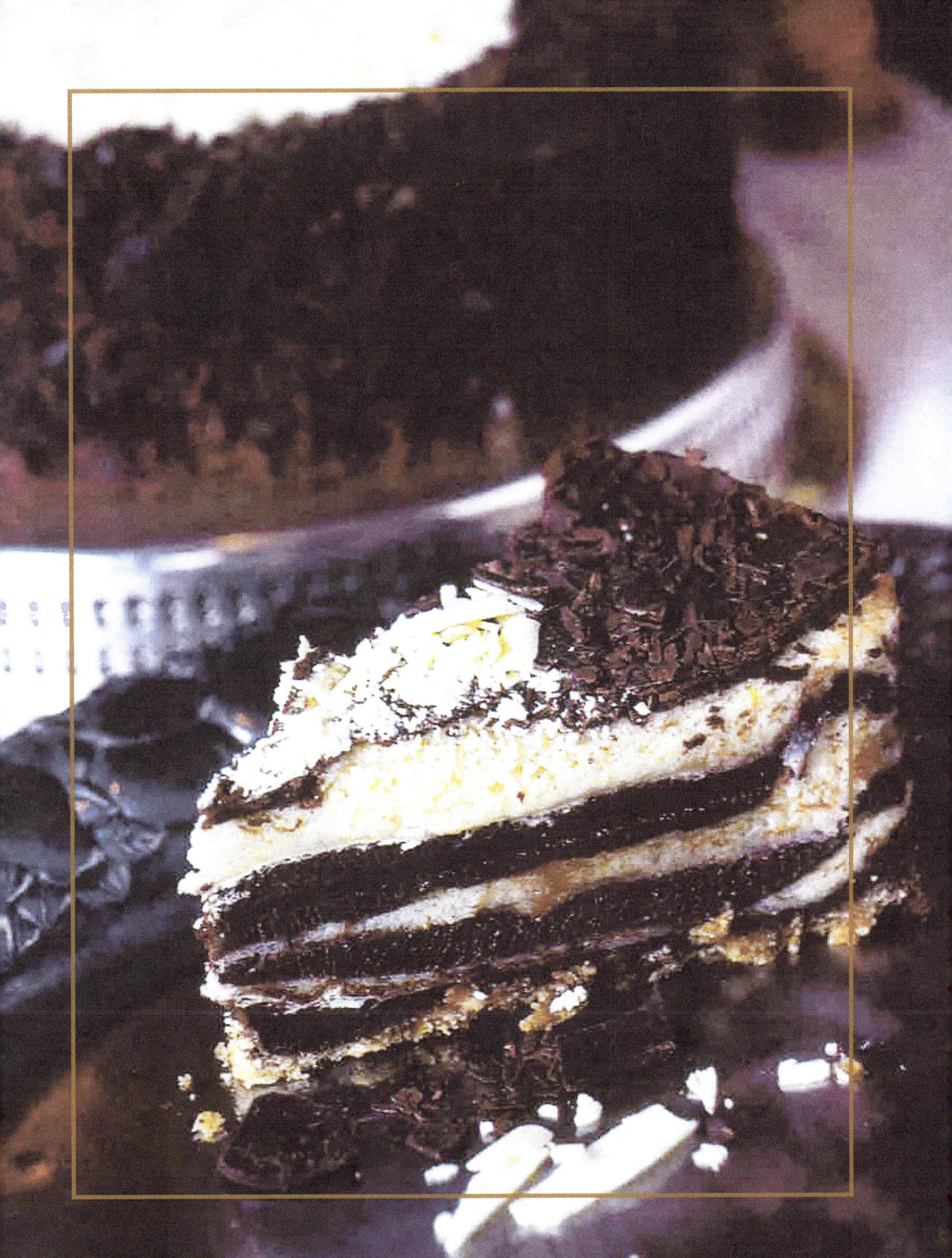

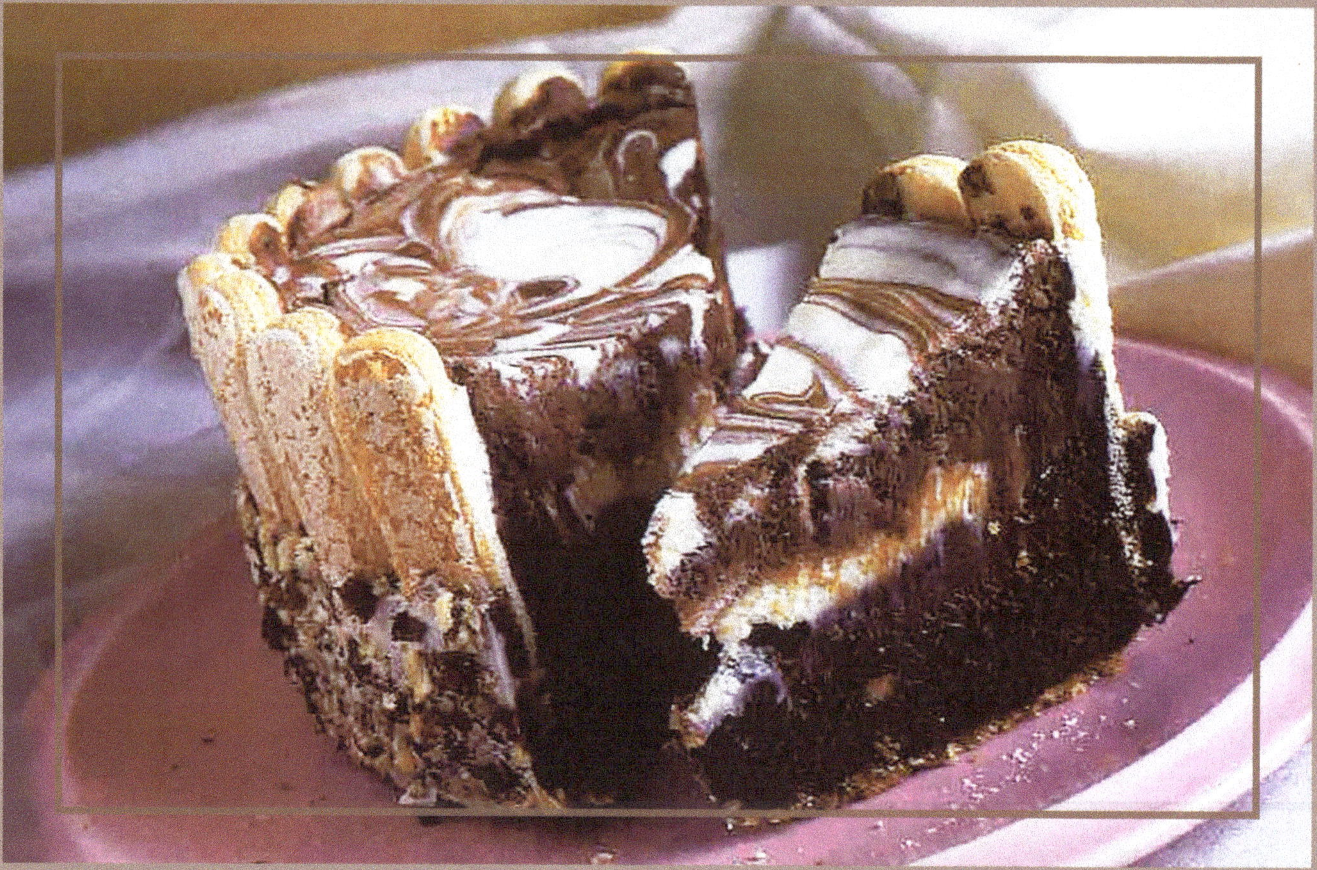

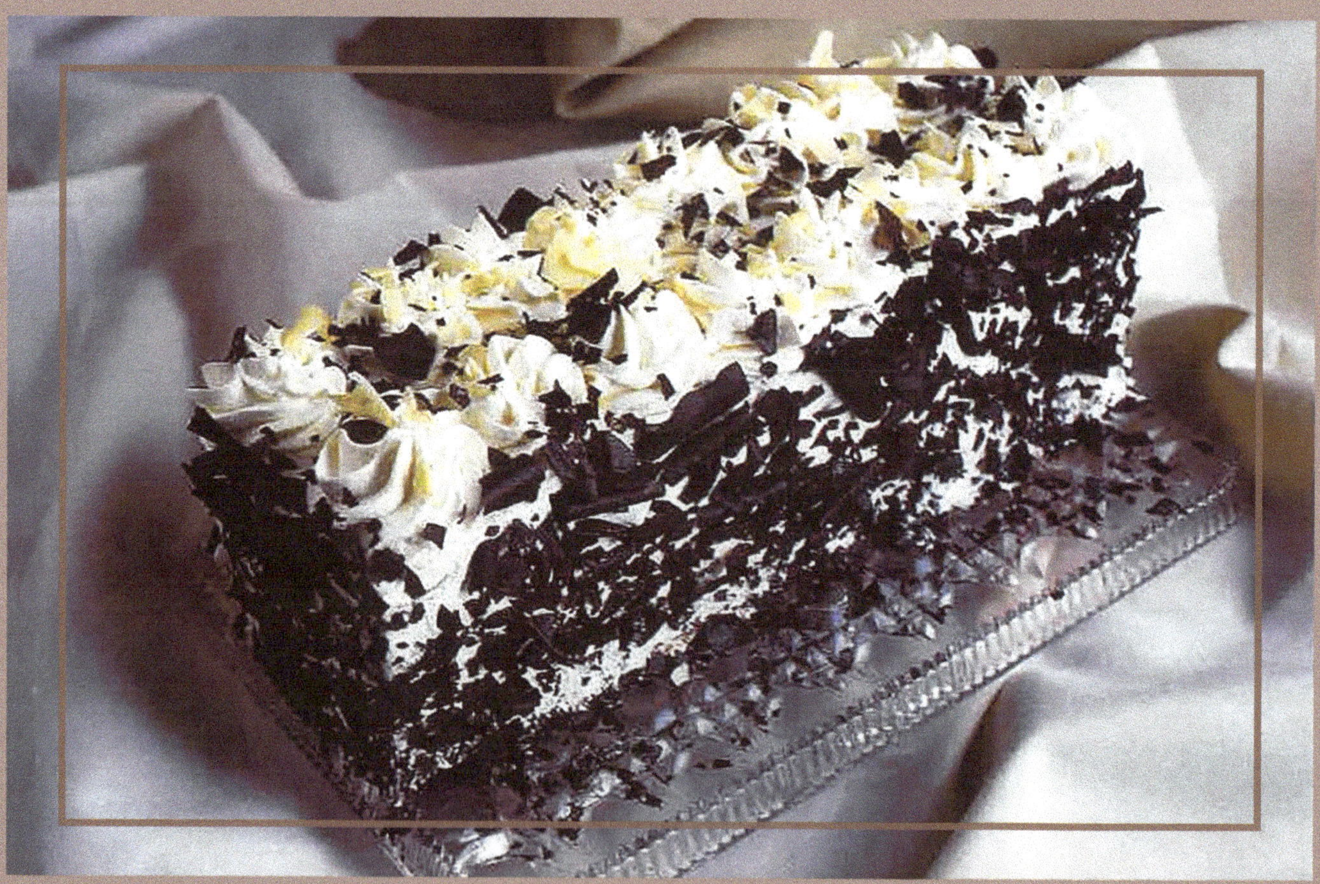

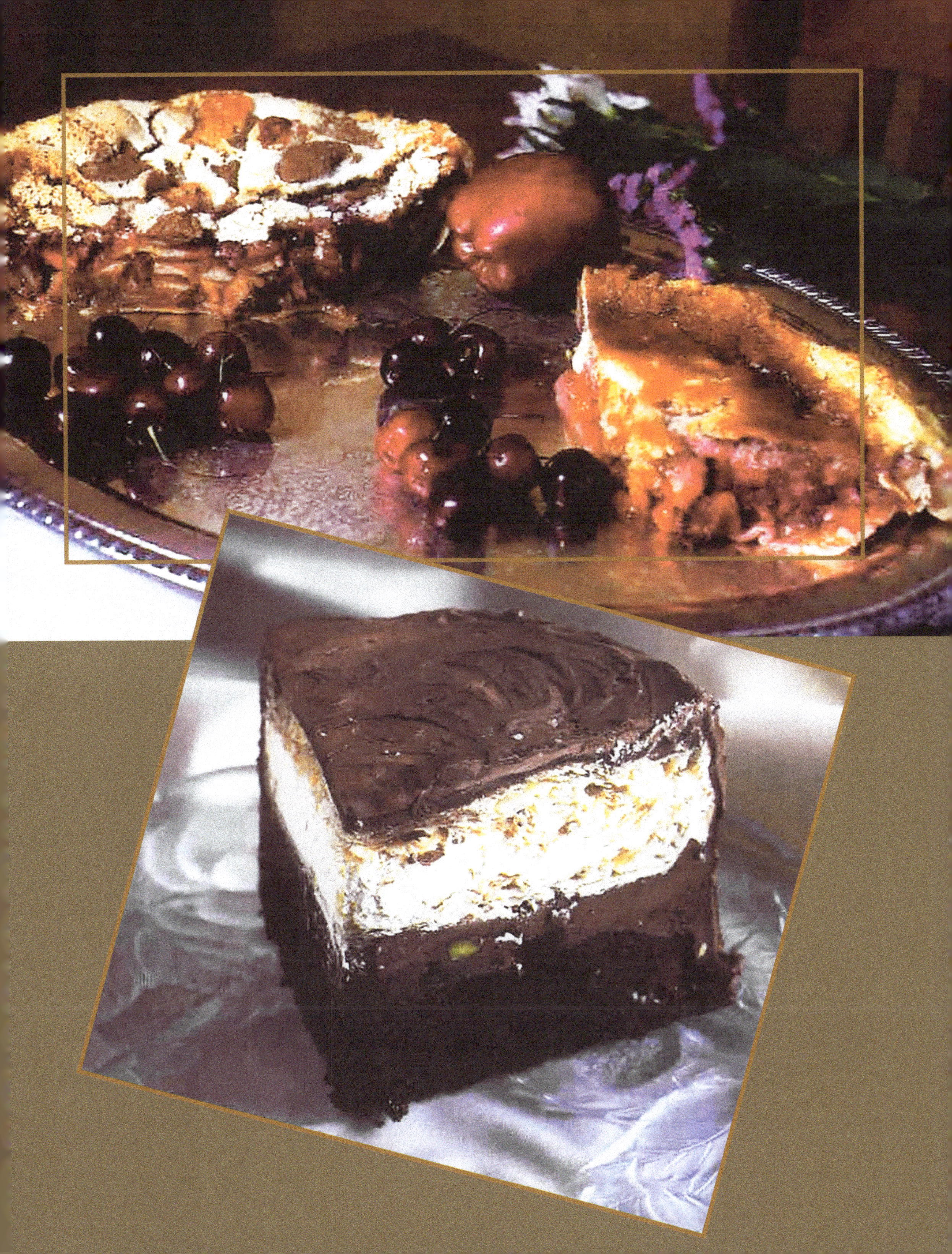

Multi-Nut Baklava

A package of phyllo pastry thawed overnight in the refrigerator

Preheat oven to 350-degrees

Cinnamon Syrup

Prepare syrup

1 cup water
½ cup honey
2 cinnamon sticks
4 whole cloves
1 tbsp lemon juice
1 tbsp grated orange peel
¼ cup sugar
½ tsp ground cinnamon
¼ tsp ground cloves

In a small boiling pot, bring mixture to boil. Reduce heat and simmer for about 10 minutes

Set aside and let cool.

Filling

8 oz sliced almonds
8 oz walnut, coarsely chopped
8 oz pecan pieces
½ cup sugar
2 tbsp cinnamon

Blend in a mixing bowl.

8 oz unsalted butter, melted

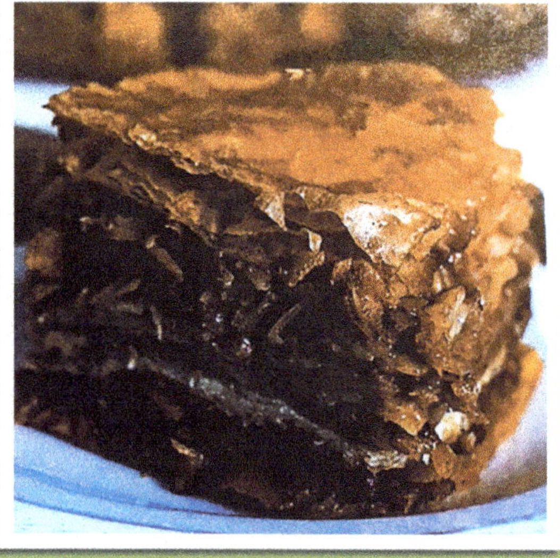

The phyllo pastry, approximately 24 sheets.

Lightly brush a 9" x 13" x 2" baking pan with some of the melted butter. Place phyllo dough on a working surface and cover it with a towel. Take one phyllo, folded in half, and place it in the pan.

Folding the phyllo in half fits the size of the pan.

Brush the top of the phyllo sheet with the melted butter. Repeat using 8 sheets of the phyllo.

Distribute about half of the mixture evenly over th top layer of phyllo.

Continue assembling 8 more sheets of the phyllo, one sheet at a time, brushing with butter. Distribute the other half of the mixture evenly over the top of the second layer of phyllo.

Finish the remaining 8 sheets of the phyllo pastry following the same process.

Using a sharp knife, cut the pastry into diamond-shaped pieces.

Bake in the preheated oven for 40 to 45 minutes until the top is golden brown.

Remove from the oven and pour the syrup all over the hot baklava.

Allow the baklava to sit for at least two hours before serving.

Makes about 36 servings.

Multi-Nut Baklava

Ladyfingers

Preheat oven to 350-degrees
4 eggs
½ cup white sugar
Separate the eggs, placing the whites into a mixer bowl and the yolks in a separate bowl
Beat the white eggs with the sugar for 2 to 3 minutes. Fold in the egg yolks. Turn the speed to low.
1 cup all-purpose flour
1 tsp teaspoon baking powder
½ tsp vanilla extract
Add and blend well
Lightly butter 2 baking sheets
Transfer mixture to a pastry with a large straight tip and bag and pipe the batter to create 4" long cookies onto the baking sheet.
Powdered sugar
Dust the top of the tops of the ladyfingers with the sugar
Bake 16 to 18 minutes
Makes about 40 ladyfingers

Precious Memories

In many cultures, the cuisine is as essential as religion, politics, and history. In my opinion, there is no celebration of life's special moments without food. Food offerings express love and hospitality; therefore, most familiar tastes of the past are associated with life's intriguing moments. The childhood aromas, tastes and textures of foods are ingrained into our senses, and often transport us back to a cherished place and time. Those who were fortunate to taste such special foods remember the surroundings and the people who prepared such stimulating aromas.

Those precious memories recollect the charming places when parents, grandparents and friends cultivated the culinary art and raised it to a memorable, succulent level. I am one of those fortunate people who grew up around such an environment. This is the main reason that I cherish our family's celebrations, knowing that the young ones will carry these special moments for the rest of their lives.

Every once in a while, we have to take time out of our busy days and celebrate life's special moments, to feed the soul and the body with familiar indulgences. There is no better way to celebrate these special times than with family and friends; with the house full of enticing aromas and tables laden with special foods. The tastes and aromas remind us of togetherness and precious moments of the past.

Now there are new tastes to be introduced. Our family has grown large and engaging. Our special dinners are not dinners for two or four; now we almost fill out a small restaurant.

The writing of this book has been rewarding for me on so many levels; above all it is a labor of love. But now I must go. Tonight, there is another family birthday to celebrate. There will be new and familiar tastes; more memories for the young ones to cherish. I hope you do the same. Go ahead and create new flavors, add new precious memories with your family and friends.

I know that the art of fabricating seductive aromas and memorable tastes is complex in culinary art. Creativity seems more challenging in culinary art than any other because it involves the satisfaction of all the senses and the involvement of thousands of ingredients. And, it concerns the selection of foods, the manner of preparation, the savoring of the foods, and the ceremony of eating; these are the four steps that make up a healthier cuisine.

I hope my new recipes and knowledge about those four steps will help you to create new tastes and new precious memories.

Amaretti Cookies

Preheat oven to 325-degrees
3 egg whites
1 cup of sugar
Beat in a mixer on medium speed for 2 to 3 minutes.
1 tbsp lemon zest
½ teaspoon amaretto liqueur
2 cups almond flour
½ cup almond meal
Add to the mixer and blend well at low speed.
Lightly butter 2 baking sheets.
Scoop the amaretti cookies to about 1" balls.
Extra sugar
Roll the balls into the sugar, coat lightly with sugar. Place on the baking pans.
Press to gently flatten.
Bake for 20 to 23 minutes.
Makes about 32 cookies

Orange Oatmeal Cookies

Preheat oven to 350-degrees
1 cup unsalted butter
1 cup brown sugar
1 cup of sugar
Place in the mixer's bowl and cream together on slow speeh until smooth.
3 eggs
Add and blend on slow speed.
1 tsp vanilla extract
1 tsp baking soda
1 tsp. baking powder
2 cups flour
1 tsp cinnamon
2 tbsp orange peel
3 cups oats
Add to the mixer and blend.
Scoop cookie dough onto baking sheets.
Bake in the preheated oven for 10 to 12 minutes.
Makes about 36 cookies

To Have or Not To Have

Dessert is the lyrical point of the meal. Its addictive taste is used by mothers all over the world to bribe their children to obey. At a dinner party, every guest wonders with anticipation if there is a dessert at the end. Dessert is a function of pure gratification. I've seen it in my restaurant hundreds of times. "We are on a diet," the guests would say. But after eating a vegetable salad with low-calorie dressing, they would approach the dessert cases to their moment of intense pleasure, never mind the concentration of calories. Dessert is a prize earned for themselves.

"This is the last piece of dessert I'll eat for a long time," I heard them say, but next time sitting in front of the dessert case, they forgot their promise. Eating a rich dessert gives a sinful pleasure, but later on, brings despair: The next time we want to have dessert, we must decide between the feeling of satisfaction for the addictive taste or the joy of victory for overcoming the temptation.

"Nearby our taverna in Kiato, there were other restaurants and bakeries with windows full of luscious pastries and ice cream shops to entice children and adults alike. Tempting aromas of various foods draped the neighborhood. There were freshly baked bread and roasted nuts, the exquisite fragrance of chocolate, the distinctive smell of garlic and the exotic scent of cinnamon. The fusion of aromas persuaded my young mind and slowly awakened a mortal fever for food flavorings. Fast forward decades later, I use the earth to grow flowers, vegetables and fruits and I have increasingly become conscious of the quality and origin of foods."

— From my book, My Heroes, My Town

Chocolate Chip Cookies

Preheat oven to 350-degrees
1 cup unsalted butter
½ cup brown sugar
1 cup of sugar
½ cup coconut sugar
Place in the mixer's bowl and cream together on slow speed until smooth.
3 eggs
Add and blend on slow speed.
1 tsp vanilla extract
1 tsp baking soda
1 tsp baking powder
3 cups flour
1 ½ cups walnuts, chopped
2 cups chocolate chips
Add to the mixer and blend.
Scoop cookie dough onto baking sheets.
Bake in the preheated oven for 10 to 12 minutes.
Makes about 36 cookies

Oatmeal Cookies, Gluten-Free

Preheat over to 375-degrees
1 cup unsalted butter, low-fat, organic
1 cup coconut sugar
½ cup xylitol sugar
Place in the mixer's bowl and cream together on low speed.
2 eggs
⅛ tsp pure vanilla extract
Add and blend on slow speed.
½ cup oat flour
1 ¼ cups brown rice flour
¼ cup tapioca flour
1 tbsp arrowroot
1 cup quick oats
1 tsp baking soda
½ tsp cinnamon
½ tsp nutmeg
Add and blend on slow speed.
1 cup raisins
Add to the mixer and blend.
Brush lightly with oil a baking sheet.
Use a medium ice cream scoop and form dough balls.
Space the dough balls a couple of inches apart. Bake for 10 to 12 minutes.
Makes 20 medium size cookies

One of the most special parts about Nick is that he continually experiments to come up with complex original recipes to add to his already stunning selection of hundreds of recipes.
— Western Express

"Nearby our taverna in Kiato, there were other restaurants and bakeries with windows full of luscious pastries and ice cream shops to entice children and adults alike. Tempting aromas of various foods draped the neighborhood. There was freshly baked bread and roasted nuts, the exquisite fragrance of chocolate, the distinctive smell of garlic, and the exotic scent of cinnamon. The fusion of aromas persuaded my young mind and slowly awakened a mortal fever for food flavorings. Fast forward decades later, I use the earth to grow flowers, vegetables and fruits and I have increasingly become conscious of the quality and origin of foods."
— From my book, My Heroes, My Town

Coconut Date Cookies, Gluten-Free

Preheat over to 375-degrees
1 cup unsalted butter, low-fat, organic
1 cup coconut sugar
½ cup xylitol sugar

Place in the mixer's bowl and cream together on low speed.

2 eggs
⅛ tsp pure vanilla extract

Add to the mixer and blend well

1 ½ cups brown rice flour
¾ cup coconut flour
¼ cup tapioca flour
1 tbsp arrowroot
½ tsp baking soda
¼ cup shredded coconut, unsweetened
¾ cup pitted dates, chopped
⅛ tsp nutmeg

Add and blend on slow speed.

½ cup white chocolate chips

Add to the mixer and blend.

Brush lightly with oil a baking sheet.

Use a medium ice cream scoop and form dough balls.

Space the dough balls a couple of inches apart. Bake for 10 to 12 minutes.

Makes 20 medium size cookies

Almond Butter Cookies, Gluten-Free

Preheat over to 375-degrees
¾ cup unsalted butter, low-fat, organic
1 cup coconut sugar
½ cup xylitol sugar

Place in the mixer's bowl and cream together on low speed.

2 eggs
¼ cup almond butter

Add and blend well.

1 ¼ cups brown rice flour
¾ cup gluten-free flour
¼ cup tapioca flour
1 tbsp arrowroot
½ tsp baking soda
¼ cup almond meal

Add to the mixer and blend.

Brush lightly with oil a baking sheet.

Use a medium ice cream scoop and form dough balls.

Space the dough balls a couple of inches apart. Bake for 10 to 12 minutes.

Makes 20 medium size cookies

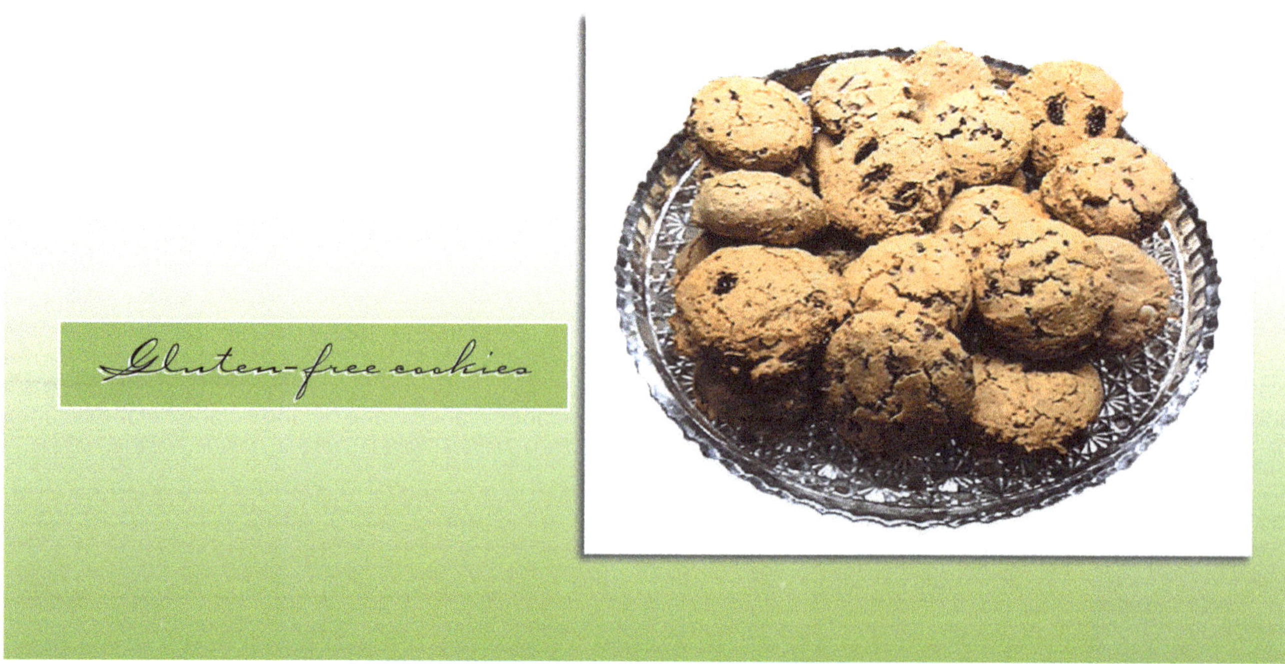

Chocolate Chip Cookies, Gluten-Free

Preheat over to 375-degrees
1 cup unsalted butter, low-fat, organic
1 cup coconut sugar
½ cup xylitol sugar

Place in the mixer's bowl and cream together on low speed.

2 eggs
⅛ tsp pure vanilla extract

Add to the mixer and blend well.

1 ¼ cup brown rice flour
¾ cup white rice flour
¼ cup tapioca flour
1 tbsp arrowroot
½ tsp baking soda

Add and blend on slow speed.

½ cup mini semisweet chocolate chips

Add to the mixer and blend.

Brush lightly with oil a baking sheet.

Use a medium ice cream scoop and form dough balls.

Space the dough balls a couple of inches apart. Bake for 10 to 12 minutes.

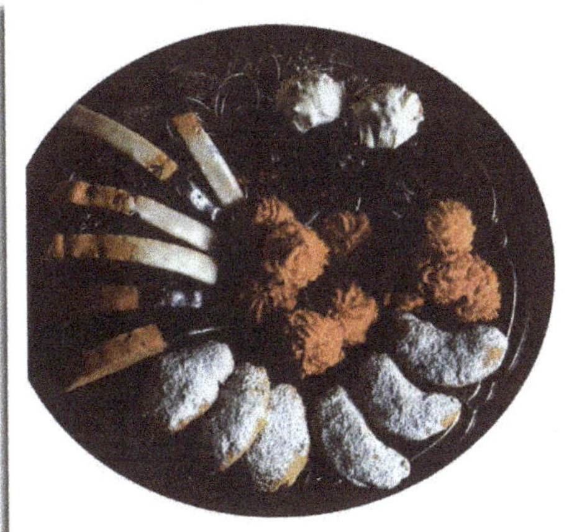

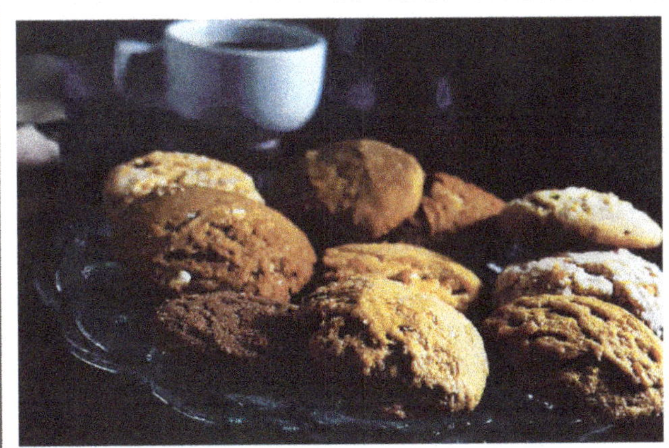

Instructions on how to bake the biscotti

Remove dough and divide it into four parts. Lightly knead each portion and roll into a cylinder, about 16″ long. It is best (and easier) to use two 12″ x 17″ baking pans. Lightly brush the baking pan with olive oil and place the rolls on the baking pans, about 4 inches apart from each other. Press gently to flatten the top of each turn and form a half oval shape. The rolls should be 16″ long and 4″ wide.

Bake in 375-degree preheated oven or about 20 to 25 minutes.
Remove from oven, let cool for a few minutes.
Turn your oven to 300-degrees.

Once cool enough to handle the dough, carefully remove, one piece at a time, place on a cutting surface and with a sharp knife, gently slice the dough into about 3⁄4 inch slices. Place the biscotti slices flat on the baking pan, return to the oven and bake for about 10 minutes longer. Turn each biscotti to expose the other cut side and continue baking for another 10 minutes, until the biscottis turn light brown.

Remove from the oven and let cool before removing from the baking pan.

Chocolate Almond Raisin Biscotti

Preheat over to 375-degrees
6 oz. unsalted butter
2 cups of sugar
Place in the mixer's bowl and cream together on low speed.
⅔ cup olive oil
7 eggs
7 cups flour
1 tsp nutmeg
1 tsp vanilla extract
2 tsp baking powder
2 cups slivered almonds
2 cups raisins
8 oz semisweet chocolate chips
Add in and mix well.
See instructions on how to bake the biscotti (page 134)

Coconut Rum Biscotti

Preheat over to 375-degrees
6 oz. unsalted butter
2 cups of sugar
Place in the mixer's bowl and cream together on low speed.
⅔ cup olive oil
7 eggs
7 cups flour
1 tsp nutmeg
1 tsp vanilla extract
2 tsp baking powder
2 cups pecan pieces
2 cups toasted coconut
Add in and mix well.
See instructions on how to bake the biscotti (page 134)

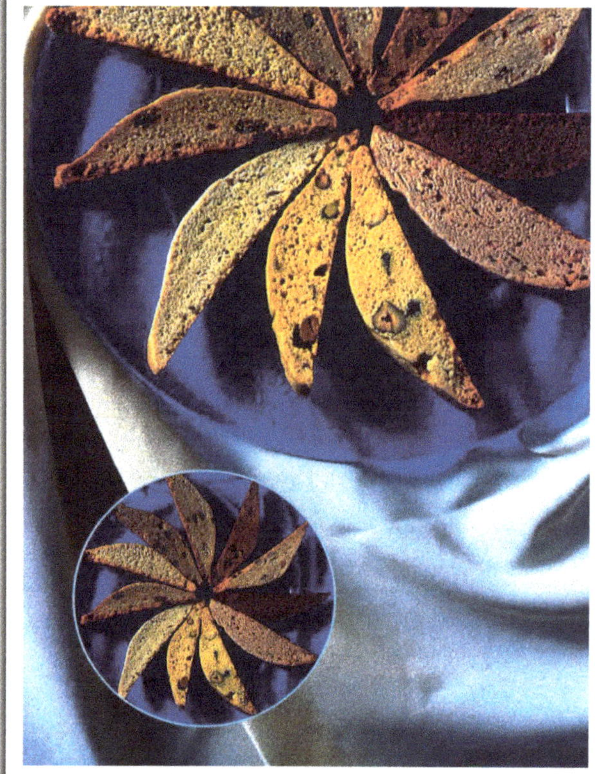

Anise Biscotti

Preheat over to 375-degrees
6 oz unsalted butter
2 cups of sugar
Place in the mixer's bowl and cream together on low speed.
⅔ cup olive oil
7 eggs
7 cups flour
1 tsp nutmeg
2 tsp ground anise
Add in and mix well
Follow the instructions on how to bake the biscotti.

ABOUT BISCOTTI

Biscotti is an old-time Southern European treat, unknown to the American public until the coffee shops became a trend in America. Biscotti is a natural partner to coffee. Its texture should be crisp and dipping it in coffee softens and enriches its flavor. Biscotti keeps well for a long time in an airtight container. But I doubt they will stay on your counter for more than a few days because they are addictive. Baking times vary due to their size and the oven used. When baking the dough rolls, make sure they are baked enough to be sliced easily. When you "dry" the biscotti in the second phase of baking, the color should be light brown when done. You can turn them midway through the second phase of baking if you like them equally brown on both sides. If they seem a bit soft when done, do not be a concern. Biscotti hardens once cooled. They taste better the second day and much better the third day.

I use both butter and olive oil in my biscotti recipes to achieve a rich taste and good texture. Butter will provide a rich flavor, but without the oil, biscotti will be hard. The oil will give it the crumbly crunch texture.

I like to dip one side of the almond biscotti with dark chocolate icing or one side of pistachio biscotti with white icing or both sides of the hazelnut biscotti one with dark icing and the other with white icing. But don't stop there; use your imagination and dip any biscotti with your icing of choice.

Chocolate Almond Raisin Biscotti

Preheat over to 375-degrees

6 oz. unsalted butter
2 cups of sugar

Place in the mixer's bowl and cream together on low speed.

⅔ cup olive oil
7 eggs
7 cups flour
1 tsp nutmeg
1 tsp vanilla extract
2 tsp baking powder
2 cups slivered almonds
2 cups raisins
8 oz semisweet chocolate chips

Add in and mix well.

See instructions on how to bake the biscotti (page 134)

Coconut Rum Biscotti

Preheat over to 375-degrees

6 oz. unsalted butter
2 cups of sugar

Place in the mixer's bowl and cream together on low speed.

⅔ cup olive oil
7 eggs
7 cups flour
1 tsp nutmeg
1 tsp vanilla extract
2 tsp baking powder
2 cups pecan pieces
2 cups toasted coconut

Add in and mix well.

See instructions on how to bake the biscotti (page 134)

Almond Biscotti

Preheat over to 375-degrees
6 oz. unsalted butter
2 cups of sugar
Place in the mixer's bowl and cream together on low speed.
⅔ cup olive oil
7 eggs
7 cups flour
1 tsp nutmeg
1 tsp vanilla extract
2 tsp baking powder
3 cups slivered almonds
Add in and mix well.
See instructions on how to bake the biscotti (page 134)

Hazelnut Biscotti

Preheat over to 375-degrees
6 oz. unsalted butter
2 cups of sugar
Place in the mixer's bowl and cream together on low speed.
⅔ cup olive oil
7 eggs
7 cups flour
1 tsp nutmeg
1 tsp vanilla extract
2 tsp baking powder
3 cups hazelnuts
Place in the food processor and pulse 2 to 3 times.
Add in and mix well.
See instructions on how to bake the biscotti (page 134)

Chocolate Espresso Biscotti

Preheat over to 375-degrees
3 oz semisweet chocolate
Melt in a double boil
6 oz. unsalted butter
2 cups of sugar
Place in the mixer's bowl and cream together on low speed.
⅔ cup olive oil
7 eggs
7 cups flour
1 tsp nutmeg
1 tsp vanilla extract
2 tsp baking powder
The melted chocolate
¼ cup strong coffee
1 tsp cinnamon
2 tsp cocoa powder
Add in and mix well.
See instructions on how to bake the biscotti (page 134)

Kahlua White Chocolate Biscotti

Preheat over to 375-degrees
¾ cup white chocolate
Melt in a double boil
Preheat over to 375-degrees
6 oz. unsalted butter
2 cups of sugar
Place in the mixer's bowl and cream together on low speed.
½ cup olive oil
6 eggs
7 cups flour
1 tsp cinnamon
1 tsp. nutmeg
1 tsp vanilla extract
2 tsp baking powder
⅛ cup coffee
⅛ cup Kahlua
The melted white chocolate
Add in and mix well.
See instructions on how to bake the biscotti (page 134)

Anise Biscotti, Gluten-Free

Preheat oven to 375-degrees
½ cup unsalted butter, low-fat, organic
¼ cup olive oil
1 cup coconut sugar
Blend well with your mixer on slow speed.
4 eggs
Add to the mixing bowl and continue mixing on slow speed.
Once eggs are blended with butter and oil, turn off the mixer.
2 cups gluten-free flour
1 ½ cups white rice flour
1 cup brown rice fl our
1 cup almond flour
¼ cup tapioca
¼ cup arrowroot
2 tsp baking powder
1 tsp baking soda
1 tsp nutmeg
Add to the mixing bowl and blend on slow speed.
⅛ tsp anise extract
1 tsp ground anise seeds
Add and continue mixing until all ingredients are blended well.
See instructions on how to bake the biscotti (page 134)

Almond Biscotti, Gluten-Free

Preheat oven to 375-degrees
½ cup unsalted butter, low-fat, organic
¼ cup organic extra virgin coconut oil
1 cup coconut sugar
Blend well with your mixer on slow speed.
4 eggs
Add to the mixing bowl and continue mixing on slow speed.
Once eggs are blended with butter and oil, turn off the mixer.
2 cups gluten-free flour
1½ cups white rice flour
1 cup brown rice flour
1 cup almond flour
¼ cup tapioca
¼ cup arrowroot
2 tsp baking powder
1 tsp soda
1 tsp nutmeg
Add to the mixing bowl and blend on slow speed.
⅛ tsp vanilla extract
1 cup slivered almonds
Add and continue mixing until all ingredients are blended well.
See instructions on how to bake the biscotti (page 134)

It is a must to try Nick's dazzling desserts. I'll wager that no one will be able to resist his Symphony of Chocolate cake. It is dark, white and chestnut chocolate veiled with an orange cinnamon, white chocolate icing.

— Phoenix Downtown

Biscotti Dough, Gluten-Free

Use this recipe for more biscotti variations. Add flavors or other add-ons.

½ cup unsalted butter, low-fat, organic
¼ cup organic extra virgin coconut oil
1 cup coconut sugar

Blend well with your mixer on slow speed.

4 eggs

Add to the mixing bowl and continue mixing on slow speed.

Once eggs are blended with butter and oil, turn off the mixer.

2 cups gluten-free flour
1 ½ cups white rice flour
1 cup brown rice flour
1 cup almond flour
¼ cup tapioca
¼ cup arrowroot
2 tsp baking powder
1 tsp baking soda
1 tsp nutmeg

Add and continue mixing until all ingredients are blended well.

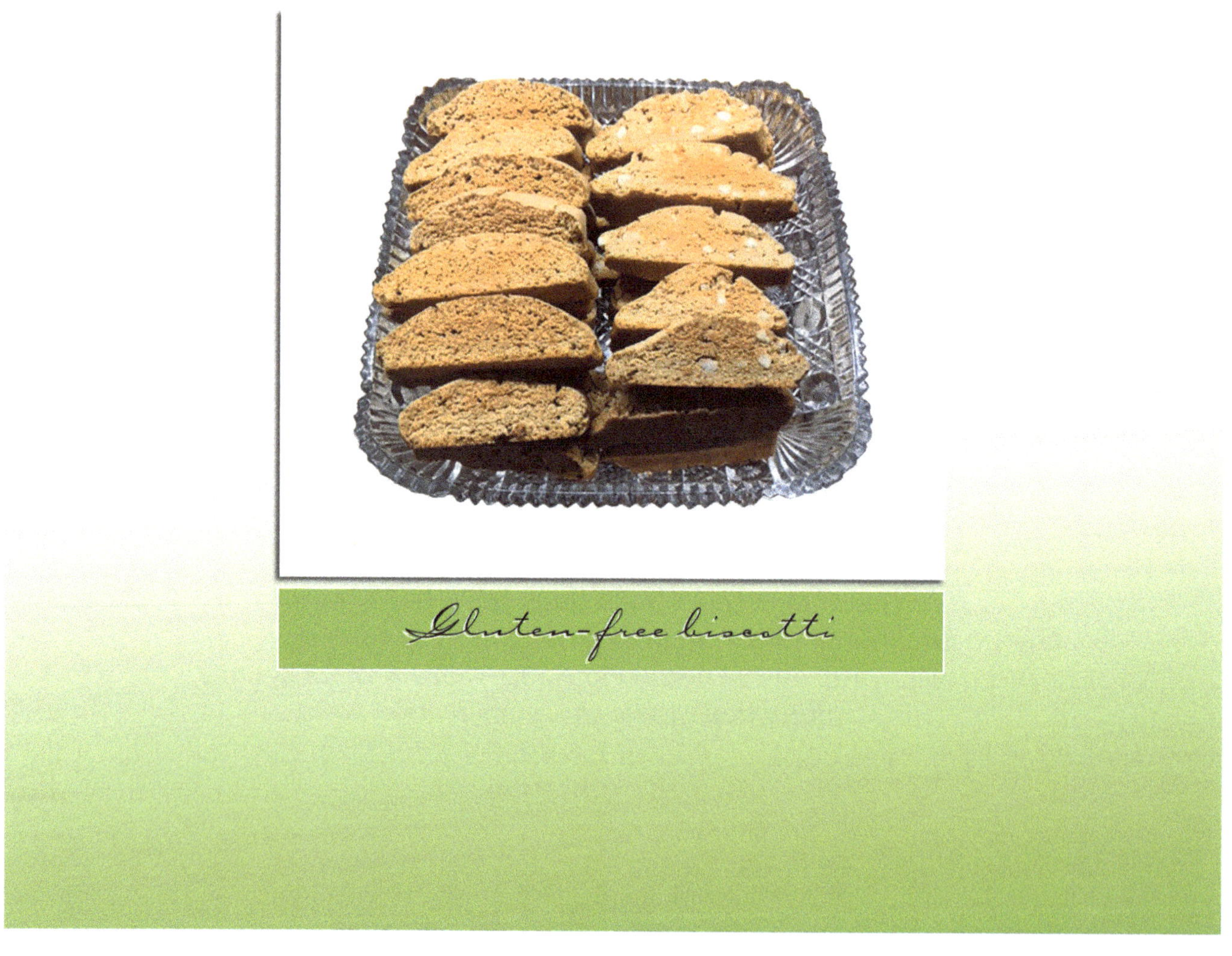

Gluten-free biscotti

Walnut Cinnamon Sheet Cake

Preheat oven to 375-degrees
5 eggs
1 cup coconut sugar
Beat at high speed mixer until stiff.
1 cup coconut milk
Turn mixer on slow speed and add the milk.
Mix for 1 to 2 minutes.
2 ½ cups walnuts, grated
2 tsp cinnamon
1 ½ tsp ground cloves
2 tsp baking powder
2 tbsp orange peel
3 ½ cups flour
2 tsp baking soda
1 tsp baking powder
Add to the mixer and gently mix well.
Lightly buttered a 9" x 13" x 2" baking pan.
Pour batter into the pan.
Bake in the preheated oven for 45-50 minutes.
Remove from pan and let cool
Slightly cut into desired size pieces.

Syrup
1 ½ cups sugar
4 cups water
1 cup honey
1 tbsp lemon peel
Bring to a boil, reduce heat and let boil for 3 minutes.
Pour half of the syrup over the filling.
1 cup chocolate chips
Place remaining syrup over low head.
Add the the chocolate and stir until melted.
1 cup walnuts, in small pieces
Add to the syrup.
Spread chocolate mixture over the filling.

Apricot Honey Sheet Cake

Preheat oven to 375-degrees
5 eggs
1 cup sugar
Beat at high speed of your mixer until eggs thicken. Remove from mixer.
1 cup semolina
2 ½ cups flour
2 tsp baking powder
2 tbsp orange peel
1 cup almonds,
Pulse 2 to 3 times in your food processor
Add to the bowl with eggs and mix by hand.
¾ cup milk at room temperature
¾ cup orange juice
1 tsp vanilla extract
Add to the bowl and mix lightly.
Lightly buttered a 9" x 13" x 2" baking pan.
Pour batter into the pan.
Bake in the preheated oven for 45-50 minutes.

Syrup
1 cup sugar
2 cup water
Boil for about 4 minutes.
8 oz unsalted butter
2 tbsp lemon juice
2 tsp lemon peel
Add to sugar water, stir until butter melts. Cool syrup to room temperature. Cut cake into desired sizes, pour ¾ of the syrup over pastry, slowly and carefully.
2 cups of toasted almonds
Sprinkle on top of the cake.

Remaining syrup
¼ cup of orange juice
2 cup of apricots, chopped
Blend together and spread over cake.

"Each one of us bent our heads in prayers of thanks to the Grecian God of Dessert."
— Java Magazine

Baked Custard in Phyllo

A package of phyllo pastry thawed overnight in the refrigerator

Preheat oven to 375-degrees

½ gallon of whole milk

Bring to a gentle boil in a boiling pot.

½ lb unsalted butter

Add in, stir until the butter melts, remove pot from heat.

8 eggs
1 ½ cups sugar
1 tsp vanilla extract

Beat in a mixer until stiff, add them slowly into hot milk, stirring well.

½ cup semolina
¾ cup flour
½ cup almond flour

Mix together; add to milk mixture stirring with a wire whip. Let mixture cool.

24 phyllo dough sheets
1 cup melted unsalted butter

Lay 12 phyllo sheets, buttering each one of them, in the bottom of a 9" x 13" x 2" baking pan.

Make sure th phyllo sheets overlap the edges of the pan.

Pour in the mixture. Fold the overlapped phyllo dough on top of the mixture.

Lay remaining phyllo on top, buttering each one of them, tucking the edges of the phyllo into the side of the filling. With a sharp knife slit the top phyllo into diamond shapes.

Bake in the preheated oven 45 to 50 minutes.

Remove and let cool.

Syrup

1 cups sugar
½ cup honey
1 ½ cup water

Boil for 5 minutes. Pour over phyllo. Let cool before serving

Phyllo Rolls

Preheat oven to 350-degrees

Filling

2 lbs walnuts. Pulse 3 to 4 times in a food processor.
2 tsp cinnamon
2 tsp ground cloves
1 cups sugar
4 oz unsalted butter, melted

Mix all ingredients in a mixing bowl.

8 sheets of phyllo dough
6 oz unsalted butter, melted

Put two phyllo on a working surface. Brush the top phyllo with butter.

Divide the walnut filling into four parts.

Spread one part of the filling lengthwise on the edge of phyllo. Roll the filling in to the phyllo.

Place the first long roll in a 12" x 18" baking sheet.

Repeat with the rest of the Phyllo, creating three more rolls.

Pour melted butter over the phyllo rolls.

Bake in the preheated oven for about 35 to 40 minutes, until phyllo is golden brown.

Honey Syrup

Prepare while the Phyllo rolls are in the oven.

1 cup sugar
1 cup honey
2 ½ cups water
1 tbsp lemon juice
1 tbsp orange juice

Bring to a boil in a sauce pan.

Turn heat to low and simmer for about 10 minutes.

Remove baked phyllo from the oven.

Pour syrup over the phyllo rolls. Let cool.

Cut the phyllo rolls into small pieces, approximately 3-inches long and serve.

"Each one of us bent our heads in prayers of thanks to the Grecian God of Dessert."

— Java Magazine

Kataifi

Preheat oven to 350-degrees

Filling

8 oz grated almonds
8 oz grated walnuts
2 tsp cinnamon
1 tbsp lemon peel
2 tbsp orange juice
1 cup sugar

In a mixing bowl, mix ingredients well.

Syrup

1 cup sugar
1 cup honey
2 cups water

Bring to a boil in a sauce pan.

Turn heat to low and simmer for about 10 minutes.

Set aside

16 oz unsalted butter, melted
16 oz kataifi dough

Place approximately one ounce of lightly buttered dough flat on a working surface. Scoop 2 tablespoons of filling on the dough and roll loosely. Place roll on a buttered baking sheet and repeat the process until dough is all used. Pour remaining butter on top of kataifi and cover with foil.

Bake in the preheated oven for about 20 minutes.

Remove foil and continue baking for another 25 to 30 minutes, until kataifi is golden brown.

Remove from oven and pour syrup over kataifi rolls.

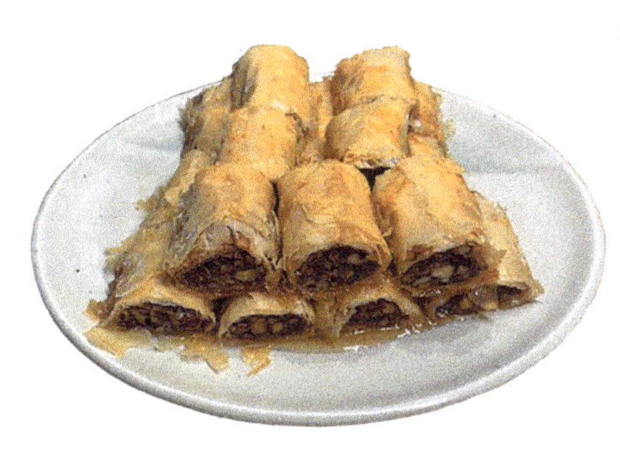

Chocolate Pistachio Phyllo

Preheat oven to 350-degrees

16 oz pistachios, thickly chopped
1 tbsp cinnamon
1 tbsp ground cloves
¾ cup sugar
2 oz unsalted butter, melted

In a mixing bowl, mix ingredients well.

8 sheets of phyllo dough
4 oz unsalted butter, melted

Put two phyllo on a working surface. Brush the top phyllo with butter. Divide filling into 4 parts.

Place one part the filling on the bottom center of the phyllo.

Fold in the sides of phyllo to cover the filling, then roll up to make a roll. Repeat with the rest of the phyllo. Place rolls into baking pan.

6 oz unsalted butter, melted

Pour over the rolls. Bake in the preheated oven for a bout 30 to 35 minutes, until rolls are golden brown.

Syrup

Prepare while the Phyllo rolls are in the oven.

1 cup sugar
1 cup honey
2 ½ cups water
1 tbsp lemon juice
1 tbsp orange juice

Bring to a boil in a sauce pan.

Turn heat to low and simmer for about 10 minutes.

Remove baked phyllo from the oven.

Pour syrup over the phyllo rolls. Let cool.

Icing

¼ cup heavy cream

Heat gently in a saucepan.

4 oz semisweet chocolate chips

Add to the saucepan. Stir to melt the chocolate.

Pour over the pistachio rolls.

Phyllo Rolls

Croissants

Makes approximately 30 croissants

¾ oz yeast
1 ½ cups milk

In a bowl, dissolve the yeast in the milk. Set aside.

3 tbsp unsalted butter, room temperature
½ cup sugar

Blend in your mixer on high speed for about 1 minute.

Add the milk with the yeast and blend.

4 cups flour

Add the flour and blend for another 4 to 5 minutes.

Cover bowl with a towel and let it rise for about 1 hour until the dough is doubled in size. Place the dough in a lightly floured pan and refrigerate for about 1 hour.

Rolling the dough

1 ¼ cups butter, cut into large pieces

On a lightly floured working surface, roll the dough into a rectangle. Place half of the butter in two-thirds of the dough and fold into fifths starting with the side that is not buttered. Roll out the dough once and fold into thirds. In this stage, cover and refrigerate the dough for about 1 hour. Follow the same process again using the other half of the butter.

Roll the dough into a rectangle approximately 12" x 36" and about ⅛" thick. Cut the rectangle lengthwise to make two strips. From each strip you should make 15 triangles. (If you like a bigger croissant, you can make the dough strips wider).

To roll the triangles into croissants, first make a small cut in the center of the bottom of the triangle and roll from the base towards the point of the triangle. Bend the edges inwards to make crescent shapes. Place the croissants in a lightly buttered baking sheet, leaving enough space between them to rise. Cover and let rise for about 1 hour.

Bake in a preheated 400-degree oven for about 16 to 18 minutes.

Flavored options

For the following recipes, instead of cutting the two strips of dough into triangles cut them into diamond shape. Place the filling given in the recipes below and fold the edges as if you were closing an envelope. Let rise for one hour at room temperature. Brush with a beaten egg and bake in a 400-degree oven for 15-18 minutes.

Chocolate Croissants

Place on each croissant 2 tsp of semisweet chocolate chips in the middle of the dough and fold.

Turkey and Swiss Croissants

Place on each croissant2 slices of turkey breast and 2 slices of Swiss cheese in the middle of the dough and fold.

Spinach and Feta Croissants

Place on each croissant 2 tbsp of spinach and 1 tbsp feta cheese in the middle of the croissant and fold.

I use the croissant dough to make cinnamon rolls.

In the middle of the 2nd century B.C., grinding grains was developed to make excellent flour. The Greek master bakers began an era of bread making which spread throughout the Roman Empire. Late in the 1st century B.C., there were over 300 bakeries in Rome alone, all run by Greek bakers. There was even a bakery college, formed in that era, where master bakers developed passwords to protect trade secrets.

I found that the Croissant Dough (page 142) makes great cinnamon rolls. The following recipes make approximately 12 to 14 rolls.

Cinnamon Rolls

Open dough to approximately 6" x 24" and 1/8" thick

8 oz unsalted butter, melted

Pour butter on top of dough.

1 ½ cups sugar

¾ cup cinnamon

Mix well and spread on top of dough.

Roll the dough lengthwise into a large roll.

Slice into 2" rolls. Place the rolls with one cut end down on a lightly buttered 18" x 12" baking pan. Cover and let rise for about 1 hour.

Bake in a 375-degree oven for 18-20 minutes.

Let rolls cool.

Icing

1 ½ cups powdered sugar

1 tbsp water

Blend well in a mixing bowl.

3 oz white chocolate, melted

1 tbsp sour cream

Add in and mix well.

Spoon icing on top of the rolls.

Pecan Rolls

Open dough to approximately 6" x 24" and 1/8" thick

8 oz unsalted butter, melted

1 ½ brown sugar

3 cups pecan pieces

Mix well and spread on top of dough.

Roll the dough lengthwise into a large roll.

Slice into 2" rolls. Place the rolls with one cut end down on a lightly buttered 18" x 12" baking pan. Cover and let rise for about 1 hour.

Bake in a 375-degree oven for 18-20 minutes.

Let rolls cool.

Icing

1 ½ cups powdered sugar

1 tbsp water

Blend well in a mixing bowl.

3 oz white chocolate, melted

1 tbsp sour cream

Add in and mix well. Spoon icing on top of the rolls.

Cinnamon Rolls Variations

Replace the filling and icing with the following.

Filling Variations:

Add to the Cinnamon Roll recipe:
1 cup of caramel sauce *(see page 106)* and 2 chopped apples.
Or 8 oz semisweet chocolate chips and 1 cup of walnuts pieces.
Or 2 cup raisins and 1 cup pecans pieces.
Or 8 oz white chocolate chips and 1 cup chopped dates.

Icing Variations:

2 cups powder sugar mixed with ¼ cup milk and 1 tsp vanilla extract.
Or 6 oz melted semisweet chocolate blended with 3 tbsp sour cream.
Or 6 oz cream cheese
1 ½ cups powder sugar
¼ cup milk
1 tsp vanilla extract mixed together.

Cocoa Tree

The cocoa trees have grown deep in the Amazon forest, between stiffing greenery and the multitude of singing colored birds. The bark of the cocoa tree is a dark green color with silver patches. The tree's trunk is slender, smooth, towering gracefully into a canopy of thick foliage. Its leaves are oblong and they carry small white and pink flowers in dense clusters. The cocoa tree bears large fruit, called pods, which contain the precious cocoa beans. Cocoa pods have no stems, they sprout out from the trunk and grow to various sizes. The pods have a reddish-violet color when young, but by the time they are ready to be picked, they have turned to a yellowish-orange color. The cocoa tree is delicate and protected by nature's wonder: other trees that always seem to surround it and grow taller to protect it from the hot sun. Without shade, the cocoa tree would not thrive. Very little has changed throughout the years in the technique to pick the pods. At the time of picking, the air resounds with a machete on timber.

Cocoa plantations are buried by the dense foliage, deep in the jungle. The majority of plantations are not very large, two to four acres at most. In the region of the tropical Amazonian forest, its birthplace, the cocoa tree grows wild at giant trees' foot.

The temperature is always 70-degrees to 90-degrees F. After the Mayans and the Aztecs cultivated the first cocoa tree, cultivation thrived in Central and South America, especially Brazil. It moved to the Caribbean Islands of Trinidad, Haiti, the Dominican Republic, Martinique, and Jamaica. In the 19th century, Brazilian samplings of cocoa trees planted on the African coast, first in the island of Sao Tome, then in Bioko and from there to West Africa, the Ivory Coast, Nigeria, and Cameroon. Today, it is in Java, Sumatra, Sri Lanka, New Guinea, Samoa, Indonesia, the Philippines and Southeast Asia. Brazil, Malaysia, and the Ivory Coast are the leading producers of cocoa beans. They produce almost 50% of the world's supply. However, Central America still possesses the best plantations, those who provide the finest cocoa beans and are high priced by chocolate manufacturers all over the world. Cocoa has never forgotten its origins. All cocoa trees belong to the theobroma genus; the name derived from the Greek words, Theos meaning God and Broma, meaning Beverage, meaning "the drink of the gods."

The Criollo tree is the original "chocolate tree" of the Mayans. It produces the finest cocoa beans, very aromatic with a slightly bitter taste and delicate flavor. The chocolate manufacturers use these beans in combination with other varieties to create different types of chocolate. This delicate cocoa tree has a low yielding and their cultivation requires meticulous care. This exceptional cocoa is only produced on a small scale today. It accounts for no more than 10% of the world's production and cultivated in regions where cocoa originated: Mexico, Guatemala, Nicaragua, Venezuela, and Columbia.

The Forastero tree produces the majority of the African cocoa crop. The Spanish introduced Forastero on the island of Sao Tome during the Colonial era. It gradually spread to the western side of Africa. This tree also cultivated in Brazil, Central America, and the West Indies. The Forastero grows faster than the Criollo and produces more fruit. It accounts for about 75% of the world's production. This bean has a strong, bitter flavor and an acid aroma. It frequently used in blends. Then there is the Trinitarios, which is a crossbreed between Criollos and Forasteros. This one originated in the island of Trinidad, from which it takes its name. At the beginning of the 18th century, a hurricane destroyed the plantations in which the Spanish colonists had cultivated Criollos because of the soil and the climate of this Caribbean island. After the hurricane, the islanders planted Forasteros. Some Criollos had survived the wrath of nature and so the new group of varieties was born from natural inter-crossing.

Trinitarios produce cocoa beans with high-fat content and represents about 15% of the world's production. Today, they are cultivated mainly in Central and South America, Sri Lanka, and Indonesia. However, the best Trinitarios cocoa beans are grown in their native land. Each region produces beans with unique characteristics and different aromas. Chocolate, like wine, has its mythical places of cultivation, comparable to the great wine-producing vineyards. One of these places is Chuao in Venezuela. The legendary Chuao bean produced there is a chocolate connoisseur's dream. It has a fine delicate aroma, but it is rare because the beans from that plantation blended with other varieties from the region before being exported. The Chuao plantation was cultivated in the 17th century on the coast near Caracas, at the steep mountains' base, that drop sharply into the Caribbean. One can only get into this place by boat following the wild coastlines.

In Chuao, nothing has changed for centuries. On the shore is the landing stage from which the ships transport the beans. Up in the mountains, wood houses appear, scattered around. In the forest, where the air is humid and the sun is hot, under the tall mango trees, bamboo groves and serrated foliage, cocoa trees appear protected from the sun. Deeper in the forest, the vegetation is dense and many more cocoa trees appear. On the plantation, the routine is identical as it is in every plantation throughout the world. The cocoa trees pruned by men who move slowly between the trees. The pruning allows the branches to form a canopy of foliage to protect the fruit. The ground around the cocoa tree regularly weeded. The quality of the chocolate depends on the meticulous care of the tree. In the wild, the cocoa tree can grow up to 30 feet high, but on the plantations are pruned down to about 20 feet so that the cocoa pods are easier to reach. The buds emerge from the bark. The flowers appear at the beginning of the rainy season. In regions where there is no seasonal change, the flower appears year-round. The cocoa pods develop from a fertilized flower. Only one out of about 100 flowers destined to create fruit. The cocoa pods grow straight out of the trunk and tum golden in the sun. Cocoa pods are tough and have an elongated, pointy shape. It seems almost impossible that such fruit could come from such a delicate flower. The following cycle is uninterrupted. Pods grow among the flowers in all stages of development. It takes six to seven months for the pods to reach their full size, about ten inches long. Twenty or 40 precious almond-shaped seeds concealed inside, surrounded by bittersweet pulp. The tree's productivity depends on its age, the variety, the care, and the soil. In South America, a tree yields about 35 pods. In Africa, it produces about 20 pods. A healthy cocoa tree lives an average of 60 years. For centuries, the plantation workers have carried out the same routine tasks. The heat is almost unbearable. If it were not for the nearby ocean's breeze, it would practically be impossible to endure. The forest is alive with birds singing, animals running, and humans moving between the foliage, pruning, weeding, waiting for the precious bean to fertilize. The samplings of the cocoa tree are planted carefully together in a line. After a few months, they bedded out under a shade tree. They flower two or three years later, but they bare fruit only after four years.

Vanilla was unknown to most of the world until the 16th century. The delicious aroma vanilla develops as if it is a miracle of nature. At first, the delicate white flowers, which come from a tropical climbing plant, are scentless. After the long thin pods fell to the ground and fermented, people noticed that they developed a delicious aroma. The pods gave flavor to cocoa drinks used by the Aztecs. The vanilla trees are found in Central America and Northern Africa. There are several kinds of vanilla plants in the tropical forests of Central America. Growing pure vanilla away from Central America seemed impossible. The bees of the forest that provided the honey for the Aztecs and a distinctive and skillful act of nature fertilized the vanilla by entering the flower part through its thin skin.

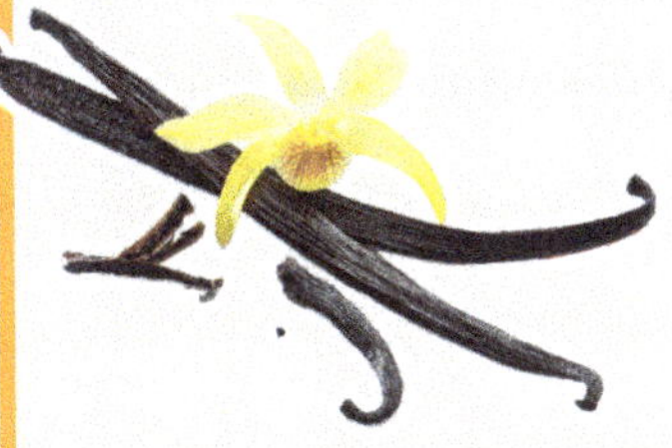

Home cooking is making a comeback

There was a time when families gathered around the dinner table to share a meal. A time when the dining table was most likely the only time of the day when a family could reconnect. And then, things changed. Our busy lifestyle was undoubtedly one of the factors which lead us to find alternatives to easier and quicker meals for the family. And so began the emergence of fast food and casual restaurants. The home dining table was replaced with drive in food pick-ups and other quick options for meals. This is the main reason that has caused obesity to reach an all time high. However, research shows that recently there is a new trend towards dining at home.

Today there are more convenient ways to cooking at home, it has become easier to find ideas about new recipes and to learn about the food quality. Sometimes you do not need research to understand a trend; the evolution of the home kitchen is the best indication of the importance of home cooking. The forgotten area of the home, with the dark brown cabinets of long ago, evolved into being the heart of the house. Open kitchens connected to the dining rooms have become the new living rooms. It is where people gather and cross paths. In the past, cooking was a thing to do, a chore, but today, the kitchen has become a place of creative art. I believe that people today are placing much more emphasis on what they eat and how they live, and the realization that food brings family and friends together is finally sinking into the social consciousness. There is no question eating at home is a better approach for your health, economically and socially. When a plate of food reaches the restaurant table, you do not know how your food was prepared and what quality ingredients were used. There is nothing wrong to occasionally enjoy indulgent food in a favorite restaurant. However, eating at home allows you to control your portion sizes and you know exactly what is on your plate. The toxicity in cooking is exceptionally high with the oils that most restaurants use for frying foods, especially the deep-fried ones. It is not likely that the restaurant will use healthy oils – such as pure coconut oil, extra virgin olive oil or pure avocado oil. The use of cheap iodized salt in excess is common in the restaurant kitchen also. Hidden added sugars, and compounds to enhance flavor are usually included in many restaurant sauces. In addition to the health risks when eating out too often, it is far more expensive. It is not that the restaurant purposely charges a high price; it is because restaurants must raise their prices to keep up with rising labor, rent and overall overhead costs. Besides the social benefits of eating at home, countless studies over the years have asserted that families who sit down and enjoy meals together at a table tend to be healthier. Eating at home can feel like a daunting task, especially if you are new to cooking or you have limited time to prepare a meal. My advice is to start small and work up to more involved dinners. In this book, many recipes take less than thirty minutes to prepare. The secret is to have an organize kitchen and have all the ingredients needed at hand. I've heard people say that eating out is a treat. While that can be true, I beg to differ. I believe that eating a home-cooked flavorful, healthy meal is the ultimate treat. The notion that all meals must be prepared by laboring in the kitchen for hours is also a myth. My new book can be a guide to introduce new flavors and healthier alternatives to your family. Learning new ways to blend various herbs and spices, the use of natural, healthier ingredients and the knowledge of food chemistry will limit your time in the kitchen.

A study published in June 2018, by the NPD Group, a leading global information company, states that last year over 80% of meals were prepared and eaten at home. The study also shows that eat at home meals will grow over the next five years. In addition, in-home meal preparation is also aided by the modern conveniences of grocery delivery. Today, the meals prepared at home, are a much higher percentage than a decade ago, according to research from NPD Group Inc.

I've heard plenty of criticism that the younger generations are eating out too much and are developing unhealthy eating habits. Despite the criticism that millennials are always going out to eat, it is encouraging to know that they are the driving force for the shifting environment to healthier eating. According to a study released on September 22, 2016, by OTA, the Organic Trade Association, parents in the 18 to 34-year-old age range are now the biggest group of organic buyers in America. Millennial parents account for 52% of organic buyers, Generation X parents made up 35% of parents choosing organic, and Baby Boomers 14%. Organic sales in the U.S. in 2015 posted new records, up to a robust 11% from the previous year, according to OTA's 2016 Organic Industry Survey.

In 2018, U.S. organic food sales saw exceptional growth. According to Nielsen Homescan household projected data, organic food sales during the 52 weeks ending November 28, 2018, rose nearly 9% over the previous period. Millennials and Hispanics made significant contributions to the sales spike, spending more during this period than the last, respectively.

In another indication that home cooking is making a comeback is the increased cookbook sales. Publisher's Weekly reports that sales of print cookbooks rose 21% in 2018 compared with 2017, according to data collected by NPD Bookscan.

There are many reasons why several reports showing that healthier foods are steadily on the rise. A meal at home is fresher, more nutritious and higher quality while eating in a friendlier environment with social activities. It is after all the home cooking and dining that helped to push organic sales to unprecedented levels. The U.S. organic market in 2018 broke through the $50 billion marks for the first time, with sales hitting a record $52.5 billion, up 6.3% from the previous year, according to the 2019 Organic Industry Survey released by the Organic Trade Association.

The changes in eating mentality and behavior shouldn't come as a surprise. The new generations are better informed and better educated about nutrition. The future of healthier foods is looking bright. As I mentioned in an earlier post, knowledge is power and today we have plenty of knowledge.

> "Foods have such an intense emotional significance that they are often linked with events with nothing to do with nutrition. In all societies, both simple and complex, eating is the primary way of initiating and maintaining relationships. In cultures where eating is a ceremony, eating alone is unthinkable. The fact of sitting down to eat together conveys an essential statement about society. The culture of a society transmits to children through eating with the family. It is a setting in which personalities develop, kinship obligations emerge and reinforce the group's customs. The association between eating and human behavior can be seen clearly in isolated and straightforward societies where eating is not considered a biological necessity for sustaining life, nor do they consciously recognize certain foods as having a higher nutritional value than others. They eat not merely because they have an appetite but because eating is a social necessity. Giving food is a virtuous act, and the man who distributes large amounts of it is a good man. For all that we denigrate the magical beliefs connected with food in simpler societies, it should be remembered that some of us throw salt over a shoulder to ward off bad luck, or eat fish in the belief that it is a superior brain food, or order oysters with the hope of inspiring sexual potency. A people's niche in the environment is determined as, indeed as it is for other animal species, by people's eating behavior. That is because eating inevitably brings humans into broader contact with their total environment, not only with their natural surroundings but also with their social, economic, and political relations with neighbors."

Index

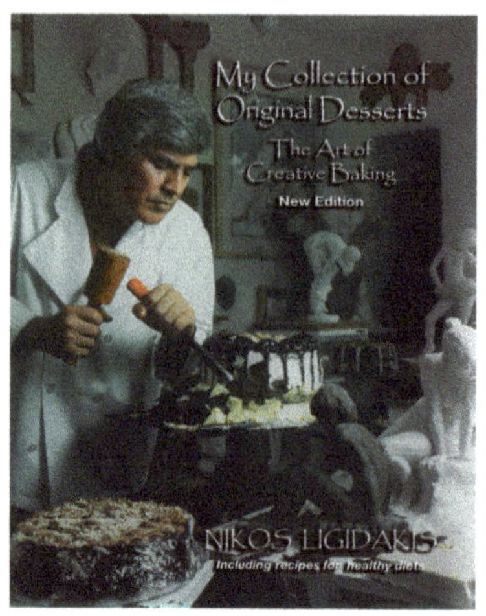

My Collection of Original Desserts

The Art of Creative Baking.

Silver Medal – 2020 Readers Favorite Book Awards
Gold Level 1 – 2020 Mom's Choice Awards

Who doesn't like dessert? But does anyone consider that food, especially dessert food, has a character all of its own. Food character includes "the essence of flavors and the perception of tastes." Desserts are more than just a sweet ending; it is a "symphony of flavors." And there is a misconception that desserts have to be sinfully sweet. In reality, they can be healthy. There are ways to make the most sinful-looking, delicious concoctions with healthier sweeteners and alternate flours, among other things. The key is knowing how and when to make the substitutions; in other words, knowing what foods work well together.

Nikos Ligidakis is an award-winning chef who has studied in great depth the wonders of food creations. He is known for his exotic creations, for his fresh, stunning works of culinary art. He is also known as an author who shares his knowledge of food with great pride and an accumulation of years of study. In other words, he knows his food. His recent book, My Collection of Original Desserts: The Art of Creative Baking, is a passionate look at sweet endings. The book begins with a background on the author and his aim of baking excellence. It then progresses into a concise sharing of his culinary knowledge: a list of ingredients and ingredient alternatives, how each ingredient works with other ingredients, culinary do's and don'ts, a fascinating account on what he terms "The Chocolate Addiction," and so much more. Then come the recipes, complete with mouth-watering images of the finished creations. The recipes are well laid out with concise and thorough instructions. This chef/ author obviously uses his imagination and his expertise to create some of the most exquisite sweet delights. This book is a must-have for any cookbook collector or anyone adventurous enough to make the ultimate dessert.

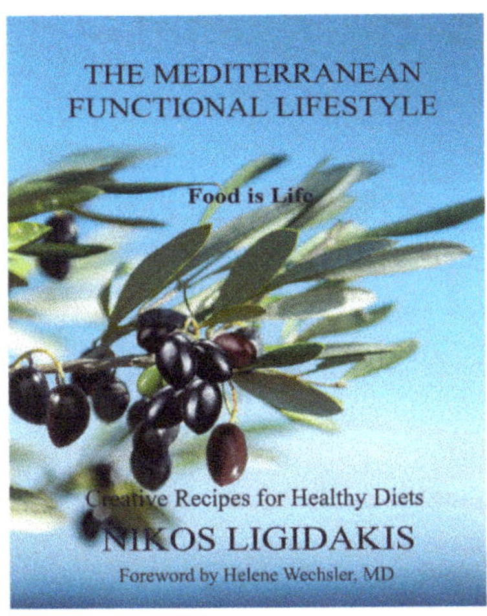

The Mediterranean Functional Lifestyle

Creative Recipes for Healthy Diets by Nikos Ligidakis

Gold – 2019 Nautilus Book Awards Program
Award-Winning Finalist – 2020 International Book Awards
Silver Medal – 2019 Readers Favorite Book Awards
Bronze Medal – 2020 Living Now Book Award
Award-Winning Finalist – 2020 Best Book Awards
Gold Medal – 2020 Mom's Choice Awards

The Mediterranean Functional Lifestyle by Nikos Ligidakis. "We've all heard the expressions, 'This book changed my life!' and 'Changing the world, one book at a time.' *The Living Now Book Awards* are designed to honor those kinds of life-changing books, and to bring increased recognition to the year's best lifestyle, home-style, world-improvement and self-improvement books and their creators."

"The Mediterranean Functional Lifestyle: Creative Recipes for Healthy Diets by Nikos Ligidakis is a gift for anyone who wants to eat and stay healthy. This book brilliantly showcases the old adage that 'we are what we eat.' The author shares more than 250 original recipes for healthy dieting, designed for people who are focused on elimination diets, gluten-free diets, vegetarian, vegan, and many more. The author shares information about and provides a cooking philosophy and diet mostly shaped by what the earth provides. It was not about one particular food with unique benefits but rather eating mostly plant-based, nutrient-dense foods and limited amounts of meats. Insights into the Early Hippocratic doctors establish a strong connection between their eating habits, their diet, and the Mediterranean diet. In the preface, Helene, the wife of the author, starts by telling readers their experience with the elimination diet and how they eliminated sugar, alcohol, dairy, eggs, corn, and gluten for three weeks. By the end of the third week, they lost weight and had much more energy. This book contains their secrets. I have read many cookbooks and have consulted them when I badly needed to cook, but The Mediterranean Functional Lifestyle is a treasure trove that doesn't just teach readers how to cook, but also how to create healthy meals. Readers will understand the nutritional value of fruits, vegetables, nuts, spices and herbs that are presented in this book. Nikos Ligidakis shares his creative ways of cooking and presents recipes that are clearly described and with easy steps to prepare them. These recipes include healthy foods like arugula, artichokes, beets, broccoli, cabbage, capers, carrots, cucumber, mushrooms, and many others. This book will not only keep those who use it healthy, but it will increase their strength levels and overall wellness. I enjoyed the creativity when it comes to the recipes, the fluidity in expression, and the strength of the writing. I also loved that while the recipes are easy to prepare, the author has done a great job of researching the biological and health properties of the spices and the foods. A gem of a book that is highly recommended."

Nikos Ligidakis

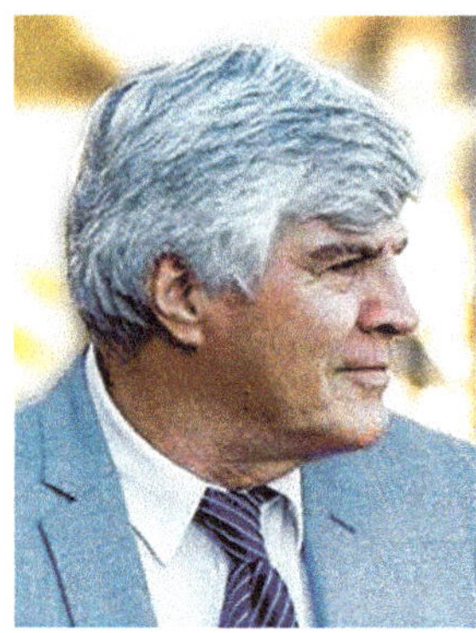

Award winning author, Nikos Ligidakis, writes with clarity and passion in an ardent voice, not to just recount adventures, but with an expression of feelings, to encourage the reader to think, to find hope in the eternal struggle for the meaning of life and the awareness of harmony.

Today Nikos devotes his life to coaching new authors encouraging and assisting them to write and publish their books. Nikos has founded several charitable organizations with the most notable his Thanksgiving Project to Feed the Hungry, a program that provided food to tens of thousands during its 21-year run. His selfless work with people has earned him several humanitarian awards over the years.

"As a writer, my aspiration has always been to share my perspective on what it means to be a human being, in all its complexities. I wanted to tell a story that reflects a comparative importance of political structures, religions and histories of the past. My books represent a lifelong dream of putting into narrative form, my many observations of the brilliance and kindness of the human spirit: people at their worst and people at their best. It is my intention to engage the reader in the process of observing history in both times past and in current day happenings for the sole purpose of gaining greater clarity in the shaping of one's own approach to life and the deepening of individual insight."

— Nikos Ligidakis

Nationally recognized chef Nikos Ligidakis demonstrates in his books his priceless culinary knowledge. There is sufficient information in this book to help you enhance your cooking skills. Ligidakis is a native of Greece, who gained national acclaim for combining the full tantalizing flavors of the Mediterranean region with an imaginative presentation. His success is credited to the fact that he created a cuisine that is both exotic and familiar. Nikos has become a legend locally both for his selfless charitable involvement and his idiosyncratic style of cooking. He prides himself on his culinary creativity, use of quality ingredients, freshness, consistency, and the fact that he prepares everything from scratch.

Nikos has been lauded in virtually every print publication in the greater Phoenix area, and in many national ones. He has been profiled numerous times on all of the valley's television stations and has received awards for his cooking, writing and charity work.

www.ingramcontent.com/pod-product-compliance
Lightning Source LLC
LaVergne TN
LVHW060616110826
845154LV00003B/100
* 9 7 8 0 5 7 8 6 6 4 8 6 6 *